Presidential Elections

Strategies of American Electoral Politics

Presidential Elections

Strategies of American Electoral Politics

SECOND EDITION

Nelson W. Polsby & Aaron B. Wildavsky

University of California, Berkeley

Charles Scribner's Sons / New York

For Linda and Carol

Preface to the Second Edition

IN PREPARING the Second Edition of this book, we received a great deal of help, mostly intentional and direct, and some hindrance, mostly unintentional and indirect. In both categories, we place the candidacy of Barry Goldwater for the Presidency. The Goldwater nomination made the 1964 election the most peculiar election of modern times—and it forced us to rewrite the entire book. The silver lining in this black cloud was the fact that the Goldwater candidacy also gave us an opportunity to rethink our interpretation of Presidential elections from start to finish. We believe that, on the whole, what we said in early 1964 stands up well, and we are able to affirm this in the light of a comprehensive consideration of the election of 1964. Our review of the literature has, however, led to certain changes of emphasis. Important recent research and the experience of 1964 have led us to give greater significance to the ideological commitments of party activists. Similarly, we have developed further our views on the reform of the Electoral College, reconsidered the significance of national conventions as decision-making bodies, and examined more closely alternative strategies that may be employed in choosing a Vice-Presidential candidate.

Although for some years we taught on opposite sides of the continent, it was our good fortune to spend a year as neighbors while this book was being revised. In this connection, Nelson W.

Polsby wishes to thank the Center for Advanced Study in the Behavorial Sciences for its hospitality in 1965–66. Our manuscript received a most helpful editorial critique from Miriam Gallaher of the Center and from Jean Zorn; Bryson Collins and Joan Warmbrunn prepared it for the publisher with care and efficiency; Robert P. vom Eigen worked devotedly on our revised and expanded Index.

Both of us have published preliminary thoughts on the 1964 election: Nelson W. Polsby, "Strategic Considerations," in *The National Election of 1964*, ed. Milton C. Cummings (Washington: Brookings Institution, 1966) and Aaron Wildavsky, "The Goldwater Phenomenon: Purists, Politicians, and the Two-Party System," *Review of Politics* 27 (July 1965), 386–413. We want to extend our thanks to the editors of both these publications and to the Institute of Governmental Studies at the University of California (Berkeley) for indispensable financial support that facilitated the research on the Goldwater phenomenon.

Finally, to our wives who warned that collaboration with either of us was impossible (and how would *they* know?), we rededicate this book.

N.W.P.
A.B.W.

June, 1967
Middletown, Connecticut
Berkeley, California

Preface to
the First Edition

THIS BOOK has had a long, and for us a very happy, gestation. Each of us has had over the last decade a chance to watch from a distance several Presidential elections; we have from time to time examined the scholarly literature on the subject, collected data on our own, and tried to think systematically about them independently of one another. In the winter of 1956–57, while we were graduate students at Yale, our collaboration began, with an effort at disentangling the theoretical and practical implications of then current proposals for party reform. Since then, we have repeatedly returned to American electoral politics in conversation and in our thoughts and writing. Despite considerable differences in the ways in which we express ourselves, and occasional differences in the emphases we would give to different events, we have been able to arrive at agreement on virtually all of the issues raised in this book. It is a totally collaborative effort in that we ourselves would have difficulty tracing the genesis or development of ideas contained here to one or the other of us.

Along the way, we have incurred many intellectual debts, separately and jointly. Some of our obligations are mentioned in the footnotes, but others, of a more personal kind, should be noted here. Nelson W. Polsby wants especially to thank Malcolm

C. Moos, Harvey Wheeler, and Ralph M. Goldman, who originally got him interested in Presidential election politics, and who helped to guide his first preliminary researches into the decision-making of the Democratic National Convention of 1952. Robert A. Dahl stimulated an approach to political analysis that led to a paper describing the logic of national convention behavior. This paper appeared as "Decision-Making at the National Conventions," *Western Political Quarterly* 13 (September 1960), 609–619. Lewis A. Froman, Jr., collaborated with him on a paper which served as forerunner and prototype of the treatment in this volume of the Electoral College. He also received excellent assistance from Margaret MacGregor Spellman, Carolyn Stoakes, Sheila Jones, and Martha Leiserson, who typed several versions of our manuscript, and from Bruce Franklin, Paul D. O'Brien, John R. Hanson, Peter Fritts, Charles L. Zetterberg, and Michael Austin, who ran down footnotes, read proof, and performed other odious chores cheerfully and well. Much of this work was made possible by a Ford Foundation Grant to Wesleyan University.

Aaron Wildavsky wants to thank the students in his senior seminar at Oberlin College for their stimulating discussion and for the preparation of a series of papers on past national conventions. He is grateful to the Eagleton Institute of Politics for a National Convention Fellowship which enabled him to study the behavior of the Ohio delegation at the 1960 Democratic Convention. The results of this enterprise were published as "'What Can I Do?': Ohio Delegates View the Convention," in Paul Tillett, ed., *Inside Politics: The National Conventions, 1960* (Dobbs Ferry, N. Y., 1962). While at the convention, he benefited from conversations with James D. Barber.

Together, we are grateful for the lasting inspiration and repeated encouragement of our teachers, David B. Truman and Allan P. Sindler, and, for excellent critical readings of earlier versions of this work, to Richard F. Fenno, Fred I. Greenstein, Lewis A. Froman, Jr., H. Douglas Price, Milton C. Cummings,

Jr., Michael Leiserson, Duane Lockard, Allan P. Sindler, Herbert E. Alexander, Elmer E. Cornwell, and Paul G. Willis.

It is customary for joint authors each to receive half the credit for their work, but to be blamed for all its errors. In this instance, as, we are sure, in so many, the credit deserves to be even more widely dispersed. We need hardly volunteer to our readers information about the sources of error.

N.W.P.
A.B.W.

July, 1963
Washington, D.C.

Contents

Chapter 3 The Campaign   122

Chapter 4 The 1964 Election   169

Presidential Elections

Strategies of American Electoral Politics

Introduction

Political Strategies and Presidential Elections

THIS BOOK is about the winning of the Presidential office. In spite of the great and lonely eminence of the Presidency, this office exists within a cultural and political tradition that guides and shapes the ways in which the Presidency is won and, later, the ways in which Presidential power is exercised. But we will not speak further here about the exercise of executive power. Rather, the task before us is to make plain the context within which the battle for Presidential office is waged, to discuss the strategies of contending parties and, if possible, to explain why some strategies are used by some contestants and other strategies by others. In this way we hope to elucidate a significant area of our common political life.

Our thesis is a simple one: The strategies of participants in a Presidential election make sense, once we understand the web of circumstances in which they operate. This principle applies to candidates and their managers, to delegates at nominating conventions, to party workers, and to voters. Strategies are courses of action consciously pursued toward well-understood goals. Watching strategies shows how political leaders use the constraints and opportunities of their environment to achieve their goals.

Both the political strategies of participants in Presidential elections and the circumstances that give rise to them are relatively stable, persistent features of our political system. We have had a two-party political system with the same two major parties for a little over a hundred years. Presidential nominees have been picked by national party conventions for an even longer period.[1] Presidential candidates have always been faced with such problems as deciding whether a greater or lesser emphasis on their party affiliation will help them gain more votes. Contemporary evidence that party preferences are not distributed evenly among the electorate helps explain, for example, why the strategy of recent Democratic candidates has been to place great stress on their party label, while Republicans are normally inclined to minimize their connection with their party.

Political strategies that persist over a period of time are reasonably easy to identify, even when they are colored by the distinctive styles and personalities of particular candidates. We hope, therefore, to achieve a level of discussion that goes beyond the special circumstances of 1968, or any other year, and say something about American Presidential elections in general.

The study of politics has progressed to the point where political scientists can now make available such a discussion. In large measure, an improved description and analysis is possible because of the efforts of dozens of scholars who have reported upon and investigated, with ever-increasing detail and accuracy, the component parts of the American political system. The task of this book will be to synthesize these reports for the enlightenment and use of interested citizens. But we cannot forecast the outcome of any particular election, and we have no desire to advise people how to vote.

In the first chapter we identify characteristics of the American political system which make up the strategic environment within which the pursuit of the Presidency takes place. Strategies are optional methods of pursuing one's goals, under certain limiting conditions. The would-be President must come to terms with voters, who enter each election period as complex bundles of already-formed habits, attitudes, and loyalties. The ways in which interest groups and parties activate these habits are largely out of the hands of any single participant in the process. Another element, the rules by which votes are counted, is also beyond any participant's control. Finally, we discuss the comparative availability to candidates of certain key resources, such as money and control over information.

The first chapter lays out a framework for much that follows in the second and third chapters. The latter deal, successively, with the various steps of the nomination and election processes. At this point in the book, we discuss a variety of classic strategic "moves," such as entering or not entering primaries, the candidacy of favorite sons, the starting and stopping of bandwagons at national party conventions, the selection of areas to campaign in, and the selection of issues to emphasize. In Chapters 2 and 3, we try to relate these moves to their necessary preconditions in terms of resources, and also to relate them to their probable consequences.

Chapter 4 deals with the election of 1964 in the light of the previous chapters. Essentially, we have to explain how the Republicans in 1964 came to nominate Senator Goldwater, even though this was, in the terms of our theory—and as the election outcome demonstrated—clearly a self-defeating strategy.

In the fifth chapter, we discuss significant proposals for altering the strategic framework of Presidential elections—proposals for reform that would in some respects reconstitute the party system and redistribute resources among contestants for the Presidency. Reform proposals are often debated rather abstractly on their presumed merits, without being related to any concrete consequences. We hope to provoke fresh insight on the subject of party reform by looking at these reforms in the light of the new distribution of benefits and handicaps which they propose to allocate to various participants in Presidential elections.

Finally, in Chapter 6, we attempt to state in general terms

what the ballot means in a political system like ours. Here we urge reconsideration of two stereotypes: one which insists that democracy cannot exist without strict majority rule, and another that suggests that public officials in our system receive many specific and meaningful policy directives from the electorate. We try to show that while our political system discourages both strict application of majority rule and mandates on specific policies, it is still meaningful to speak of our form of government as democratic, open, and responsive—as well as flexible, tough, stable, and resourceful.

Presidential elections are important to us as citizens. They determine who will guide our future. They also remind us of our heritage of political responsibility and freedom, a heritage which, in a troubled world, seems to us increasingly precious.

NOTES

1. See Paul T. David, Ralph M. Goldman, and Richard C. Bain, *The Politics of National Party Conventions* (Washington, 1960) for a lengthy treatment of the history of national party conventions.

Chapter 1

The Strategic Environment

ALL POLITICAL STRATEGIES are worked out within a framework of circumstances which are, in part, subject to manipulation but to even a greater degree are "given." Needless to say, this fact of life also applies to the strategies of aspirants to the Presidency, who must construct extremely complex plans of action within a context of hundreds of thousands of relevant circumstances, most of which lie beyond their control. Some of these circumstances are contingent and relate to the strategies being pursued by other active participants in the election process and to the resources at their command. Other circumstances are more stable and have to do with features of the American political system that have persisted over time. These features provide advantages and handicaps differently to Democrats and Republicans, to incumbent Presidents and challengers. It is these relatively persistent "givens" that we shall deal with in this chapter. We shall discuss the behavior of American voters and how the parties "reach" them, the party system, and party finance, the rules for counting votes in the Electoral College, and the nature of political information. Our point of view in dealing with these elements of the political system will be to show how they shape the decisions of Presidential election strategists.

VOTERS

Precisely what part does the voter play in American politics? This depends entirely on his interest and activity. Most people, however, are not interested in most public issues most of the time.[1] In our society, it is apparently quite possible to live comfortably without being politically concerned. Political activity is costly. It eats up time and energy at an astounding rate. To be informed on strategic problems in nuclear politics or on the operations of a municipal electric plant is not a matter of a few moments of reflection; many hours must be spent. One must ordinarily attend meetings, listen to or participate in discussion, write letters, attempt to persuade or be persuaded by others, and engage in other time-consuming labor. This means foregoing other activities, like devoting extra time to the job, playing with the children, and watching TV. But, so far as we can tell, these other activities rather than public affairs are the primary concerns of most people, and the costs of participation in public affairs appear, for most people, to be greater than the returns. Only a few people receive financial rewards or hold jobs or are acclaimed in the public arena—considerations which might lead them to devote the time and effort required to participate. It is only in regard to a few issues, at best, that most citizens find it worthwhile to participate in politics compared to other sectors of life.

Even so, there are a few people who are continuously interested in a wide variety of issues. These are usually public officials, interest group leaders, newspaper editors, and academics—all people whose occupations require their interest. There are a larger number who have specialized interests in specific policy areas. These may include public and private officials, members of civic organizations and interest groups, citizens who are directly affected, and a sprinkling of others who make a hobby of being interested, including seekers after causes and people who like to get their names on letterheads.

The fact that individuals do vary enormously in their degree of interest has profound implications for political life. For interest is a necessary condition of influence. The interested tend to go to meetings where public affairs are discussed and decided. They tend to belong to political parties and to work in various ways to help the party of their choice. They cultivate their access to public officials. They tend to care more about the outcomes of public policies and to communicate their concerns to decision-makers. And so, they become more influential.

Differences in interest also influence voting behavior: People who are interested in politics tend to vote and those who are disinterested tend not to vote.[2] Who are in these two groups? In general, the better educated people are more active and interested in public affairs. They also tend to be people who are better off financially.[3] This is, of course, also the population from which the Republican party draws disproportionate support, which consequently gives a substantial advantage to the Republican party among voters who tend to turn out most reliably for Presidential elections. On the other hand, the low turnout groups (normally Democratic) tend to be numerically greater than the high turnout groups. Furthermore, traditionally Democratic groups may be clustered in such a way as to maximize their strength in Presidential elections by being located in areas which are favored by the Electoral College system of vote-counting. We shall return to this topic later.

How do voters make up their minds whom to support? By far the majority of people vote according to their habitual *party* affiliation.[4] In other words, most people will have made up their minds how to vote in 1968 before the candidates are chosen, because they always support a particular party. These party regulars are likely to be more interested and active in politics and have more political knowledge than the "independents." [5] But they rarely change their minds. They tend to listen to their own side of political arguments and to agree with the policies espoused by their party. They even go so far as to "block-out" information which they perceive to be unfavorable to the party of their choice.[6]

If party is so important in giving a structure to a voter's picture of reality, and in helping him choose a Presidential candidate to vote for before the candidate is even nominated, we had best inquire where people get their party affiliations from. There seems to be no simple answer to this. The party affiliations of most voters seem to be governed by a number of forces. An individual lives in a social context and inherits a social identity from his parents that contains a political component. People are Democrats or Republicans, in part, because their families and the other people they interact with are Democrats or Republicans.[7] Most individuals come into close contact only with people who are predominantly one or the other.[8] And just as people tend to share characteristics with their friends and families such as income and educational level, religious affiliation, area of residence, and so on, they also tend to share party loyalties with them, too.[9]

Now, of course, we all know of instances where people do *not* share various status-giving characteristics with their parents and at least some of their friends, and so it should come as no surprise that sometimes children do not share the politics of their parents. In fact, political differences tend to run together with the other kinds of differences as well. But, by and large, voters retain the party loyalties of the primary groups of which they are a part.

The result of this process is to give each of the major political parties reservoirs of voting strength they can count on from year to year. Republicans traditionally do well in the small towns and rural areas of New England, the Middle Atlantic states, and the Middle West. They draw their support from people who are richer, better educated, occupy managerial or professional positions or run small businesses, tend to live in or to move into the well-to-do suburban areas, and are predominantly Protestant. Democrats draw great support from the large cities outside of the South and the rural areas in the South. Poorer people, wage earners, union members, Catholics, Negroes, Jews, and the new (that is, since 1900) immigrant populations of Irish and Polish ethnic origins—all contribute disproportionately to the Democratic vote.[10]

One may ask, how did these particular groups come to have these particular loyalties? We must turn to history to find answers to this question. Enough is known about a few groups to make it possible to speculate about what kinds of historical events tend to align groups with a political party.

Let us take a few examples. We all know about the "Solid South," which ever since the Civil War has been predominantly Democratic in its Presidential voting. To this day, resentment against the harsh Reconstruction period under the leadership of the Republican party is reflected in the election returns. Less well known is the fact that the South was not unanimous in its enthusiasm for the Civil War, or in its resentment of Reconstruction. In many states of the old South, there were two kinds of farms: plantations on the flat land that grew cash crops, used slaves, and, in general, before the Civil War, prospered; and subsistence farms in the uplands that had a few or no slaves and, in general, were run by poorer white people. This latter group formed the historical core of mountain Republicanism that still can be discovered in Presidential elections today, in western Virginia and North Carolina, eastern Tennessee and Kentucky, and southeastern West Virginia.[11]

The voting habits of Negroes, where they have voted, have been shaped by several traumas. The Civil War freed them and made them Republicans. The Counter-Reconstruction disenfranchised them, and the industrial revolution brought them North, where a crushing burden of economic destitution was added to racial discrimination. The differing effects of the Great Depression of 1929 on Negro voters in the North brought them into the New Deal coalition, and the Northern Negro has remained Democratic ever since.[12]

If, for some people, the historical events of the Civil War

and the Depression shaped their political heritage, for others the critical forces seem less traumatic and more diffuse. It is possible perhaps to see why the poor become Democrats, since the Democratic party has in recent years been so welfare-minded, but why do the rich lean toward the Republicans? Perhaps, in part, this is a reaction to the redistributive aspirations of some New Deal programs and the inclination of Democratic Presidents to expand the role of government in the economy. But in all probability it is also a response to the record of the Congressional wing of the Republican party which so thoroughly dominated the post-Civil War era of industrial expansion. In this era, Republican policies vigorously encouraged risk-taking by private businessmen, granted them Federal aid in a variety of forms, and withheld Federal regulation from private enterprise.

Sometimes party affiliation coincides with ethnic identification because of the political and social circumstances surrounding the entry of ethnic groups into the country. In southern New England, politics was dominated by the Republican party and by "Yankees" of substance and high status during the decades following the Civil War. During these decades, thousands of Irish people streamed into this area. The Democratic party welcomed them; the Republicans did not. Soon the Democratic percentage of the two-party vote began to increase, and Irish politicians took over the Democratic party.[13]

In the Middle West, events such as the American involvement in two wars against Germany under Democratic auspices seem to have shaped the political preferences of Americans of German descent.[14]

Specific *candidates* of special attractiveness may under certain circumstances sway voters to leave the party of their choice. The extraordinary elections of President Eisenhower are a recent example of this. His appeal to Democrats was quite amazing. But this was possible partially because these Democrats did not perceive President Eisenhower as a partisan figure, and so it is not surprising that his personal popularity did not greatly aid other Republicans who ran with him, or the Republican party, once he no longer headed the ticket.[15]

Most of the time *issues* have much the same sporadic and peripheral effect as candidates. Let us see why. We can say to begin with that at least three preconditions must be satisfied for a voter's opinion about an issue to change his vote.[16] First, a voter must know about the issue; second, he must care about it at least a little; and third, he must be able to distinguish the positions of the parties and their candidates on the issue. Data from public opinion polls tell us that most people are not well informed about the content of issues most of the time.[17] All but major public issues are thus eliminated for most people. And even these major issues may enter the consciousness of most people in only the most rudimentary way.

It makes a difference whether a person has a weak preference on an issue, or whether he breathes fire when the subject is mentioned. The number who care, even a little, is substantially less than those who know about issues.

Once a voter has some grasp of the content of a public policy, and learns to prefer one outcome rather than another, he must also find public leaders to espouse his point of view. Finding differences on policy issues between parties is not always easy. Party statements on policy may be vague because leaders have not decided what to do. They may deliberately obfuscate an issue for fear of alienating interested publics. They may try to hold divergent factions in their parties together by glossing over, as best they can, disagreements on many specific issues. Even when real party differences on policy exist, many voters may not be aware of them. The subject may be rather esoteric to the common understanding, or the time required to master the subject may be more than most people are willing to spend. By the time we get down to those who know *and* care *and* can discriminate between party positions on issues, we usually have a small proportion of the electorate, rarely larger than 30 per cent.[18] What can we say about these people?

The most obvious characteristic they share is interest in and concern about issues and party positions. But these are precisely the people who are most likely to be strong party identifiers, men and women who are characterized by a deep devotion to party, which makes it most unlikely that they will shift allegiance just because of a disagreement on one or two issues.[19] The number of issue-oriented "independents" who are left must be very small. And it is not unlikely that these people are distributed about equally on both sides of major policy questions so that the total number of votes changed by the impact of any specific issue is bound to be minute.

We still have some preconditions to satisfy, however, before even these changes can be accepted as certain. One is that there must not be other issues which are also highly salient to voters and which work the other way. For if voters were willing to change their votes on one particular issue, why should they not switch their support back because of another? There are usually many issues in a campaign; only if all or most of the issues pointed voters in the same direction, would they be likely to switch their votes. But what is the likelihood that parties will arrange their policies along a broad front so as to force large numbers of "independent" voters from or into the fold? It is low—but not impossible. In 1964 the Republicans may have done so. We will examine this question in detail in Chapter 4.

Although it is true that the less knowledge a person has about public affairs, the more likely he is to vote for a candidate of the opposite party, it is important to distinguish between those who only have a little knowledge and those who have none at all. For, the man utterly without any contact with the political world, except at the polls, has no reason whatsoever to change his customary party vote. Thus changes in vote from one party to another are likely to be concentrated among those who receive a little but not a great deal of information about parties, issues, and candidates.[20]

A recent study seeks to demonstrate that there is considerable issue content in the citizen's behavior at the polls, by showing that those who change party from one election to the next are generally sympathetic to some key policies of their new party. The standpatters, on the other hand, generally are in sympathy with major policies of their party.[21] Whether the citizen is taught what to believe by his party or finds a party in accordance with his beliefs cannot be determined from evidence presently available.

We can now see that a strong issue orientation is likely to guide voting decisions under some circumstances. One set of circumstances occurs when one issue becomes so intensely important that the voter is willing to lay aside his party preferences and his preferences on other issues. An unpopular war, severe economic deprivation (whether or not it is related to governmental policies), a fixation on a subject like keeping water free of fluoride have at times led to the required intense feeling. The pocketbook nerve seems especially sensitive.[22] Another possibility occurs when a party is seen to change across the spectrum of policies or the voter himself undergoes such a broad-scale change of heart. Finally, in a historical sense we can say that issues may have a lasting impact on voting behavior through the ways in which they shape the party affiliations of whole generations of voters. But few issues have the power to do this; and unless they occur under obviously dramatic circumstances, they are hard to identify except long after the fact.

This picture of the relation between voters and issues is somewhat unreal, in any case. For as far as we are able to tell, voters adopt most of their issue orientations at the instigation of the parties: Strong party identifiers are more likely to learn more about issues and to care more about them, in part, precisely because it reinforces their party identification.[23] This means that there are few issues that are not made by parties and political leaders, and hence few party identifiers are lost as a result of the policies adopted by the party of their choice.

Merely to list the functions which party identification performs for the voter—reducing his costs of acquiring political information, telling him what side he is on, organizing his information, ordering his preferences, letting him know what is of prime importance—is to suggest the profound importance of parties in the voter's mind. Politics is amazingly complex; there are scores of possible issues, a myriad of relevant political personalities, and often many choices to be made on Election Day. The voter who follows his party identification, however, can vastly simplify the choices he must make and thus reduce to manageable proportions the amount of time he spends on public affairs. He need only follow his party's nomination to arrive at a voting decision. When issues arise, the voter with strong party identification need not puzzle over every one. He can, instead, listen to the pronouncements of his party leaders who inform him about what issues are important, what information is most relevant to these issues, and what position he ought to take. Of course, the citizen with greater interest in public affairs will want to investigate a few matters for himself. Even so, his party identification provides him with important guides for the many other matters on which he cannot possibly be well informed. Indeed, all of us, including full-time participants like the President, have to find ways to cut information costs on some matters.[24] For most people who vote, their identification with one of the two major political parties performs that indispensable function.

If parties and their leaders make the issues and give them meaning for most people, then fundamental *changes* in party allegiance among large numbers of people are not likely to arise from their reasoned look at issues. A depression, a civil war, events felt immediately and personally by millions have precipitated the great changes in party allegiances, not debates on the merits of this or that comparatively minor matter. The sheer, brute impact of great events does more to change votes over the long run than any single policy problem.

INTEREST GROUPS AND VOTING BLOCS

Interest groups are collections of people who are similarly situated with respect to one or more policies of government and who organize to do something about it. The interest groups most significant for elections in our society are those having the following characteristics:

1) they have a mass base, that is, are composed of many members;

2) they are concentrated geographically, rather than dispersed thinly over the entire map;

3) they represent major resource investments of members—such as in the case of the *producers* of bicycles, whose entire livelihoods are tied up in the group involved, as against the *consumers* of bicycles, for whom investment in a bicycle is not anywhere near as important;

4) they involve those characteristics of people which give them status in society—such as their race and ethnicity.

Interest groups may be more or less organized, and more or less vigilant and alert on policy matters that concern, or ought to concern, them. They are not necessarily organized in ways that make them politically effective; very often the paid lobbyists of interest groups spend more time trying unsuccessfully to alert their own members to the implications of government policies than they spend lobbying with politicians.[25]

In American politics, interest group activity is lively and ubiquitous, even when it is not particularly effective or meaningful in terms of policy outcomes. We shall be concerned with interest groups in three ways: First, we must recognize that membership in these groups may be quite important in giving voters a sense of affiliation and political position. In this respect, interest groups act much the way parties do, helping to fill in the voter's map of the world with preferences, priorities, and facts. Secondly, interest groups are important with respect to their partisan political activities; they may actively recruit supporters for candidates and aid materially in campaigns. Thirdly, interest groups may influence party policy by making demands with respect to issues in return for their own mobilized support.

The extent to which interest groups can "deliver" the votes of their members, however, is always problematic; to a great extent interest group leaders are the prisoners of past alliances their group has made. Even so, the Negro vote, the farm vote, the labor vote, and many other "votes" are bandied about as though they were political commodities which could be manipulated easily in behalf of one or another candidate for public office. So long as the use of election statistics and opinion polls was in its infancy, claims to guarantee support or threaten to withdraw it could be accepted or rejected on intuitive grounds where no man could claim much greater competence than another. The appearance of voting studies and the development of the arts of statistical manipulation have created new opportunities for the purveyors of bloc votes and new difficulties for the interested but necessarily amateur citizen and public official. How are they to evaluate these important political claims backed up by impressive and complicated arrays of data?

The usual argument is that if one or another candidate captures the allegiance of a particular bloc, that bloc's pivotal position in a state or large population will enable the fortunate aspirant to capture all of the electoral votes and thus win the election. It is incorrect to speak of any one combination of states totalling more than a majority of electoral votes as in any sense more critical, valuable, or pivotal than any other such combination. In a fairly close election the defection of any number of combinations of states to the other side would spell the difference between victory or defeat.

An important point to remember is that appeals to various groups are necessarily conditioned by time, place, and circumstance. There is little doubt that under *some* conditions during *some* elections *some* social characteristics of voters and candidates may have *some* relevance to the polling results. Finding the conditions under which specified social characteristics become relevant to voter choice is most difficult. The problem cannot be solved by slogans advertising the alleged potency of this or that group at the polls. We know that in a competitive political system various participants (parties, interest groups, leaders) put forward candidates and issues designed to capture the allegiance of various groups of people. Rarely is it possible to appeal to one group and one group alone, not only because there are so many different groups, with all sorts of conceptions of policy, but also because each individual may have many social characteristics which are potentially relevant to his voting decision. While some men may be so single-minded that they have only one interest that is important in determining their vote—color, religion, ethnic background, income—most of us have multiple interests which sometimes conflict. Much depends on the movement of events which may bring one or another interest to the forefront of the voter's consciousness and incline him toward the candidate he believes best represents his preferences on that matter.[26] In addition, the appeals which were relevant at the turn of the century have slowly lost their effectiveness and have given way to a period when national, economic, and foreign policy issues or matters of style of living in the suburbs have assumed primary importance to many children of immigrant parents. Long-term social trends, as well as the strategies of candidates, have much to do with the impact of appeals to bloc votes.

In this context we can appraise the impact of John F. Kennedy's appeal to his fellow Catholics in the 1960 election.[27] Let us distinguish between two kinds of claims. One is the minimal claim that Kennedy's Catholicism helped him more than it hurt him in the election. This is correct. And it is largely correct because Catholics are disproportionately located in areas where they could contribute to Kennedy's majorities in states with large electoral votes.[28] If the claim is expanded to state, however, that something called the "Catholic vote" was the single factor which gained Kennedy's victory, then it is incorrect.

Two hard facts stand out from the welter of imponderables in the 1960 Presidential election: (1) there was probably a Catholic vote of some magnitude; (2) the increase in the votes of Catholics as compared to 1956 was not sufficient in and of itself to ensure Kennedy's victory. He also needed increases in the Democratic votes of Negroes, Jews, and other groups.

Both poll and electoral data strongly suggest that there was both a Catholic vote and an anti-Catholic vote in the 1960 election. According to the Gallup poll, the percentage of Catholics supporting the Democratic candidate rose from 51% in 1956 to 78% in 1960. Moreover, 62% of the Catholics who voted for Eisenhower in 1956 actually voted for Kennedy in 1960, while only 3% of the Catholics who voted for Stevenson in 1956 switched to Nixon in 1960. Although we do not know how many of the Catholics who voted for Eisenhower and Kennedy would also have voted for a Protestant Democrat in 1960, it seems safe to assume that by no means all would have done so. The presumption that there was a Catholic vote is further strengthened by the 1960 election returns which show that there is a high and positive correlation between the percentage of Catholics in a state and the percentage gain for the Democratic party over 1956. While part of these results may be accounted for by other demographic variables such as urbanization, it appears unlikely that this conclusion about the Catholic vote will be shaken.

These figures, it must be said, do not necessarily validate the claim that Catholics had been moving from the Democratic party and that the presence of a Catholic candidate brought them back into the fold. Another Gallup poll shows that 75% of the Catholics who voted in the 1958 Congressional election supported Democratic candidates, a total just three percentage points less than Kennedy received in 1960. It is possible, therefore, that the relatively low vote of Catholics for Adlai Stevenson represents a switch to the magical name of Eisenhower rather than a desertion of the Democratic party.

Unfortunately, we are not in a position to say whether or not Kennedy lost a considerable number of votes from Protestants. Gallup tells us that Kennedy received 38% of the votes by Protestants, while Stevenson received only 37% in 1956. But we know from other surveys that Stevenson's overall personal popularity in 1956 lost ground from 1952. In addition, he faced the handicap of running against the extraordinarily popular incumbent, President Eisenhower. Any Democratic candidate in 1960 was expected to do better than Stevenson did in 1956. Since we are not permitted the luxury of running a laboratory test in which a Protestant Democrat runs against Nixon, there appears to be no certain way of determining how many Nixon voters who are Protestant would have gone Democratic if Kennedy had not been on the ballot. The closest thing to such a test is a study done by the Simulmatics Corporation which predicted electoral outcomes from survey data on voting intentions carefully broken down into the characteristics of voters. The analysis concluded that

> The religious issue cut both ways. Not only did some Protestants reject Kennedy but also some Catholic Republicans swung to him. . . . The shift of one in ten American voters on religious grounds cost Kennedy one and a half million votes, or 2.3% of the total vote. But while Kennedy lost in the popular vote, he gained in electoral votes on the religious issue. The best-fit simulation indicates that Kennedy achieved a net gain of 22 electoral votes because of the religious issue. . . . The bunching of the Catholic shift in large, closely fought, industrial states and the location of much of the Protestant shift in "safe" Southern states gave Kennedy this net advantage despite a popular vote disadvantage. By our calculations, Kennedy lost, by the religious issue, the following states he otherwise would have won: Kentucky (10), Tennessee (11), Florida (10), Oklahoma (8), Montana (4), Idaho (4), Utah (4), California (32), Oregon (6), Virginia (12), and

Washington (9). He won the following states he would otherwise have lost: Connecticut (8), New York (45), New Jersey (16), Pennsylvania (32), Illinois (27), and New Mexico (4).[29]

A study has also been made which shows that Democratic candidates for Congress in Wisconsin suffered defeat in close districts probably because of Protestant defection due to Kennedy's candidacy.[30] Finally, a plausible guess has been made by the Michigan Survey Research Center. It estimated what the "normal" votes of Catholics and Protestants for Democratic Presidential candidates would be. Then, calculating the 1960 divergence from this hypothetical "normal" pattern, they concluded that Kennedy was shy about 2.2% of the two-party vote, a large proportion of the defections coming from the South.[31] On balance, it appears that Kennedy was hurt somewhat in the Southern and Border states and perhaps in the Midwest and Mountain states as well, but he more than made up for it in the Northern and Midwest industrial states whose electoral votes were far larger.

In terms of popular votes, Kennedy received 49.7% to Nixon's 49.6% out of a total vote of 68,832,670, a hair-breadth margin if there ever was one. The exceedingly close popular and Electoral College vote makes it unlikely that increased votes by Catholic voters alone could have been sufficient to give Kennedy victory. Virtually any group—Jews, or Negroes, for example— could claim that a shift of their few thousand votes in a few critical states made the difference between victory and defeat.[32]

Two brief examples may be cited to support this conclusion. Illinois and Texas together account for 51 electoral votes. Out of the approximately 4.7 million votes cast in Illinois, Kennedy's margin of victory was 8,858. Where a shift of 4,500 votes by any group would have been enough to spell the difference, it would not be difficult to find any number of groups which could be considered necessary for the victory. Gallup reports that on a national basis the votes of Jews increased from 75% to 81% Democratic over 1956 and the votes of Negroes from 61% to 68%.

Evidently Kennedy needed the additional votes from the Jews and the Negroes who live in Illinois in order to have won there. In Texas, Kennedy's margin was 46,233 out of 2.3 million votes cast. There could easily have been a shift by as many as 25,000 Texas Negro voters toward Kennedy.[33]

What, then, do the 1960 election returns have to teach us about the requirements for future non-incumbent Democratic Presidential candidates? If a candidate wants to get elected President on the Democratic ticket he had better get many more votes from Catholics, Jews, Negroes, and other groups traditionally providing support for his party than was the case in 1956. If the best he can do is to get 38% of Protestant voters, he had better look for exceedingly strong support from other groups. Common sense suggests that if a candidate can increase his support among Protestants he need not be so dependent upon other groups. As a postscript to Kennedy's victory we might add that it is also advisable to be personally attractive, energetic, photogenic, wealthy, skillful, determined, and to run against Richard Nixon rather than Dwight Eisenhower.

The picture of voters and interest groups we have drawn thus far can be generalized. Presidential elections and election campaigns are events which activate the personal loyalties of voters. The amount of new information about candidates or issues which citizens need in order to participate at the minimal level of voting, or in order to hold casual conversations about the election, is slight, because the political component of their personal identities is reasonably stable and familiar to them. Party loyalty and membership in interest groups provides a short cut to voter preferences, and minimizes the costs of getting information about the specifics of the issues and candidates in any particular election year.

Interest groups are intermediary agencies that help voters to identify their political preferences quickly. They perform this function in two ways: by actively soliciting their members' interest in behalf of specific candidates and parties, and, more importantly, by providing still another anchor to the voter's identity. This helps the voter fix his own position quickly and economically, in what otherwise would be a confusing and contradictory political environment.

PARTIES

A third aspect of the social framework which will help us to account for the strategies of participants in Presidential elections is the nature of political parties in this country. These can best be explained as organizations devoted to maintaining or increasing their own opportunities to exercise political power.

By "political power" we mean the ability to make decisions, or to influence the making of decisions of government. Instrumental to this goal is the achievement of access[34] to those offices and officials legally entitled to make governmental decisions. Access, in turn, depends in part upon one's participation in staffing the government, either by selecting officials to fill appointive offices (patronage) or by significantly influencing the nomination and election of elected officials. Since elected officials are usually empowered to select appointed officials, access to them is often instrumental to the dispensation of patronage. There are, of course, numerous ways of gaining access to public officials, but the original selection of these officials is the primary avenue of access used by political parties.[35]

At each level of government, the elected chief executive (Mayor, Governor, President) generally has the most political power, and as a result the party organizations depend more upon controlling these offices than on any other source for their political power. In addition, parties are accountable for the activities of chief executives elected under their endorsement. Accountability means that when the party endorses a man, it designates him as its agent before the electorate. The fortunes of the party depend on the success of party candidates. Candidates come and go, but parties and electorates remain. The party organizations, therefore, are quite concerned about selecting suitable officeholders since it is assumed that the actions and identities of these men will in the long run marginally determine the extent and location of the party's appeal within the electorate, and its record of success at the polls.

Just as the party is greatly dependent, at any moment, upon its incumbent officeholders for its political power, these officeholders in turn often have great discretion in the distribution of rewards to the party, and it is expected that they will seek to strengthen themselves within the party organization by the judicious dispensation of favors and patronage. As men who have won office at the head of party tickets, elected chief executives will probably come closer than other individuals to possessing the kinds of control over the party organization that will make it possible for them to impose their own preferences on party organizations.

State party organizations are not simple in their internal workings. Sometimes elected chief executives run them; sometimes they are run by coalitions of party chieftains representing the local organizations of several large cities or counties. Sometimes party officials and elected officials work cooperatively; sometimes they work at cross purposes. A strong national committeeman in a state party organization whose party, nationally, occupies the Presidency may find his position amplified as *the* avenue of access in the distribution of Federal largesse if there are few officeholders elected in the state with whom he might have to share power. On the other hand, there are instances of Governors who felt their chances of continuing personal victory would improve if they thoroughly disassociated themselves from the party whose label they nominally bore, causing the party organization in the state to shrivel on the vine. A strong party organization, well led, can enforce on an executive choices suitable for the party's purposes that conflict with alternative choices more likely to enhance the executive's position regardless of its effect on the party. Leaders of party organizations are frequently at odds with the party's elected officeholders for a variety of reasons. Many elected officials see their party leaders as potential threats to their positions; many party leaders see the officeholders as ungrateful louts with whom the organization is unfortunately saddled.

Even so, what party leaders ordinarily care about most is getting their men into office and keeping them there. Other considerations are usually secondary. Party leaders are neither for nor against policies in the abstract; they are concerned with policies as means to the ends of officeholding. If new policies help win elections, they are for them; if they help lose elections, they are against them.

Though party leaders try to espouse policies which they believe will enhance their political power and try to avoid very unpopular points of view, this does not mean that they are necessarily indifferent to the substance of policy questions. Because they are more interested and active than most citizens, they also tend to care more about the policies with which they have to deal. In fact, some politicians who hold public office make a specialty of being policy-oriented. At times they may deliberately incur some unpopularity in order to serve their policy preferences, although they are unlikely to go so far as to knowingly lose the election for which they are a candidate. The experience of the 1964 election, which we take up at length in Chapter 4, provides an extreme case, which is instructive in this connection. But in general, party leaders regard policy to a certain extent as a result of an interaction among legitimate political demands—as a bargainable product—and not as a set of logical or ideological imperatives.[36]

Political parties in America are not organizations with elaborate procedures of membership, dues, and formal organizational structure. They are constituted differently in different localities and exist primarily to make nominations for and elect candidates to a variety of state and local elective offices. They are regulated by state law, and are often quite cohesive up to the state level.

But the state parties are joined together nationally only in loose federations. They meet formally by sending delegates to national committee meetings, and, most importantly, by coming together at national conventions to nominate a President.[37]

It is often said that our political parties are decentralized. How do we know this? Perhaps the most obvious indicator is the fact that the major parties are organized on a geographic basis in which the state units are the constituent elements. The state party organizations choose their representatives to national party bodies; the national committees and conventions do not choose officers of state parties. In a negative sense, the permanent national party organizations are not in a position to help the state parties; they have neither the funds, nor personnel, nor contacts to contribute substantially to the nomination or election of candidates for Congress or local office who must run within state boundaries. The operation of the so-called Presidential coattail is problematical at best;[38] it does not help state parties and candidates who must try to win every year in numerous elections at the state and local level. At best, coattails operate every four years and then only if there happens to be a strong Presidential candidate on the ballot.

The state parties, however, have substantial powers enabling them to share in the making of national policy. Their Representatives and Senators in Washington compete for the distribution of Federal resources and for the assignment of advantageous positions on Congressional committees. The states have their own sources of patronage and, through their Congressmen and Senators, a share in Federal patronage. The very circumstance that the states are separate legal entities engenders a drive for autonomy as those who hold places of prestige and profit in the state governments and parties seek to protect their jurisdictions, much as the framers of the Constitution hoped they would. Federalism, however, is much more than a legal fact. The states are given great vitality because there are distinct, numerous, and vigorous ethnic, religious, racial, and economic groups who are disproportionately located in specific geographic areas and who demand separate recognition. State organizations, therefore, become infused with the purposes of groups of citizens who use their state parties for the recognition and enhancement of their separate identities and needs. Italians in Rhode Island, Jews and Negroes in New York, Germans in Wisconsin, wheat growers in Kansas, and many others make the idea of a decentralized party system a living reality.[39] The state parties are composed of different personnel, with somewhat different interests to protect and demands to make. Control over these organizations must be exercised from within each state, since the various states do not control one another, and the national party cannot exercise this control. This, we take it, is the very essence of what is meant by a decentralized party system in which power is dispersed among many independent state bodies.

Thus, our national parties are coalitions of state parties which meet every four years for the purpose of finding a man and forging a coalition of interests sufficiently broad to win a majority of electoral votes. This means bringing into the coalition state parties and party factions—Southern and Northern Democrats, coastal and Midwestern Republicans—who disagree on some major policy issues. As a result, it is necessary to compromise and, sometimes, to evade issues which would split the parties and lead to drastic losses of support. A man and a set of policies, however loosely joined, must be found that can blend disparate party elements for the purpose of securing electoral victory.

The major parties, as we have seen, cull their electoral support from somewhat different groups in the population. *But,* no party has a monopoly of support from any of these groups; each party draws significant, and often indispensable, support from almost all the categories.[40] How could Republicans hope to win without some support from wage earners, or Democrats without some votes from business and professional people? The parties are sufficiently variegated to draw support from many quarters. In a close election the ability of a party to increase its support within one group from, say, 20% to 30% may be crucial, even though that group still votes overwhelmingly for the opposition. The strategic implications of these remarks color all of national campaign politics: The parties try to do things which will keep happy the groups consistently allied to them without alienating other groups unduly.

Thus the temptation for parties to avoid specific policy commitments in many areas is very great. The American population is so extraordinarily varied—crisscrossed by numerous economic, religious, ethnic, racial, sectional, and occupational ties—that it is exceedingly difficult to guess at the total distribution of policy preferences in the population at any one time, except for questions that have already been settled between the parties like Social Security and unemployment compensation. It is even more difficult to predict how these aggregations of actual and potential interest groups might react to shifts in party policy positions, and still more hazardous to prophesy what different policy commitments might do to the margin of votes required for victory. This pervasive problem of uncertainty makes the calculation of gain from policy positions both difficult and risky and suggests that the self-interests of the parties and candidates in keeping office might best be served by vague, ambiguous, or contradictory policy statements which will be least likely to offend anyone. The advantages of vagueness on policy are strengthened by the facts that the vast majority of citizens are not interested in policy or are narrowly focused on a few things, and that only a few groups in the population demand many specific policy commitments from their parties and candidates.

Yet, despite all this, political leaders and parties do make policy commitments which are often surprisingly precise, specific, and logically consistent. There are meaningful differences between the parties in the realms of welfare, natural resources, public power, medical care under Social Security, Federal aid to education, and other domestic policies. Thus, we must consider not only why the parties sometimes blur and avoid commitments on issues, but also why they often commit themselves to policies more than their interest in acquiring or retaining office would appear to require.

Part of the answer may arise from the fact that the parties serve slightly different functions for their own activists than for people who vote but are otherwise largely disengaged from politics. Party activists are people who are much more interested in politics and attentive to political issues, than the general population is. The interest and attentiveness of political activists leads them to formulate and elaborate political opinions and preferences. Their desires to make these preferences internally consistent and consistent with the preferences of the party of their choice and the mutual reinforcement of activist opinions when activists interact with one another would certainly lead to demands upon the party leadership for policy positions which are reasonably clear and forthright.[41]

There are notable differences between the parties in the social identities of party activists. Activist Democrats are far more likely to come from working-class backgrounds; activist Republicans, on the other hand, are disproportionately middle class. These differences may be reflected in the noticeable tendencies for the two parties to support policies intended to benefit the members of the social strata from which their active members are drawn.[42]

The interest groups most closely allied with each party also make policy demands upon them which must be met to some extent. While it is true that voters are generally disinterested in specific policies, interest group leaders and their paid bureaucracies are manifestly concerned. If they feel that the interests they represent are being harmed, they may inform their members or even go so far as to withdraw support from the party at a particular election. Should voters find that groups with which they identify are opposed to the party with which they identify, they may temporarily support the opposition party, or they may withdraw from participation and not vote at all. Consequently, the party finds that it risks losing elections by ignoring the demands of interest groups. Since the demands of many of these groups conflict, however, the parties have no choice but to mediate among them, hoping to strike compromises which, though they give no one group everything, give something to as many groups as they can.

Finally, throughout the years the opposing political parties have become identified with somewhat different policies. When new candidates arise they may bring with them somewhat new policy preferences. But there are bound to be many areas of policy on which they are not informed or do not have strong preferences. In such cases the existing set of policies traditionally associated with the parties provides the candidates with a useful economizing device. They can accept the going positions and concentrate on the policies which they may wish to revise, supplant, or present anew. This tack is bound to be popular with the party faithful who have been brought up on the rallying cries of the past, who have learned to prefer what their party prefers, and who respond with vigor and enthusiasm to the cues provided by mention of their party's chief stocks in trade. Just as voters commonly use parties as a means of cutting their information costs on issues and candidates, and activists use them as reference groups, so may candidates use the parties' traditional policy positions to ease their burden of calculation.

THE ELECTORAL COLLEGE

Another element of the strategic environment within which the drama of a Presidential election is played is that peculiarly American institution, the Electoral College. American Presidential elections are not decided by popular vote, but rather the popular votes are collected within each state, and each state casts all of its electoral votes for the candidate receiving the most popular votes within the state. This "winner take all, loser take nothing" approach is called a "unit rule." [43] We will explain some consequences of this rule presently.

Each state is allowed as many electoral votes as it has Senators and Representatives in Congress. Thus, all states, no matter how small, have at least three electoral votes. This means that mathematically, sparsely populated states are overrepresented by the Electoral College. In 1964, 67,259 Alaskans influenced the disposition of three electoral votes, which gives a ratio of one electoral vote for every 22,419 voters. In New York, on the other hand, 7,166,015 voters went to the polls and voted for 43 Electors, a ratio of one electoral vote for every 166,651 voters. In California, 7,050,985 voters for 40 Electors produces a ratio of one electoral vote for every 176,275 voters.[44] One might conclude, therefore, that each Alaskan had about eight times as much influence on the final outcome as each Californian. But this is not entirely valid.

Why not? Because the unit rule of the Electoral College provides that the candidate having the most votes in a state receives the entire electoral vote of the state. This means that each Alaskan was influencing the disposition of all three of Alaska's electoral votes, and each Californian was helping to decide the fate of all *forty* of California's votes. Ask any politician whether he would rather have three votes or forty—the answer is immediately apparent. In fact, the present method of electing the President tends to give greater power to the large, urban states, not the small, rural states, because the large states can deliver to the winner large blocks of the votes he needs to win. Consequently, Presidential nominees tend to come from big states and tend to run on platforms likely to appeal to big city interest groups. They concentrate their campaigns in the big centers of population, and, as politicians know, they stand or fall on the big state votes. This feature, interestingly enough, is the mirror image of the situation in Congress. Where the unit rule of the Electoral College gives extra weight to the voices of large, urban, two-party states in the Presidential nomination process, the seniority rules of Congress and the rules strictly allocating jurisdiction to Congressional committees have over the years worked to give one-party areas the most power, and these have, until quite recently, tended to be disproportionately rural and small-town in their composition.

THE DISTRIBUTION OF RESOURCES

Certain resources which, at any given time, are disproportionately available to Democrats and Republicans play a significant part in the strategic environment. For example, possession of the Presidential office, skill in organization, knowledge of substantive policies, reputation for integrity, facility in speechmaking, ability to devise appealing campaign issues, wealth, stamina—all can be drawn upon to good advantage in a Presidential campaign. There are, it is clear, more resources available to the parties than any one book could deal with exhaustively. But some resources are obviously going to be more important than others, and the importance of different resources varies from occasion to occasion. It would be sensible to regard as especially important those resources which one side effectively *monopolizes* —such as the Presidential office—and those resources which can be easily *converted* into other resources, or directly into public office—such as money, which can be used to buy competent staff, newspaper space, and so on.

Although political resources are distributed unequally between the parties, in a competitive two-party system such as ours the inequalities do not all run in the same direction. Sometimes the Republicans reap the benefits; sometimes the Democrats do. One result of these inequalities of access to different resources, however, is that different strategies are more advantageous to each of the two parties. Let us examine three resources commonly held to be extremely important in the strategic environment of the Presidential election—money, control over information, and the Presidential office—in order to see what effects they have on election strategies.

Money

Presidential campaigns are terribly expensive. Radio and television appearances, newspaper advertising, travel for the candidate and his entourage, mailings of campaign material, buttons and placards, maintaining a network of offices to run the campaign, taking polls—all cost a great deal of money. It is estimated that the various committees (the Republican and Democratic national committees, the House and Senate campaign committees of both parties, and various *ad hoc* volunteer committees that spring up in each campaign) at the national level spent approximately $25 million in 1960 and over $29 million in 1964.[45] There is no sign that costs are decreasing. And substantial sums were also spent by state and local organizations in behalf of the Presidential candidates. Total political costs for all candidates at all levels of government amounted to something like $140 million in 1952, $155 million in 1956, an estimated $175 million in 1960, and approximately $200 million in 1964.[46] The huge costs involved inevitably raise serious questions about the relationship between wealth and decisions in a democracy. Are Presidential nominating and electoral contests determined by those who have the most money? Do those who make large contributions exercise substantial or undue influence as a result of their largesse? Is the victorious candidate under obligation to "pay off" his major financial contributors? Do those who pay the piper call the tune?

First, let us establish some basic facts. Republicans do spend more than Democrats in most places, but the difference is not as overwhelming as some would suppose. The Democratic percentage of major party expenditures from 1932 to 1964 has varied from a low of 35% in 1940 (when Roosevelt won) to a high of 45% in 1960 (when Kennedy won).[47] Although the Johnson forces spent more money in 1964 than Kennedy's had in 1960 (the

Democrats in 1964 managed to spend $12 million), Goldwater forces spent $17.2 million, significantly more than Johnson's.[48] Thus, total expenditures of both parties are high in absolute terms, but outlays per voter per party are quite modest, running in the 1960 election to about 16 cents for each of the 68.83 million voters.[49] "Contrary to frequent assertion," says an author who has made a comprehensive study of party finance, "American campaign monies are *not* supplied solely by a small handful of fat cats. Many millions of people now give to politics. Even those who give several hundred dollars each number in the tens of thousands." [50]

Since 1956, roughly 10% of the population has been contributing in Presidential election years. Data from the Survey Research Center show that 10% of a national population sample said they had contributed in 1956, 12% in 1960, and 11% in 1964. Translating these numbers into individuals, we find that 8 million people in 1956, 10 million in 1960, and 12 million in 1964 contributed to political campaigns.[51] It remains true, however, that the bulk of the money to run campaigns comes from people who contribute over $100. For the years before 1956, two-thirds of the campaign war chests at the national level were made up of contributions of over $500, and an additional one-fifth came from contributions of over $100. At the local level, where approximately six-sevenths of election expenses are met, the proportion of gifts over $500 declines to one-half or one-third. The figures on contributors for 1952 will perhaps give some idea of the numbers. Around 3 million people made some contribution. At least one gift of $100 was made by 150,000 contributors, $500 by 20,000 of these people, and $10,000 or more was given by 200 of these individuals.[52]

The most obvious and most important conclusion in our view is that money does not buy election victories. The candidates and party with the most money do not always win. Otherwise, Republicans would have won every election in the last thirty years, and we know, in fact, that the Democrats have won with the sole exception of the two terms of Dwight Eisenhower. Nor does there seem to be a correlation between the amount of money spent and the extent of electoral victory in national elections.[53] This is the more surprising because one would expect that money would flow into the coffers of the party which was believed to have the best chance of victory. There does not seem to be a single Presidential election in this century which any competent observer believes would have turned out differently if the losing candidate had spent more money than the winner. We can at once eliminate all the Democratic victories because the Democrats spent less than the Republican losers. Dwight Eisenhower was so popular that his two elections now seem to have been certain, whether he had a substantial campaign surplus or not. No doubt part of the reason he had as much money to run with as he did was his personal appeal to the people who contribute to campaigns, and they might well have given to him even if he had run as a Democrat. The Republicans who won in the period from 1900 to 1928 did so with substantial majorities as befits the party which then enjoyed the allegiance of a preponderant part of the voting citizenry. The problem, then, is not to explain why money is crucial but, on the contrary, to explain why it is not.

No one doubts that money is important; parties and candidates, not to speak of ordinary mortals, can hardly function without it. If a candidate could not raise any money, or only a pitifully small amount, he would be dreadfully handicapped and might not be able to run at all. But this situation has never arisen after the national convention has made its choice. The crucial question is not the total spent by each candidate but the *difference* in the amounts they spend. The first part of our explanation, therefore, is that the differences in spending have not been so great as to give any candidate an overwhelming advantage. So long as the poorer candidate can raise the minimum amount necessary to mount a campaign—that is, to hire employees, distribute literature, go on the radio and television a few times, get around the country, and so on—he can do most of what he has to do. Another way of putting this would be to say that above the minimum amount necessary to run a campaign the additional expenditures do not appear to confer significant advantages. Like other goods, money is subject to diminishing returns. People may get tired of being bombarded with literature and harangued by speakers. The candidates sometimes worry about over-exposure lest they go the way of certain television celebrities who were seen once too often. Criticism of "trying to buy the election" may arise if too much time is taken on television. Indeed, there may be resentment at favorite programs taken off the air to accommodate a candidate who seems to have had more than his say. We know that many voters are relatively impervious to bombardment by the opposition, and all the handouts in the world will not make them change. The actual result of extensive assault by the richer party may be to increase the polarization of the electorate as those who oppose that party find additional reasons to intensify their opposition.

Given the necessary minimum amount of money on his side, the less affluent candidate can count on a good deal of free publicity. Presidential campaigns are deemed newsworthy by the press and are extensively reported. While Democrats may get somewhat less space than Republicans in papers, they still get some, and they do better in the magazines and on the air. Thus, they get through to their supporters. To some extent the candidates can make news. John Kennedy's grappling with the religious issue, Harry Truman's assaults on the opposition, Dwight Eisenhower's dramatic promise to go to Korea made headlines at little or no financial cost. The television debates in 1960 between Nixon and Kennedy attracted millions of viewers, numbers far in excess of the usual political broadcasts for which fees have to be paid.

The factor of skill must also be considered. Money can be spent for unrewarding purposes which actually rebound against the candidate. Democratic strategists during the 1930's were delighted at the expenditures made by the Liberty League on behalf of the Republican candidate, because they considered it to be an ideal target for their charges that the Republicans were the party of privilege. Money may be expended unwittingly getting the opposition to the polls. A poor performance on television may do the candidate no good no matter how much is spent. The man who says the wrong thing may deeply regret the wealth which made it possible for him to disseminate his statement widely.

Other things being equal, of course, it would be nice to have more money to spend than the other fellow. But conditions are rarely, if ever, equal. The fundamental party allegiances of the population, the state of the economy, religious and ethnic affiliations, personalities of the candidates—all appear to be more significant in determining the outcomes of elections than the differences in total party spending. Despite the understandable cries of harried party money-raisers, the Democrats always seem to come up with enough to get by. There is always the hope of victory. The winner can expect to have his deficits covered at the next round of party "victory" fund-raising drives. It remains true that the most expensive election is the one you lose.

Money is probably more important at the nominating rather than the electoral stage. Eisenhower and Taft spent about $2.5 million each on their nominating campaigns in 1952.[54] The candidate who wishes to enter primaries and conduct a national drive to obtain delegates may be dissuaded through lack of the minimum amount necessary to get started. The lower visibility of primaries and the lesser attention paid to them by citizens may give an advantage to those with more to spend. Money, however, is only one factor. Estes Kefauver put on a vigorous campaign despite his relative lack of wealth. Had he not been bitterly opposed by party leaders, or had he won all the primaries he entered, as Kennedy did, he might have won the nomination. As it was, Kefauver lost to Stevenson whose command of wealth was the least of his political assets.

Other candidates may, however, have been adversely affected

by lack of funds. Nelson Rockefeller is a curious example. Apparently he decided not to contest the Republican nomination in 1960 in part because he could not raise the cash.[55] During the 1960 Kennedy-Humphrey primary campaigns in West Virginia, charges of vast Kennedy spending were made. Certainly, Kennedy's ready cash did him no harm. In retrospect, however, it does appear that he was decidedly more popular with the voters than his rival, Hubert Humphrey. Would more money have enabled Humphrey to turn the tide? Humphrey's campaign was badly managed and severely underfinanced and in part this led the press to accord him less serious treatment than he might otherwise have merited. Had Humphrey had as much money to spend on campaigning as Kennedy, for as long a period of time, the tide might conceivably have run in the other direction. There were, nonetheless, other candidates—Johnson and Symington, for example—who had plenty of money but who chose not to contest the primaries.[56]

It is exceedingly difficult to get reliable information on an event that involves a decision *not* to act. Such an event would be a decision by a political candidate not to run because he could not raise the money. There is, of course, no literature on this subject. But there have undoubtedly been some men whose inability to raise the cash has proven fatal to their chances of being considered for the nomination. While this is most regrettable, a more important question concerns whether there has been systematic bias in favor of or against certain kinds of men that consistently alters the outcome of Presidential nominations. We can immediately dismiss the notion that the richest man automatically comes out on top. If that were the case, Rockefeller would have triumphed over Goldwater, Taft over Eisenhower, and neither Nixon nor Stevenson would have been nominated.

The ability to raise money is not only a matter of personal wealth but of being able to attract funds from others. Does this mean that only candidates attractive to the wealthy can run? It might be said that the problem is not so much whether it helps to be rich but whether men who favor the causes of the rich have the advantage over those who favor the poor. There is little evidence to support such a view. Given the nature of the American electorate, no candidate would openly admit to being the candidate only of the rich. Candidates holding a variety of views on economic issues—most of which are highly technical—manage to run for the nominations of both parties. If candidates are generally chosen from among men who differ but little on most substantive issues the reason is not because the rich are withholding their money from more radical candidates but rather because the distribution of opinions in the electorate renders the cause of such men hopeless. Our conclusion is that it is nice to be rich; some men who lack funds may be disadvantaged. From the standpoint of the total political system, however, the nomination process does not appear to bar types of men who are otherwise acceptable to the electorate.

Although the difference in ability of the two parties to raise money is not in any sense a critical determinant of national elections, large sums of money are necessary to run campaigns. May not those who contribute or raise money in large amounts thereby gain influence not available to others? Aware that the answer to this question is not a simple one, we would say, "Yes, but not overly much." What contributors or fund raisers (the financial middlemen) get to begin with is access to centers of decision-making. Control over money certainly makes it easier to get in and present one's case. Men of wealth, however, are likely to have substantial economic interests which would provide them with good access whether or not they made contributions. If no significant interest feels disadvantaged by what these contributors want, they may well be given the benefit of the doubt. But in matters of great moment, where the varied interests in our society are in contention, it is doubtful whether control over money goes very far with a President. There are many reasons for this.

In the first place, there are many issues on which a candidate is likely to be already publicly committed. Suggestions that a candidate change his position during the campaign are likely to be met with little favor. If the matter is important enough to be mentioned it has to be considered in relation to its vote-getting potential. Forced to make a choice, nominees are far more likely to prefer votes to dollars. And even if a miscalculation is made *in public*, candidates generally prefer not to reverse their field and appear vacillating and inconsistent. Money may be given in the expectation of future favors. To spell this out in detail would appear unseemly, however, and is likely to be rejected outright. The moral sense of the candidates would most likely forbid such a thing; if not, the good political sense of their advisors would suggest that the consequences of discovery are much worse than any possible benefits. Thus, any strings attached to a gift are likely to be vague and cloudy, subject to all sorts of interpretations.

Once a President assumes office, he is in a much stronger bargaining position. Contributors are likely to need him much more than he will need them; he can do more to affect their fortunes than they can to affect his. A President may at that point refuse to acknowledge any alleged agreement of policy concessions in return for contributions. Wealthy contributors frequently give to both parties and, in any case, are often found on opposite sides of public issues. For candidates to give in to one of them may simply incur the wrath of others.

A decline in contributions from one source may be made up by funds from another. The President's need to gain or maintain support from the voters, the limits placed on his powers of decision by what Congressmen, bureaucrats, and interest groups will accept, his own preferences, all serve to place drastic limits on benefits contributors get from campaign contributions. In brief, money simply becomes much less important to the things a President needs to do while he is in office. Contributors may be heard to complain in the hurt tones of Henry C. Frick, who after visiting Theodore Roosevelt at the White House, said, "We

bought the son of a bitch and then he did not stay bought." [57]
The foregoing analysis should help to explain why Presidential
politicians do not "stay bought" whatever their debt to their
financial supporters.

Though it is true that the parties usually seem to raise enough
money to get by, finding money is likely to be a traumatic experience. There is a day-by-day scramble which must be enervating.
The Republicans are somewhat better off, not only because of
their ability to collect in the business community, but also
because they go about the task much more systematically than
do the Democrats. Personal solicitation has been found to be
the best method of collecting funds. So Republicans arrange for
comprehensive coverage on a local basis of all likely contributors,
and they have a good deal of central coordination which assures
that the national organization receives its share. Democratic
efforts are, to say the least, chaotic. Aside from the union strongholds, contractors, and textile people, they do not have a visible
group in many parts of the country whom they can count on to
give a little. Unlike the Republicans, they have not hired a
professional moneyraiser, sympathetic to their cause, who will
take on the job over a long period of time. [58] As a result, each
financial campaign tends to be run by different people who have
to start from the beginning. Experience is not accumulated as
it might be. When Adlai Stevenson was nominated in 1952, he
downgraded large contributions and appointed Beardsley Ruml
who tried to get most of what he needed from small contributions.
Ruml did get more than usual from that source but not nearly
enough. [59] Edwin Pauley, who raised funds for Truman, was an
oilman who had a wide acquaintanceship among men of wealth
and who was adroit in having his claims recognized by groups
like road builders and construction firms who could expect to
benefit from Democratic policies. Until the Kennedy campaign,
the Democrats continued to live, at best, from hand to mouth,
day to day, crisis to crisis. President Truman in 1948—few wished
to contribute to a sure loser—found himself stranded without

funds in the middle of Oklahoma on his campaign train. Where-upon the Governor and a few others on that train decided that this could not be allowed to continue and found the money. Again, the essential wherewithal was forthcoming but the attend-ant tension is hardly the best atmosphere in which to conduct a political campaign.[60] In 1964, "when Republican chances of vic-tory over Johnson were never rated much brighter than those of a snowflake in Austin," the Republicans raised more money than they had in any previous campaign. And, contrary to previous campaigns, the money came not from big business but primarily from "small donations sent in by hundreds of thousands of con-tributors, many of whom had never before contributed to a national campaign." The GOP collected 651,000 small, individual contributions in 1964.[61]

The fund-raising dinner has in recent years become a major source of money. To the accompaniment of rubbery chicken or, in the more affluent affairs, good steak, the well-heeled come to listen to exhortations at up to $1000 a plate. The advantages of this system to the parties are many. Attendance is visible. Those who do not come may be conspicuous by their absence. Those who wish to be regarded favorably by the parties' officeholders may decide that it is a good idea to come. Dinners are easy to organize, and a large profit is usually cleared. Such disadvantages as there may be to this system do not seem to accrue to the party coffers so much as to the party faithful. These loyal souls may, if fund-raising meals continue to proliferate, find it necessary to give up one of their expensive hobbies, politics or eating.

Control Over Information

Control over information is another major political resource. Information does many things besides help voters to change their minds—that rare phenomenon. It helps people keep in touch with the progress of the campaign, gives the party faithful indications of the effectiveness of their side, acquaints voters with the major arguments that the candidates are making. Information helps to guide and channel both the enthusiasm and content of participation, and therefore control over information and its dissemination is a significant political resource.

As we scan the major media of information it appears that, generally speaking, newspapers are a good deal more partisan in their straight news coverage than are the radio and television stations. A political party that feels discriminated against over the air can take its case to the Federal Communications Commission which may require the offending station to make a prompt restitution of the balance of coverage, on pain of removal of the station's license to broadcast.[62] There is no such legal limitation on the "freedom" of newspapers and magazines to be one-sided in the presentation of the news, and, indeed, it has again and again been discovered that the printed media avail themselves rather extensively of this freedom. Many newspapers enjoy monopoly positions in their communities, and most of the political information available comes from the press. For these reasons the character of press coverage of Presidential elections is a matter of strategic importance.

It will come as no surprise to regular readers of the newspapers to learn that partisanship in news coverage generally tends to favor that side which is most often endorsed editorially by the press, namely the Republicans. Repeated studies have shown that the Republicans are normally the favorite party of the newspaper executives who determine editorial policy in most newspapers. And they have also shown that whatever biases exist in news reporting, in the placing of stories in the papers, in the location and size of headlines, and so on systematically favor the Republicans.[63] Only the election of 1964 provides an exception. But even then, the Democrats had only a slight edge, with President Johnson supported by 440 of the daily newspapers in the *Editor and Publisher* survey to Goldwater's 359. [64]

Yet, paradoxically, Democratic candidates for President do not seem to be harmed excessively by pro-Republican sentiments in the press, even among voters who rely heavily upon newspapers as sources of civic information. In recent decades Democrats like Franklin Roosevelt, Harry Truman, and John F. Kennedy have gained office despite the fact that a vast majority of the press, sometimes approaching 90% in terms of circulation, was against them. Turning to issues, we discover that many controversial programs like medical care for the aged, public power, and federally-aided housing are much more favored by the citizenry than by the newspapers.[65]

Two possible ways of explaining this anomaly suggest themselves. Perhaps the press is not primarily concerned with politics, or perhaps there are slips in communication between what a newspaper wants its readers to do, the readers' perception of these desires, and the readers' eventual action at the polls. We shall examine these factors in order to arrive at an appraisal more consistent with the behavior we observe in the press and at the polls.

The days of the crusading editor who owned his own paper and used it as a vehicle to propagate his own political doctrines are largely gone. In our time, newspapers with substantial circulations are much more likely to be part of a corporate chain devoted primarily to making money for their stockholders.[66] The costs of publication are high. In order to show a profit, papers must have a substantial circulation and a good deal of advertising. This is difficult to achieve in the midst of competition among several papers and accounts for the trend toward consolidation. Reader attention is gained by emphasizing stories with high human interest appeal—sports, crime, local personalities, and the high jinks of movie stars. Political news, though it does have a place, is subordinate because most readers are not terribly interested in politics. An excessive emphasis upon public affairs, therefore, is unlikely so long as appeal to readers is a prime consideration. This factor certainly has drawbacks for civic education. But for present purposes, it means that the possibilities for political propaganda are much less than they otherwise might be, because public affairs do not get much space.[67] Advertising is gained by convincing businessmen that it will pay them in terms of increased sales. The periodic appeals of conservatives requesting business-men to place or withhold advertising as a form of political coercion usually fall on deaf ears, because the motives of those who pay are commercial rather than political. Both the paper and its advertisers are likely to shy away from many forms of political controversy; it tends to make enemies rather than friends and is commonly believed to be "bad for business." The result is that much of the time newspapers are rather bland. Such political opinions as they do express are watered down so as not to give offense. Their political opinions, far from being their central concerns, tend to be sporadic and aimless, rather than representing a coherent political ideology.[68]

These tendencies are strengthened by a prevailing belief that papers ought to be nonpartisan in their news stories and present both sides of the issues of the day. However much the norm of impartiality may be honored in the breach, it provides a standard which serves to some extent to hold down partisanship. More than that, the belief that it is a newspaper's function to report what happens rather than to editorialize in its news columns has many other attractions for editors. It enables them to escape to some extent from the hostilities engendered by political contro-versy; it lessens problems of editorial judgment, thus decreasing the amount of work they have to do; it enables them to select items that they think will enhance their readership; it provides editors with a rationale for defending themselves against the charge of giving too much prominence to causes and candidates which may be unpopular with advertisers or some influential readers. This norm leaves the papers open to manipulation by political strategists who can create sensational news stories. During the heyday of Senator McCarthy, for example, newspaper-men slowly became aware of the extent to which they had aided him by publicizing his charges, because they were "news," rather than ignoring or carefully evaluating them.[69] During Presidential campaigns, application of the same standard gives the candidate who is opposed by newspapers the opportunity to enter at least some of its news stories because whatever he says is "news." If he should be an incumbent, his exposure will be greater because the President of the United States, as the outstanding public official and symbol of the nation, gets attention for the smallest things that he and his family do.

The desire to cut costs has at least one consequence favorable for increased impartiality in news stories. There is today increasingly greater reliance on material put out by the giant news services, the Associated Press, United Press International, and to some extent the New York *Times*, Los Angeles *Times*, Washington *Post*, and Chicago *Daily News* news services. These news-gathering agencies serve an exceedingly wide clientele which includes a broad spectrum of opinion. They are instructed, therefore, to prepare stories which will prove acceptable to various shades of opinion.[70] Presenting what happened with a minimum of slanted commentary is a good way to do this, though the wire services are by no means perfect in this respect. The final product, however, is closer to the canons of impartiality than would be the case if each paper prepared stories in accordance with its editorial position.

While it remains true that candidates favored by newspapers receive better treatment and somewhat greater coverage than others, there is one compensating factor in Presidential campaigns which has not received the attention it deserves. If the papers are generally conservative and Republican, political correspondents are comparatively more liberal and Democratic.[71] The stories they send, though subject to the mercies of the rewrite man in the home office, serve to a certain extent to redress the balance on the paper. This is particularly the case in the rather subtle question of how candidates are portrayed. The feeling that some candidates are more responsive, more open, more friendly, more intelligent than others may get communicated through little human interest stories and result in an impression contrary to that preferred by the owners of the paper. Such appeared to be the case with John F. Kennedy, who was popular with the reporters; and the extra attention he received resulted in complaints from Richard Nixon, who was not so popular with them.[72]

Dependent upon business interests for advertising and devoted pretty much to the status quo, most papers usually endorse Republican candidates and favor them in editorials and (to a lesser but real extent) in their news columns. However bland this advocacy has become, it certainly has existed in all recent elections except 1964.[73] But it is a far cry from acknowledging this situation to a conclusion that citizens are actually influenced in their opinions and voting choices by the newspapers they take. We use the word "take" advisedly because the fact that a newspaper enters a home is no guarantee that its political news and editorials will be read. Most people pay little enough attention to politics; they often read nothing or just scan the headlines without taking away much of an impression. Analyses of tons of newspaper clippings showing political propaganda by newspapers means nothing insofar as the effect is concerned if these stories are never read.

When stories and editorials are perused with some care, the reader's perception of what has been written may differ markedly from the intentions of the writer on the newspaper. An editorial may not be clear in intent, particularly if it is hedged by qualifications or watered down to minimize offense as is often the case. Frequently, the reader pays attention only to those parts of the piece which substantiate his own opinions. Opinion studies have demonstrated the remarkable capacity of people to filter out what they do not wish to hear and come away with quite a different impression than an objective analysis of an editorial or article would warrant. Indeed, the reader may interpret the story to mean precisely the opposite of what it intends; a criticism of Harry Truman for being vituperative, for example, could be taken as a commendation of his fighting spirit.[74]

Stories and editorials may be interpreted as they were meant to be and still be rejected as invalid. There is a great deal of suspicion of the press in the United States. Party identification is so powerful a force that it is likely to overwhelm most anything a paper says. Obviously, millions of citizens have no difficulty remaining and voting Democratic while reading Republican newspapers. Group loyalties are another force which may lead to rejection of opinions in newspapers. Face-to-face groups in unions, on the job, in fraternal, religious, and ethnic organizations may generate opinions of their own. If these differ from those in the newspaper, the members of the groups are provided with defense against the persuasion of the press. Group pressures of this kind are likely to be far more influential than what is written in a paper. The group may also reinforce what the paper says, but this represents an intensification rather than a change of opinion.[75]

No doubt the monopoly position of most newspapers in local communities makes the dissemination of opposing views more difficult than it might be in the presence of competition from a newspaper of a different outlook. But there are ways of getting around this. Other publications may enter the home: magazines and pamphlets which are religious, ethnic, union, fraternal, and even political in their focus, and these may contain contrary notions of public policy and candidate preference. True, only a relatively few persons read the political magazines. But these people are likely to be opinion leaders, people who take an active interest in public affairs and who are looked up to by others for advice. The availability, therefore, of little magazines of many shades of opinion permits the opinion leaders to receive and then disseminate information on a personal basis which may counteract whatever is in a newspaper.

Consider a puzzle concerning the political impact of the New York *Daily News,* a sensational tabloid with a circulation in the millions. It is apparent that if those who read the *News* had voted against Franklin D. Roosevelt, as the paper repeatedly recommended in vitriolic terms, Roosevelt would certainly never have carried New York City by the huge margins he did. At the same time it seems strange that so many people who not only voted for but revered FDR in New York continued to read a newspaper whose editorials bitterly attacked their hero. The Democratic readers of the *News* apparently managed to get the best of both possible worlds. They read the paper they liked and voted for the man they favored without noticing the apparent contradiction—because, for them, there was no contradiction. They either did not pay attention to the editorials, or blocked out the unfavorable ones completely, or interpreted them to mean something favorable to FDR. Voting studies document instances where people who wanted to vote for Harry Truman in 1948 convinced themselves that the incumbent President was against price controls; some people who preferred Dwight Eisenhower in 1956 apparently had no difficulty in believing that he surely favored medical care for the aged.[76]

Or, let us consider the case of the opposite of the New York *Daily News*, the good, gray, sober, responsible New York *Times*. After the *Times* came out for John F. Kennedy in the closing weeks of the 1960 Presidential campaign, various political pundits speculated as to the probable impact of the fact of this endorsement by so august and respectable a source. Our theory about voting behavior would lead us to be wary of claiming much influence for the *Times*, not because its readership was too indifferent to heed this call to reason but because of the kind of people who read this paper. One has to be terribly interested in politics to read through the *Times* as far as the editorial page. People who read that far are among the small, interested minority who comprise the core of the strong party identifiers. Precisely because of their interest, they are likely to identify with a major party and to be resistant to changing their allegiance. A call from the *Times*, therefore, however respectable, could hardly shake these devoted party people in their fundamental loyalty. The vacillating, the doubtful, and the uninformed who cannot make up their minds are far more likely to read *True Confessions* or *Modern Romance* than the New York *Times* with its surfeit of news about seemingly dull political events.

What, then, is the significance of newspapers in Presidential campaigns? We have suggested that the press is by no means immensely influential. Its major importance probably lies in two directions: presenting some kind of information about the candidates and the campaign to its readers, and intensifying the predispositions held by people who tend to agree with the paper's preferences. If one asked the candidates, they would undoubtedly prefer to have the press on their side instead of against them. But they can and do win in the face of opposition from the press. It may be that the newspaper a person reads subtly conditions his attitudes in ways now unsuspected, and that this has some effect on his opinions and voting choice.[77] There is no evidence, however, to indicate that this point has much force in Presidential elections, and evidence does exist which suggests severe limits to what newspapers can do. Undoubtedly, whatever impact the press has varies enormously with circumstances. Against a well-known and immensely popular President like Franklin Roosevelt in 1936 or Lyndon Johnson in 1964, with substantial publicity resources of his own, the impact of the press may be negligible. Against a little-known candidate like Adlai Stevenson in 1952, the attitudes communicated by the press— say, aloofness, over-intellectuality, indecisiveness—may be more significant. Yet we know from voting studies that in 1952 Stevenson was favorably regarded by Democrats who identified him with his party.[78] Perhaps the press counts for more on issues that are relatively far removed from the direct experience of the voters, such as corruption in government (where voters are prepared to believe the worst), and which may be blown out of proportion by hostile coverage. But the sheer number of different issues which may become relevant during a Presidential campaign, especially if they are "pocketbook" issues that are grasped with relative ease by voters, may also neutralize the influence of the press.

The Presidency

The Presidency is one resource which, in any given election year, must of necessity be monopolized by one party or the other. When an incumbent President seeks re-election, he enjoys many special advantages by virtue of his position. He is, to begin with, much better known than any challenger can hope to be. Everything the President does is news and is widely reported in all the media of information. The issues to which the President devotes his attention are likely to become the national issues because of his unique visibility and capacity to center diffused public attention on matters he deems important. To this extent, he is in a position to focus public debate on issues he deems most advantageous. The President can act and thereby gain credit. Should he face a crisis in foreign affairs, and these are many, he can gain by doing well or by calling on the patriotism of the citizenry to support its Chief Executive when the nation is in danger. An example of this occurred during the 1964 campaign, when United States vessels in the Bay of Tonkin were fired upon, and President Johnson took to the airwaves to promise rigorous defensive measures. In late July, just before the incident, he attracted 59% of the voters to 31% for Goldwater; in early August, just after the incident, the President's score went up to 65%, and Goldwater's declined to 29%.[79]

As the symbol of the nation, the President can travel and make "nonpolitical" speeches to subtly advance his candidacy, while his opponent is open to charges of "blind partisanship" in what are becoming unceasingly troubled times. Should his opponent claim that he can do a better job, the President need hardly make the obvious response that he is the only candidate who has had experience in a job for which there exists no completely appropriate prior training.

The life of the incumbent, however, is not necessarily one of undiluted joy. If the economic situation takes a turn for the worse, if a race riot erupts, if another nation comes under Communist influence, he is likely to be blamed as the man who was in office at the time. Whether he is really to blame or not, whether or not any man could possibly deal with an intractable world in the realm of foreign policy, he is deemed responsible and has to take the consequences. His opponent can to some extent permit himself to be irresponsible or carried away by exuberance. The President cannot detach himself from office while campaigning, however, and he must recognize that other nations are listening when he makes statements. The President's very superiority of information may turn out to be a handicap as he cannot make certain statements or reveal his sources for others without committing a breach of security. His opponent can attack his record, but the incumbent may have difficulty finding a comparable record to assail on the other side.

Yet the incumbent President's advantages are probably sufficient to overcome these disabilities; it is the candidate who seeks to succeed an incumbent of his own party who suffers the most. His is the unhappy lot, as Nixon and Stevenson discovered, of getting the worst of all possible worlds. He suffers from both the disadvantages of having to defend an existing record and of being a new man. He cannot attack the administration in office without alienating the President and selling his own party short, and he cannot claim he has experience in office. It may be difficult for him to defend a record he did not make and may not wholly care for. His is the most difficult strategic problem of all the candidates.

CONVERTIBILITY OF RESOURCES

Clearly, the social framework within which Presidential election strategies must be pursued distributes advantages and disadvantages rather importantly between the parties.

We have attempted to explain why the unequal distribution of key resources such as money and control over information do not necessarily lead to election victories for the parties and candidates which possess and use most of these resources. Might there not, however, be a cumulative effect which would greatly assist those who possessed both more money and more control over information? This effect may exist but it could obviously not be of overwhelming importance since the Democrats, who are usually disadvantaged in these respects, have won most of the recent elections. We can suggest three reasons for Democratic strength despite these disadvantages. First, the Democrats are able to convert other resources into money and control over information thereby narrowing the gap during campaigns. Second, the Democrats have superior access to other important resources —especially the numerically dominant party identifications in the voting population—which may overwhelm the Republican superiority in money and control over the media of information. Third, the Democrats are better able in general to convert some resources into others than are their opponents.

Once the Democratic party assumed the Presidency in 1933 and held it for twenty years it was able to use the resource of official position to collect more campaign funds because contributors want access to the winner and to get greater news coverage because the President's activities are newsworthy no matter what his party. The alliance of the Democrats with the large industrial unions has, at times, meant that the party received contributions in the coin of personal labor in electioneering for which the Republicans had to lay out cash or do without. The superiority (perhaps the mere existence) of Democratic organizations in cities of large population, with strategic impact on the Electoral College, has sometimes led to the availability of election workers who did not have to be paid in cash—at least not during the campaign and not at all if the party lost the election. The appeals of the Democrats to ethnic, racial, and religious groups has meant that publications of these specialized groups might serve to offset the preponderant Republican orientation of the daily press.

The fact that the Democrats have approximately a three to

two lead over Republicans in party identification is perhaps the most effective resource in the Democratic arsenal, so effective, indeed, that it is apparently more than enough to compensate for whatever advantages the Republicans gain through wealth and the mass media. For unless the Republicans manage to do something special, the voters will elect a Democrat by following their usual partisan dispositions. To be sure, other things such as turnout, for example, are not always equal; otherwise the Republicans would never win. But with respect to sheer numbers of nominal supporters the Democrats are ahead at the start.

Implicit in these remarks is the proposition that the Democrats in our era are better able to convert their resources into success at the polls than are the Republicans. That is, the party identification of a significant majority of the electorate can more easily be turned into electoral victory than can money or control over information be turned to winning the allegiance of citizens to a different party. Party identification changes but slowly and changes significantly only under the impact of events in the society which profoundly affect the mass of citizens. No one really knows short of that how to go about changing the party identifications of masses of people in the same partisan direction.

The Republicans can use their advantage in turnout to overcome the Democratic advantage in party identification. They can try to make party identification seem less relevant at election time by putting up an attractive candidate who is "above" partisanship. They can capitalize on errors by Democrats or on dissatisfaction with a Democratic administration. No one can claim to predict the outcomes of elections yet to come; certainly we cannot. Nothing that has been said here means that a Republican might not win handily, as Eisenhower did in two particular elections. Speaking in terms of probabilities over several elections, however, it seems to us that the Democrats are likely to win more often than they lose.

SUMMARY

As politicians develop their strategies for winning nomination and election to the Presidency, they will have to keep in mind numerous facts that are given in their political environment, and probably not subject to change by anything they may do. Among these are the facts that:

1) Most voters are not sufficiently concerned with specific policies to change their votes in response to policy appeals.
2) Rather, they vote the way they do out of party habit.
3) They may or may not *turn out* in great numbers, however, and therefore it is necessary to activate intermediary organizations and party activists in order to help turn out one's own voters.
4) Parties seek to win elections as their major goal.
5) Either party has a reasonably good chance to win the election: the Democrats because they are in the majority; the Republicans because they are much more likely to turn out, and because they have better access to money and greater sympathy in the press.
6) Intermediary organizations such as interest groups and party organizations can be activated by policy commitments and reaffirmations and promises of access to governmental decision-making.
7) Each of the parties consists of a loose coalition of interest groups and state and local parties.
8) The Electoral College puts a premium on votes from large two-party states.

Most or all of these basic facts are well understood by Presidential candidates and their managers. They understand that getting nominated and getting elected present two separate, though interrelated, problems. Let us now see what sorts of political strategies they devise to master these problems.

NOTES

1. In a major work on public opinion, V. O. Key, Jr. states, "For most Americans issues of politics are not of central concern. . . ." At another point Key summarizes the literature as follows: "In analysis after analysis of opinions on specific issues, sizable proportions of persons have been shown to lack an opinion." *Public Opinion and American Democracy* (New York, 1961), pp. 47, 185. When asked "What things are you most concerned with these days?" two out of three people in a representative sample of registered voters in New Haven, Connecticut, spoke of personal matters like jobs, health, and children. Only one out of five cited local, state, national, or international affairs. Robert A. Dahl, *Who Governs?* (New Haven, 1961), p. 279. A similar survey conducted in Oberlin, Ohio, shows that only 17% of a random (but representative) sample say that they are concerned with public affairs. Aaron B. Wildavsky, *Leadership in a Small Town* (Totowa, N. J., 1964). Further supporting evidence may be found in Julian L. Woodward and Elmo Roper, "Political Activity of American Citizens," *American Political Science Review* 44 (December 1950), 872–875, and Samuel Stouffer, *Communism, Conformity and Civil Liberties* (Garden City, 1955), Chapter 3. Using data from the Survey Research Center, Philip E. Converse estimates that those who are strongly ideological number about 3.5% of the voting population, and those who have some ideological capacities number no more than 12%. He finds that 17.5% of the population have attitudes with no issue content whatsoever, that 45% concentrate on matters of some immediate group interest, and that 22% are concerned largely with something in the nature of the times. See his article on "The Nature of Belief Systems in Mass Politics," in *Ideology and Discontent*, ed. David E. Apter (New York, 1964), pp. 206–261. See especially the table and commentary on p. 218.

2. See Angus Campbell, Philip E. Converse, Warren E. Miller, and Donald E. Stokes, *The American Voter* (New York, 1960), pp. 89–115. Writing of the 1956 Presidential election, for example, the authors say that "the rate of turnout among persons of high interest exceeded that among persons of low interest by nearly 30 per

cent . . ." (p. 102). See also Gordon M. Connelly and Harry M. Field, "The Non-Voter—Who He Is, What He Thinks," *Public Opinion Quarterly* 8 (Summer 1944), 175–187. The work of Angus Campbell and his associates at the University of Michigan's Survey Research Center, to which we will refer again, is based on numerous sample surveys of the entire American voting population. These studies, which have been going on since 1948, have through the years increased in breadth and sophistication and at the moment represent the largest pool of data we have on the political habits of Americans. The work of Paul Lazarsfeld, Bernard Berelson, and their associates at the Columbia Bureau of Applied Social Research has been going on since 1940. Rather than national sample surveys, the BASR group has collected data of a more focused kind, often limited to a single community. The BASR group pioneered in the use of panel surveys, which consist of series of re-interviews with a sample of respondents. For a description and critique of these and other materials we shall be using, see Peter H. Rossi, "Four Landmarks in Voting Research," in *American Voting Behavior*, eds. Eugene Burdick and Arthur J. Brodbeck (Glencoe, 1959), Chapter 1.

3. Bernard Berelson, Paul F. Lazarsfeld, and William N. McPhee, *Voting* (Chicago, 1954), p. 25; Campbell *et al.*, *The American Voter*, pp. 475–483; Key, *Public Opinion and American Democracy*, pp. 195–199.

4. Campbell *et al.*, *The American Voter*, pp. 120–145. Robert E. Lane concludes, "Over the long run party identification has more influence over a person's vote decision than any other single factor. . . ." *Political Life* (Glencoe, 1959), p. 300.

5. The authors of *The American Voter* write that in comparison to habitual party identifiers, ". . . Independents tend as a group to be somewhat less involved in politics. They have somewhat poorer knowledge of the issues, their image of the candidates is fainter, their interest in the campaign is less, their concern over the outcome is relatively slight, and their choice between competing candidates . . . seems much less to spring from discoverable evaluations of the elements of national politics." (Campbell *et al.*, p. 143.) See also Berelson *et al.*, *Voting*, pp. 25–27, and, for a somewhat different treatment, Robert Agger, "Independents and Party Identifiers," in *American Voting Behavior*, eds. Burdick and Brodbeck, Chapter 17.

6. Berelson *et al.*, *Voting*, pp. 215–233. George Belknap and Angus Campbell state that "for many people Democratic or Republican attitudes regarding foreign policy result from conscious or unconscious adherence to a perceived party line rather than from influences independent of party identification." "Political Party Identification and Attitudes Toward Foreign Policy," *Public Opinion Quarterly* 15 (Winter 1951–52), 623. Campbell and his associates speak of "the electorate's profound loyalty to the existing parties. Our [Survey Research Center] studies regularly have shown that three-quarters of the adult population grants outright its allegiance to the Republican or Democratic Party and that most of those who call themselves Independents acknowledge some degree of attachment to one of the parties. These partisan identifications . . . appear highly resistant to change." (Campbell *et al.*, *The American Voter*, pp. 552–553.)

7. The various voting studies previously cited all contain substantial discussions of this subject. See, especially, Robert E. Lane, "Fathers and Sons: Foundations of Political Belief," *American Sociological Review* 24 (August 1959), 502–511; Campbell *et al.*, *The American Voter*, pp. 146–147; H. H. Remmers, "Early Socialization of Attitudes," in *American Voting Behavior*, eds. Burdick and Brodbeck, pp. 55–67. Key, *Public Opinion and American Democracy*, pp. 293–314, sums up in these words: "Children acquire early in life a feeling of party identification; they have sensitive antennae and since they are imitative animals, soon take on the political color of their family . . ." (p. 294); see, especially, Fred I. Greenstein, *Children and Politics* (New Haven, 1965), Chapter 4.

8. ". . . People are more likely to associate with people like themselves—alike in political complexion as well as social position." (Berelson *et al.*, *Voting*, p. 83.)

9. Paul Lazarsfeld, Bernard Berelson, and Hazel Gaudet, *The People's Choice* (New York, 1944), pp. 16–28.

10. *Ibid.*; Angus Campbell and Homer C. Cooper, *Group Differences in Attitudes and Votes* (Ann Arbor, 1956); Woodward and Roper, "Political Activity of American Citizens," 872–875; Key, *Public Opinion and American Democracy*, pp. 99–120, 121–181; Berelson *et al.*, *Voting*, pp. 54–76. Unfortunately, Moses Rischin, *Our Own Kind* (Santa Barbara, 1960), has Presidential data only from the unusual Eisenhower elections.

11. V. O. Key, Jr., *Southern Politics* (New York, 1950), pp. 75–81, 223–228, 280–285.

12. V. O. Key, Jr., "A Theory of Critical Elections," *The Journal of Politics* 17 (February 1955), 3–18; Campbell *et al.*, *The American Voter*, p. 160. See, more generally, James Q. Wilson, *Negro Politics* (Glencoe, 1960).

13. See Duane Lockard, *New England State Politics* (Princeton, 1959); Dahl, *Who Governs?* pp. 33–51, 216–217; Elmer E. Cornwell, "Party Absorption of Ethnic Groups: The Case of Providence, R. I.," *Social Forces* 38 (March 1960), 205–210; J. Joseph Huthmacher, *Massachusetts People and Politics* (Cambridge, Mass., 1959), pp. 118–126.

14. Samuel Lubell, *The Future of American Politics* (New York, 1951), pp. 129–157.

15. Campbell *et al.*, *The American Voter*, pp. 55–57, 525–528, 537; Herbert H. Hyman and Paul B. Sheatsley, "The Political Appeal of President Eisenhower," *Public Opinion Quarterly* 19 (Winter 1955–56), 26–39.

16. The portions of this analysis which deal with voters and issues are taken from Chapter 8, "Public Policy and Political Preference," in Campbell *et al.*, *The American Voter*, pp. 168–187.

17. In a methodologically excellent national sample survey conducted in 1954 which was designed to discover the concerns of the American people on subjects relating to Communism and civil liberties, Samuel Stouffer found: "The number of people who said that they were worried either about the threat of Communists in the U. S. or about civil liberties was, even by the most generous interpretation of occasionally ambiguous responses, *less than 1 per cent*. Even world problems, including the shadow of war, did not evoke a spontaneous answer from more than 8 per cent." (Stouffer, *Communism, Conformity and Civil Liberties*, p. 59.) See Hazel Gaudet Erskine, "The Polls: The Informed Public," *Public Opinion Quarterly* 26 (Winter 1962), 669–677. This article summarizes questions asked since 1947 of national samples of Americans designed to ascertain their information on current news topics. Similar data for 1935–46 are contained in Hadley Cantril and Mildred Strunk, *Public Opinion, 1935–1946* (Princeton, 1951).

18. The data on which this conclusion is based refer to issues in

rather general categories such as "economic aid to foreign countries," "influence of big business in government," and "aid to education." (Campbell *et al., The American Voter*, p. 182.) It is highly probable that the proportion of people meeting the three requirements would be substantially reduced if the precise and specific policies within these general issue categories formed the basis of questions in a survey.

19. The authors of *The American Voter* tentatively conclude that in the Eisenhower years, covered by their study, "people who paid little attention to politics were contributing very disproportionately to partisan change." (Campbell *et al.*, p. 264.)

20. Philip E. Converse, "Information Flow and the Stability of Partisan Attitudes," *Public Opinion Quarterly* 26 (Winter 1962), 578–599.

21. V. O. Key, Jr., with the assistance of Milton C. Cummings, Jr., *The Responsible Electorate: Rationality in Presidential Voting, 1936–1960* (Cambridge, Mass., 1966).

22. Campbell *et al., The American Voter*, pp. 153–160; Key, "A Theory of Critical Elections," 3–18. Stouffer, *Communism, Conformity and Civil Liberties*, p. 87, says that Americans are concerned not with world problems, but with personal problems. He adds, "a 'business recession' finds a path into almost every home—whether it is that of a factory worker or that of a butcher who finds his sales of meat declining. It becomes a threat that is immediate and personal."

23. Key asserts that "as has been demonstrated, the citizen's identification with party tends to produce a tie consistent with his policy preferences." (*Public Opinion and American Democracy*, p. 460.) See also Lazarsfeld *et al., The People's Choice*, Chapter 9.

24. This notion is developed by Anthony Downs, *An Economic Theory of Democracy* (New York, 1957).

25. See Raymond A. Bauer, Ithiel de Sola Pool, and Lewis Anthony Dexter, *American Business and Public Policy* (New York, 1963), pp. 323–399, especially p. 373.

26. See Seymour M. Lipset, Paul F. Lazarsfeld, Allen H. Barton, and Juan Linz, "The Psychology of Voting: An Analysis of Political Behavior," in *Handbook of Social Psychology*, ed. Gardner Lindzey (Cambridge, Mass., 1954).

27. This discussion is drawn largely from Aaron B. Wildavsky,

"The Intelligent Citizen's Guide to the Abuses of Statistics: The Kennedy Document and the Catholic Vote," *Politics and Social Life*, eds. Nelson W. Polsby, Robert A. Dentler, and Paul A. Smith (Boston, 1963), pp. 825–844. See also Thomas Flinn, "How Nixon Took Ohio," *Western Political Quarterly* 15 (June 1962), 276–279; Philip E. Converse, Angus Campbell, Warren E. Miller, and Donald E. Stokes, "Stability and Change in 1960: A Reinstating Election," *American Political Science Review* 55 (June 1961), 269–280; Andrew R. Baggaley, "Religious Influence on Wisconsin Voting, 1928–1960," *American Political Science Review* 56 (March 1962), 66–70; and Rischin, *Our Own Kind.*

28. See Ithiel de Sola Pool, Robert P. Abelson, and Samuel L. Popkin, *Candidates, Issues, and Strategies* (Cambridge, Mass., 1964), pp. 117–118.

29. *Ibid.,* pp. 68, 117–118.

30. Baggaley, "Religious Influence on Wisconsin Voting, 1928–1960," 66–70.

31. Converse, Campbell, Miller, and Stokes, "Stability and Change in 1960: A Reinstating Election," 269–280.

32. See Wildavsky, in Polsby *et al., Politics and Social Life,* pp. 825–844.

33. At least a quarter of a million Jews and over a million Negroes live in Illinois. Over a million Negroes live in Texas, and 174,387 of them are registered to vote according to the U.S. Civil Rights Commission. ("Voting," *1961 U. S. Commission on Civil Rights Report,* 301.) The conclusion is far from implausible.

34. "Access" is the opportunity to press claims upon decision-makers. This does not imply that those who have more access are more successful in pressing their claims, but it is generally supposed that claims have a better chance of realization when they are presented repeatedly and auspiciously to decision-makers, and by "known" rather than "unknown" claimants. See David B. Truman, *The Governmental Process* (New York, 1951), pp. 264–270.

35. Our interpretation of parties is based largely on Pendleton Herring, *The Politics of Democracy* (New York, 1940); V. O. Key, Jr., *Politics, Parties and Pressure Groups,* 4th ed. (New York, 1958); David B. Truman, "Federalism and the Party System," in *Federalism Mature and Emergent,* ed. Arthur Macmahon (New York, 1955),

Chapter 8; Anthony Downs, *An Economic Theory of Democracy;* and a burgeoning literature (some of it already cited) on state and local political party organizations. See, especially, Truman, *The Governmental Process,* pp. 262–287.

36. Herring, *The Politics of Democracy,* especially pp. 272–287. See also, Edward C. Banfield, *Political Influence* (New York, 1961).

37. The structure of American political parties is treated, among other places, in Key, *Politics, Parties and Pressure Groups;* Hugh A. Bone, *American Politics and the Party System* (New York, 1955); and William Goodman, *The Two-Party System in the United States* (New York, 1956).

38. See Warren E. Miller, "Presidential Coattails: a Study in Political Myth and Methodology," *Public Opinion Quarterly* 19 (Winter 1955–56), 26–39.

39. William S. Livingston, "A Note on the Nature of Federalism," *Political Science Quarterly* 67 (March 1952), 81–95.

40. See Robert R. Alford, *Party and Society* (Chicago, 1963), Chapter 6, "The United States: The Politics of Diversity." This re-analysis of a variety of surveys suggests that class-oriented voting in the United States, while it exists, does not polarize voters to the extent that can be found in Great Britain or Australia.

41. Herbert McClosky, Paul J. Hoffman, and Rosemary O'Hara, "Issue Conflict and Consensus Among Party Leaders and Followers," *American Political Science Review* 54 (June 1960), 406–427. The authors, who compared large samples of Democratic and Republican leaders on twenty-four major public issues, conclude that "the belief that the two American parties are identical in principle and doctrine has little foundation in fact. Examination of the opinions of Democratic and Republican leaders shows them to be distinct communities of co-believers who diverge sharply on many important issues." They add, "Little support was found for the belief that deep cleavages exist among the electorate but are ignored by the leaders. One might, indeed, more accurately assert the contrary, to wit: that the natural cleavages between the leaders are largely ignored by the voters" (pp. 425–426).

42. Key, *Public Opinion and American Democracy,* p. 439, observes, "Of Democratic high participators . . . only 34 per cent fall into white-collar occupations; of the Republican group comparable in

political activity, 48 per cent are from white-collar occupations. Substantially more Democratic than Republican high participators are blue-collar workers. Occupational differences between the party identifiers become more marked as level of political participation increases."

43. The unit rule is not prescribed in the Constitution or by Federal law. Rather, it is the result of individual state action which provides, in all states, that Electors for party nominees are grouped together and elected *en bloc*, on a "general ticket" such that a vote for one Elector is a vote for all the Electors on that ticket, with the majority vote electing all Electors for the state. Senator Thomas Hart Benton said in 1824, "The general ticket system . . . was the offspring of policy. . . . It was adopted by the leading men of [ten states] to enable them to consolidate the vote of the state. . . ."

Thomas Jefferson had earlier pointed out that ". . . while ten states choose either by legislatures or by a general ticket it is folly and worse than folly for the other states not to do it." In short, once a few states maximized their impact by using the unit rule, the others followed suit. See *Motion for Leave to File Complaint, Complaint and Brief, Delaware v. New York*, No. 28 Original, U.S. Supreme Court, October term, 1966; and Neal R. Peirce, "The Electoral College Goes to Court," *The Reporter*, October 6, 1966.

44. The 1960 figures are:

Alaska: 50,773 votes, three electoral votes, or, one electoral vote for every 16,924 voters;

New York: 7,258,921 votes, 45 electoral votes, or, one electoral vote for every 161,309 voters;

California: 6,506,578 votes, 32 electoral votes, or, one electoral vote for every 203,330 voters.

45. For 1960 figures, see Herbert E. Alexander, *Financing the 1960 Election* (Princeton, 1962), p. 10. Figures for 1964 are contained in Herbert E. Alexander and Harold B. Meyers, "The Switch in Campaign Giving," *Fortune* (November 1965), 103–108.

46. Alexander Heard, *The Costs of Democracy* (Chapel Hill, 1960), pp. 7–8; Herbert E. Alexander, "Financing the Parties and Campaigns," in *The Presidential Election and Transition, 1960–61*, ed. Paul T. David (Washington, 1961), pp. 116–118; Alexander and Meyers, "The Switch in Campaign Giving."

47. Heard, *The Costs of Democracy*, pp. 18–22, 39; Alexander, "Financing the Parties and Campaigns," p. 118; Alexander and Meyers, "The Switch in Campaign Giving."

48. Alexander and Meyers, "The Switch in Campaign Giving."

49. Alexander, "Financing the Parties and Campaigns," p. 117.

50. Heard, *The Costs of Democracy*, p. 6.

51. *Ibid.*, p. 41; Herbert E. Alexander, *Financing the 1964 Election* (Princeton, 1966), pp. 68–69.

52. Heard, *The Costs of Democracy*, pp. 49–53.

53. For expenditure figures, see *ibid.*, pp. 17–24 and, for 1960, see Alexander, *Financing the 1960 Election*, pp. 9–13. The following table is adapted from figures in both these books.

	Democratic Percentage of Two-Party Vote	*Democratic Percentage of Two-Party Expenditures*
1932	59	49
1936	62	41
1940	55	35
1944	52	42
1948	52	39
1952	44	45
1956	42	38
1960	50	45
1964	61	41

On the state level, our conclusion may not be correct, however. See Murray Levin and George Blackwood, *The Compleat Politician* (Indianapolis, 1962), pp. 227–243.

54. Alexander, "Financing the Parties and Campaigns," p. 119.

55. See Theodore H. White, *The Making of the President, 1960* (New York, 1961), pp. 71–74.

56. See *ibid.*, pp. 92–110 and Harry Ernst, *The Primary That Made a President: West Virginia, 1960* (New York, 1962), especially pp. 16–17, 29–31. Several factors appear to have contributed to Humphrey's difficulty in raising money. First and probably foremost, he had very little of his own to draw upon. Second, Adlai Stevenson was being indecisive. By refusing to withdraw himself, his backers were encouraged to wait and see rather than switch monetary

support to Humphrey. Had Stevenson not been in contention, Humphrey might have gotten more money. And third, Humphrey apparently was unwilling to do things which would severely alienate the other candidates or otherwise jeopardize his future associations in the party. He may, therefore, have been restrained from actions which would have aided him. A revealing passage in White (pp. 109–110) indicates what may have been involved.

> In New York, from which so much Stevenson money had originally come to Humphrey's coffers, Governor Abraham Ribicoff, acting on Kennedy's instructions, warned all Stevensonians that if they continued to finance the hopeless campaign of Hubert Humphrey, Adlai Stevenson would not even be *considered* for Secretary of State. Where necessary, Kennedy lieutenants were even rougher; in Connecticut, Boss John Bailey informed former Connecticut Senator William Benton . . . that if he continued to finance Humphrey (Benton had already given Humphrey $5,000 earlier in the spring), he would never hold another elective or appointive job in Connecticut. . . .

57. Jasper B. Shannon, *Money and Politics* (New York, 1959), p. 35.

58. Heard, *The Costs of Democracy*, pp. 212–232.

59. *Ibid.*, pp. 249–258.

60. See *ibid.* and Shannon, *Money and Politics,* p. 59. On pages 13–65, Shannon presents a colorful history of American experience in raising money for Presidential campaigns.

61. Alexander and Meyers, "The Switch in Campaign Giving," 103–108.

62. Television stations have few programs of news commentary and these are not usually overtly partisan. (To be sure, the wealthier party may buy more TV time for its candidate, but we have already discussed the real limitations of this resource.) Radio news commentary is more ubiquitous, but, as we know, only those who initially agree with commentators are likely to tune in regularly.

63. See Nathan B. Blumberg, *One-Party Press? Coverage of the 1952 Presidential Campaign in 35 Daily Newspapers* (Lincoln, Neb., 1954); Edwin Emery and Henry L. Smith, *The Press in America* (Englewood Cliffs, 1954), pp. 714 ff. Arthur Edward Rowse, *Slanted*

News: A Case Study of the Nixon and Stevenson Fund Stories (Boston, 1957).

64. *Editor and Publisher,* October 31, 1965, p. 5.

65. See, for an example on the local level, Dahl, *Who Governs?* pp. 77, 256–267.

66. A. J. Liebling, with characteristic pungency, puts the proposition this way: "With the years, the quantity of news in newspapers is bound to diminish from its present low. The proprietor, as Chairman of the Board, will increasingly often say that he would *like* to spend 75 cents now and then on news coverage, but that he must be fair to his shareholders." *The Press* (New York, 1961), p. 5.

67. Bernard C. Cohen, in *The Press and Foreign Policy* (Princeton, 1963) presents figures from a variety of sources on foreign affairs news (Chapter 4). His conclusion: "The volume of coverage is low."

68. Following is an example, atypical but illuminating, of this aimlessness at work. Former House Speaker Joseph Martin in his memoirs describes the appearance of an editorial mildly critical of Presidential candidate Thomas E. Dewey in Martin's own newspaper (Martin was editor and publisher) on the day of Dewey's arrival in Martin's hometown during the 1948 campaign. "Behind all this fuss was a very simple explanation. Having a small staff, the *Evening Chronicle* bought 'boilerplate' editorials prepared by a syndicate. The day of Dewey's visit, the editorial in question happened to be on top of the pile, and a man in the composing room slapped it into the paper. Ironically, he was one of the most ardent Dewey supporters in North Attleboro. As for myself, I never read the editorial until it was well on its way to fame." Joseph W. Martin, Jr., *My First Fifty Years in Politics* as told to Robert J. Donovan (New York, 1960), pp. 196–197.

69. See Richard Rovere, *Senator Joe McCarthy* (New York, 1959), pp. 137, 162–169.

70. See Frank Luther Mott, *The News in America* (Cambridge, Mass., 1952), p. 110 and Emery and Smith, *The Press in America,* pp. 541 ff.

71. See William L. Rivers, "The Correspondents After 25 Years," *Columbia Journalism Review* 1 (Spring 1962). On p. 5, he says, "In 1960, 57 per cent of the daily newspapers reporting to the *Editor and Publisher* poll supported Nixon, and 16 per cent supported

Kennedy. In contrast, there are more than three times as many Democrats as there are Republicans among the Washington newspaper correspondents; slightly more than 32 per cent are Democrats, and fewer than 10 per cent are Republicans. . . . More than 55 per cent of the correspondents for newspapers consider themselves liberals; 26.9 per cent consider themselves conservatives."

72. See White, *The Making of the President, 1960*, pp. 333–338. On Barry Goldwater's press relations, see Charles Mohr, "Requiem For a Lightweight," *Esquire* (August 1965), 67–71, 121–122.

73. See the findings previously cited in footnotes 63, 64, 70.

74. Elmo Roper has observed that "On the civil rights issue [in 1948], Mr. Dewey draws the support of voters favoring exactly opposite things, and more than that, each side thinks Dewey agrees with them." Bone, *American Politics and the Party System*, p. 447.

75. This paragraph summarizes the major findings of researchers on what has come to be called the "two-step flow" of information. See Elihu Katz and Paul F. Lazarsfeld, *Personal Influence* (Glencoe, 1955).

76. Key, *Public Opinion and American Democracy*, p. 453.

77. An example would be in instances where candidates were not known to voters before the campaign, and where they ran without benefit of party labels, as in local nonpartisan elections. See Charles R. Adrian, "Some General Characteristics of Nonpartisan Elections," *American Political Science Review* 46 (September 1952), 766–776, Charles E. Gilbert and Christopher Clague, "Electoral Competition and Electoral Systems in Large Cities," *The Journal of Politics* 24 (May 1962), 323–349, especially p. 344.

78. Campbell, *et al.*, *The American Voter*, pp. 58, 530.

79. American Institute of Public Opinion Survey, released October 18, 1964. For other examples, see Nelson W. Polsby, *Congress and the Presidency* (Englewood Cliffs, 1964), p. 26.

Chapter 2

The Nominating Process

Nᴀᴛɪᴏɴᴀʟ ᴘᴀʀᴛʏ conventions are notoriously puzzling to casual observers, both foreign and domestic. The tumult and the shouting, the threats and bargains, the claims and counter-claims seem so confusing that it is tempting to say the events make little sense. It is, therefore, worthwhile to show that a great many convention practices and events can be related to basic rules and circumstances of American politics.[1] The observer who understands, for example, that parties generally look for a winner and that primaries, platforms, and demonstrations may perform important functions in communicating the strength of the various candidates, is in a much better position to appreciate what is happening than the person who attends only to the surface noise.

In our view the patterns of events at national conventions are largely a product of three factors: the goals of the politicians who do business there; the disparity between the information these politicians need in order to pursue their goals and the information at their disposal; and their power relationships. After a brief exposition of these factors, it will be possible for us to account for the strategies of the participants as they go about making the crucial choices which help determine the final outcomes.

STRATEGIC CONSIDERATIONS

Goals

The delegates to national party conventions are selected state by state, in conventions or primaries, or by a combination of the two methods.[2] They represent the outcomes of processes that are slightly different in their legal requirements and political overtones in each of the states, the District of Columbia, and the territories—all of which send delegations to both party conventions. But when delegates arrive at the convention, they enter into a social system in which their roles are reasonably regularized. Not surprisingly, they try to behave in a way that will maximize their political power. The rational dice player will place his bets in accordance with his chances of winning under the rules of the game he is playing. Similarly, the "rational" delegate will be expected to be reasonably well informed about how his behavior affects his chances of achieving his goals, and will behave in accordance with his information, his position in the game, and the goals he is intent upon achieving.

American national parties are loose federations of independent state parties representing somewhat different combinations of economic, ethnic, religious, sectional, and other interests. Therefore, the great search at most conventions is for "The Man Who Can Win," for without hope of victory, over the years there would be little reason for a heterogeneous party to stay together. Even if the parties were far more cohesive than they are today, they still could not disregard the need to get into office now and then by nominating a popular candidate.

The desire to nominate a winner is widespread, but it is not equally distributed among delegates. It is weaker among delegates with deep and intense policy commitments and stronger among those who are not so fiercely committed to specific policies. Since state parties represent various interests and live somewhat diverse lives, we find that they differ in the nature and intensity of their policy preferences. Within the Democratic party, for example, outside of the South, "Those states in which a powerful Democratic party organization predated Franklin Roosevelt tend to be moderate; those states in which the local Democratic party is a creation of the New Deal and of organized labor in politics tend to be the liberals." [3] Ideological divisions are even more pronounced within the Republican party. Certain states consistently vote for conservative candidates. "Of the 23 states that supported Taft in 1952 only one, North Dakota, failed to cast a majority of its votes for Goldwater twelve years later." [4] Along another dimension, the desire to nominate a winner is strongest among delegates from states with a high degree of party competition or where the party is weak. Both of these groups of delegates need a popular candidate, in close states to increase their vote, and in states where the party is weak to bring them some patronage. On the other hand, winners are least needed in areas where the party is overwhelmingly dominant, such as the South in the case of the Democrats, where local fortunes will continue to be good regardless of what happens in the national election. But the one-party areas have long since ceased to control the conventions and competition seems to be growing in many formerly one-party areas.[5]

Capitalizing on the understandable desire to nominate a winner, candidates seek to demonstrate that they can win and others cannot. Candidates cite polls and make complicated electoral analyses in order to convince delegates on this point. Frequently, there appear to be several strong candidates and disagreements about which one is the most probable winner often take place because the delegates have private preferences and lack enough information about what the voters are likely to do.[6]

Politicians seek to maintain or increase their own political power. In order to do so, most of them feel that they must, in general, increase the potential vote for candidates whom they sponsor. The more leaders who agree on a candidate and the more interest groups and state party organizations that are working for his election, the greater are the chances that he will win office and provide those politicians who supported him with access to political power. Party unity, therefore, is perceived by politicians as an important prerequisite to the achievement of victory. Unless party leaders achieve a consensus among themselves, the chances are diminished that they will be able to elect a President. Parties tend as a result to nominate candidates who at the least are not obnoxious to, and ideally are attractive to, as many interest groups and state party leaders as possible.[7] If winning becomes less important, or ideology more important, or both, the incentive to find a candidate with broad appeal will decline.

The members of each party may love their party on a sentimental basis. But do they love one another? The convention tests party unity by determining whether the disparate elements which make up each party can agree on one man to represent them— a man who cannot possibly be equally attractive to all of them. Party unity may aid in securing victory and this provides an incentive for keeping all the factions under the same party umbrella. But the differences among delegates may be so great that no one is quite sure whether they can agree. The much maligned party platform is exceedingly important in this regard not so much for what it makes explicit but for the fact that it is written at all. The platform tests and communicates the ability of the many party factions to agree on something, even if on some crucial points major differences have to be papered over.[8]

One of the important estimates which rival party leaders must make is how far they can go in attaining their preferences without completely alienating some faction, resulting in its withdrawal from the convention. This information may not be available until party factions begin to bargain at the convention.

Delegates not only want to unify the party around a probable winner; they also want to make certain that they have a claim on him so that he will consider their requests favorably. Thus, they seek either a candidate who is known to be friendly to them, whose policy views tend to coincide with theirs, or who will be indebted to them because they have provided support toward his nomination. Jim Farley's famous list establishing priorities for distributing patronage—FRBC (For Roosevelt Before Chicago) —illustrates this point. It helps to explain the rush to get on the bandwagon by delegates who wish access to the winning candidate. But more than one bandwagon may appear to be in the making, and delegates and their political leaders may have difficulty deciding when the best time is to make the jump and gain the greatest bargaining advantages for themselves.

It must never be forgotten that delegates come from state parties with internal lives of their own. The delegates spend over 1400 days every four years as members of their state parties and less than a week at the national convention. To commit acts at the convention—supporting a candidate unpopular in that state, insisting on a unit rule for delegation voting against the intense opposition of a strong minority—which would lead to years of bitter internal rivalry would be unwise. Yet it is not always possible to avoid mistakes. Delegates may misjudge who will run well in their state and provide a "coattail effect." Sometimes nominees run better in states which opposed them at the convention than in those which gave them support.[9] In any event, it is clear that in order to interpret or predict a state's behavior one may have to know a great deal about internal party conditions. One of the first requirements imposed on any Presidential aspirant is that he acquire information on internal party affairs which may prove indispensable to planning his strategy and may enable him to take advantage of or to avoid dangerous party splits.

We have seen that some delegates have strong policy preferences. Negroes and Southerners may care deeply about racial questions. Union officials and industrial executives may be unwilling to support candidates presumed to be hostile to the interests they represent. Delegates from the District of Columbia may consider home rule to be of paramount importance while the men from Tennessee may be adamant about public power. There are consistent liberal and conservative blocs in both major parties. To some extent, therefore, intense policy preferences may restrict the actions of delegates who share them; they may seek the man who has the best chance of winning among those candidates who meet their specifications on crucial policies.

The major goal of the Presidential aspirant in the convention is to win the nomination; but in addition he rightly regards the nominating convention as the first part of the election campaign. This means that even while prospective candidates are belaboring one another in an attempt to get the nomination, they must give due consideration to the necessity for party unity in case they win. There are several ways in which this party unity is achieved. One device available to the winner of a contested nomination is to select the disappointed Presidential aspirant with the second most votes in the convention as a Vice-Presidential nominee, as Kennedy selected Lyndon Johnson in 1960.

Incumbent Presidents and other obvious choices, such as Richard Nixon in 1960, are in a better position to treat the convention as the opening gun of their campaign. They can participate wholeheartedly in the party rituals, the speech-making, informal social gatherings, and the self-congratulation that give the party faithful at the convention a sense of identity and mission, and project over television an image of unity, purpose, and togetherness. Such nominees also can manipulate the party platform to offset their real or imagined weaknesses with the electorate and to capitalize on their strengths. In contested conventions, the platform must be negotiated among representatives of the leading contenders and major segments of the party, and so it is less easy to write a platform that the eventual winner can comfortably campaign on.

Thus, we can describe quickly the major goals of most delegates to national conventions. They want to gain power, to nominate a man who can win the election, to unify the party, to obtain some claim on the nominee, to protect their central core of policy preferences, and to strengthen their state party organizations.

For example, "My most critical problem," Richard Nixon wrote, "was to see that our Convention ended with all Republicans united behind the ticket. If this were to be accomplished, I knew I had to take some decisive action with regard to Nelson Rockefeller. . . . My goal was to beat Kennedy—not Rockefeller. . . . I felt it was essential that he be an enthusiastic rather than a reluctant supporter of my candidacy after the Convention. His differences with [Eisenhower] Administration policies had to be ironed out." So Nixon took the initiative in meeting Rockefeller and from ten o'clock one evening until 4:30 the next morning they hammered out a joint statement.[10] Afterwards, Nixon was inevitably (and as it happens quite wrongly) accused of "selling out" to Rockefeller but this did not deter him in his search for party unity. As in so many other ways, Goldwater was different in this. We shall see in Chapter 4 that it could be said that he was against unity moves as a matter of principle.

Nixon, in 1960, also wanted a reasonably strong platform on civil rights which would reflect his views and not alienate Negro voters. As a result, he had a staff member draw up a lengthy statement of his own views. During the course of the discussions on the platform subcommittee dealing with civil rights, Nixon's spokesmen actively participated in the discussion and bargaining. When it began to look as if the subcommittee report would be most unsuitable, the Nixon staff contacted the leaders of state delegations from which the members came. Nevertheless, Nixon's views became the minority report of the subcommittee by an eight to seven vote. Finally, Nixon himself was called in. He spoke to members of the full platform committee, and his staff followed up seeking pledges of support. The Nixon draft won by a vote of 55 to 45.[11] Johnson's moves to insure unity at the 1964 Democratic Convention included naming Senator Hubert Humphrey to the Vice-Presidency in order to appease the liberals and compromising on the Mississippi Freedom Democratic Party challenge to the Mississippi delegation by seating the latter but allowing the former the status of observers.[12]

Uncertainty

It is far easier to describe goals than to attain them. The attainment of each participant's goal requires a great deal of information about the future. What will the electorate do at the polls months after the convention? Who will other delegates to the convention support and for how long? What will be the effect of initial declarations and switches of support on other delegates? What bargains can a particular candidate make? What will be the consequences of the nomination for one's state party?

Answers to these and other questions about pre-convention and convention events are characteristically difficult to obtain and uncertain at best. There are good reasons for this. The answers depend, first, on national and world conditions, which we have not learned how to predict—war, depression, inflation. To pick an extreme example, the candidate who appears likely to win in peacetime may not be able to command the support of the electorate during open warfare unless he happens to be the incumbent President. Second, the answers depend on a complex series of events involving the actions, reactions, and intentions of others. To obtain a claim on the winner, a delegate (or delegation) often must contribute to his support at the convention by guessing who will win in time to "get on the bandwagon." But a delegation's estimate of who will win may be determined, in part at least, by the estimate it makes about what other delegations are going to do. And their behavior, in turn, may be influenced by what still others do or say they are going to do. This situation may result in a self-fulfilling prophecy where a delegation's estimate of who is most likely to win leads to actions which influence others in the same direction and confirms its original expectation. A third difficulty in acquiring the necessary information results because delegates are required not merely to predict an isolated set of occurrences (although this would be difficult enough) but to gauge the outcome of complex chains of events. If nominee A receives support from delegation B and wins decisively in primary C, then he will be in a position to bargain with delegation D and to use this leverage to gain support from party leader E, which, in turn, will lead to the possibility of heading off rival nominee F, and so on.

There are some potentially reliable sources of information—primaries, polls, balloting on procedural motions or on the platform, successive nominating ballots, shifts by key delegations—which are avidly observed. But these publicly available indicators of what might happen in the future do not necessarily have meaning in themselves; they are given meaning by interested observers. Unless the significance attributed to the indicators is widely shared and clear beyond any doubt, so that one overwhelming favorite emerges, the delegate is still left with the troublesome problem of interpretation.

Many of the standard indicators may be perceived to be ambiguous. Did Senator John F. Kennedy emerge from the 1960 Wisconsin primary with a margin of *only* 100,000 votes, or did he win by *the substantial margin* of 100,000? [13] Perceptions (and hence interpretations) of identical indicators may vary widely depending on the delegate's predispositions, or on the amount of reinforcement or counter-interpretation to which he is subjected. Unless a delegate's interpretation of events coincides with those made by others, his predictions and the actions based on them may be invalidated. At best, the delegates swim in a sea of uncertainty.

The belief of delegates about what is happening determines the premises of many decisions. One report on this subject was made by Colonel Jack Arvey who led the forces in Illinois which wanted to draft Adlai Stevenson in the 1952 Democratic Convention.

> Cook County Chairman Joe Gill and I were having dinner . . . when one of our ward committeemen came running over

to tell us an important roll call vote was under way on the seating of Virginia. . . . Gill and I hurried back into the hall. Illinois had already been recorded 45–15 against seating Virginia. It suddenly dawned on us what was happening. The strategy of the Kefauver backers and the Northern liberal bloc was to try and make impossible demands on the Southern delegates so that they would walk out of the Convention. If the total Convention vote was thus cut down by the walkout of delegates who would never vote for Kefauver, then the Tennessee Senator would have a better chance of winning the nomination. Our Illinois delegation quickly huddled and then changed our vote to 52–8 in favor of seating Virginia.

The eight opposed included Senator Douglas and other backers of Kefauver.[14]

Now, whether or not Arvey correctly guessed the strategy of the Kefauver forces, this anecdote provides a vivid picture of the premises on which the action of the Stevenson group was based.

Power

A relatively few party leaders control the decisions of a large proportion of the delegates to conventions. Delegates to national conventions are chosen, after all, as representatives of the several state party organizations, apportioned according to a formula laid down by action of previous national conventions. While it is true that official decisions are made by a majority vote of delegates, American party organizations are centralized at state and local levels. This means that such hierarchical controls as actually exist on the state and local level will assert themselves in the national convention. Since the probabilities are fairly good that both major parties at any given time will have succeeded in electing a substantial number of Governors and Mayors of important cities, the chances are also fairly good that a substantial number of delegates will be controlled hierarchically. Some states, of course, may be badly split with no one holding the lever to much more than his own vote.[15]

And there are also cases when effective leadership is exercised by men who are not the highest elected officials. In 1956, for example, it was quite clear that party leader Carmine DeSapio had more to say about what the New York delegation did than did Governor Averell Harriman. Leadership in the state organization may belong to a national committeeman, a Congressman, a coalition of county officials, or an elder statesman.

The power of elected leaders over their state party organizations varies as well. Governor Dewey was able to wield virtually absolute control over the New York Republican delegation when he was in office.[16] Other Governors may be able to throw their votes to certain candidates but not to others because the delegates would not permit it. The delegation may agree to stick with its leader for a specified number of ballots and no further. Then internal bargaining may take place with the Governor acting as first among equals, but no more than that. The desire to maximize the delegation's bargaining power by maintaining a united position may cause a Governor to make concessions to some of his delegates.

Barring catastrophic events—depression, war, scandal—the President's power is most certainly strong enough to assure him of renomination within the limits imposed by the Anti-Third Term (the 22nd) Amendment to the Constitution. This is not merely because his is the greatest, most visible, office in the land with all sorts of patronage and other controls over potential delegates. There is, in addition, the fact that his party can hardly hope to win by repudiating him. To refuse him the nomination would, most politicians feel, be tantamount to confessing political bankruptcy or ineptitude.

The Presidential power over national conventions has historically extended to (1) the right to renomination, or to designate the party nominee, effectively exercised in seventeen of the nineteen conventions since the Civil War in which the President interested himself in the outcome; (2) the power to dictate the party platform; (3) the power to designate the officers of the convention; (4) the power to select many delegates—especially potent in the case of Republican delegations from the one-party Democratic South, where Republican Presidents, until the passage of the Hatch Act, drew upon a corporal's guard of Federal patronage appointees to man this sizable convention bloc.

The constitutional amendment limiting Presidents to two terms may eventually change the power of a two-term incumbent radically, but we doubt it. The party still must run on the Presidential record, and the outgoing President still seems likely to control the management of the convention. Before President Roosevelt broke the two-term tradition, outgoing Presidents controlled conventions even when no one expected them to run again. And President Truman was also very influential in 1952, when he was not a candidate for re-election.[17]

In the absence of hierarchical control by an incumbent President, decision-making at conventions is ordinarily coordinated by a process of bargaining among party leaders. We think of bargaining as a method by which activities are coordinated in situations where controls between individuals approach equality, where no leader by himself can fully dominate another. Each leader represents a state party or faction within a state which is independently organized and not subject to control by outsiders. In the presence of disagreement and the absence of coercion, leaders must persuade one another, compromise, and form coalitions if they are to gain sufficient support to carry the day. Although the leaders may differ in their preferences among possible candidates, they believe that participating in the bargaining process will aid them in achieving their goals and inform them of the goals and tactics of others, which in turn may help them in attaining their goals.

Prerequisites to bargaining may be summarized as (1) no hierarchical controls; (2) interdependence of bargainers; (3) disagreement among bargainers; and (4) expectation of gain. When the President is of the opposite party, or chooses not to intervene, the convention becomes a bargaining system because no political leader besides the President is in a position to control the national convention by himself. The interdependence of party leaders may be established by reference to the custom of American democracy which allows the voters to replace the elected officials of one party with those of another at general elections. In order to mobilize enough nationwide support to elect a President, party leaders from a large number of constituencies must be satisfied with the nominee. Without agreement on a nominee, none of them is likely to enjoy access to the eventual President; hence, party leaders are interdependent and expect to gain from the outcome of the bargain. Because of the different amounts of access to different aspirants which delegates carry with them into the convention, the preferences of delegates are likely initially to disagree.[18] Most politicians believe that bargaining is necessary and not dishonorable. By challenging the moral basis of this belief, Senator Goldwater took the position in 1964 that the gains to be expected by bargaining were greatly outweighed by the loss of ideological purity and commitment.

PRE-CONVENTION STRATEGIES

The selection of a Presidential nominee is the business which dominates the convention. From this it follows that decisions preceding the Presidential nomination are important or unimportant largely depending upon their implications for the Presidential nomination. Decisions not taken unanimously which precede the Presidential nomination in the convention are almost always tests of strength between party factions divided as to the Presidential nomination. These decisions are usually more important for the information they communicate on the strength of the candidates than for their actual content.[19]

Perhaps the first strategic decision facing an avowed candidate is whether to attempt to become a front-runner by entering primaries, barnstorming the country, and publicly seeking support at state conventions. The advantage of this strategy is that a candidate may build up such a commanding lead (or appear to do so) that no one will be able (or will try) to stop him at the national convention. The disadvantage is that an open campaign may reveal his inability to acquire support or may lead other candidates to band together in order to stop him. Adoption of this position depends for its success, then, upon the front-runner's ability to predict accurately both how he will fare compared to others in open competition, and what others will be able to do when they discover his lead. He may, for example, try to anticipate whether his activity will stimulate a coalition of opponents who are otherwise unlikely to get together. If such a coalition seems likely, the candidate may issue communications playing down the extent of his support. But this tactic may discourage new supporters who would have been attracted by a display of strength. Candidates can never be entirely certain that they are striking the right balance between reticence and aggressiveness, which may explain why unabashed attempts to use bandwagon *or* dark horse strategies in relatively undiluted form are quite common.

The dark horse is an avowed candidate who avoids primaries and much open campaigning. Like Stuart Symington in 1960, or Richard Nixon in 1964, he is content to be everyone's friend and no one's enemy.[20] As Abraham Lincoln wrote to a supporter in 1860 describing his dark horse strategy: "My name is new in the field, and I suppose I am not the first choice of a very great many. Our policy, then, is to give no offense to others—leave them in a mood to come to us if they shall be compelled to give up their first love." [21] The strategy of the dark horse is to combine with others to oppose every front-runner. His hope is that when no front-runner is left he will appear as the man who can unify the party by being acceptable to all and obnoxious to none. The dangers the dark horse faces are that he will enter the convention with too little support to make a strong bid or that some other dark horse will prove preferable. How much support is enough to make a serious bid but not enough to be shot at as a front-runner? How far behind the front-runner can a candidate permit himself to get without becoming entirely lost from sight? Either an intuitive ability to guess or an exceedingly accurate apparatus for collecting information on the present strength of candidates, as well as on the likely effect of different levels of strength on other delegates, must be part of the serious dark horse's equipment.

Primaries

Primaries are important largely because the results represent an ostensibly objective indication of whether a candidate can win the election. The contestants stand to gain or lose far more than the small number of delegate votes which may be at stake. Thus a man situated as was Richard Nixon in 1960 would be ill-advised to enter a primary unless the information at his disposal led him to believe that he was quite certain to win. This stricture applies with special force to any candidate who is well ahead in delegate support. All he can gain is a few additional votes, while he can lose his existing support by a bad showing in the primary since this would be interpreted as meaning that he could not win in the election. The candidate who is far behind, or who has to overcome severe handicaps, however, has little or nothing to lose by entering a risky primary. If he wins, he has demonstrated his popularity; if he loses, he is hardly worse off than if he had not entered the primary at all. Such was the case when John F. Kennedy quieted the apprehensions of Democratic politicians about the religious issue by winning in Protestant West Virginia.[22] Goldwater needed a primary victory in California to show uncommitted delegates that he had voter appeal, even though at the start of the primary campaigns he had been a prominent candidate. He accepted the risk of losing the nomination if he lost the primary because his need for proof of popularity to get the votes necessary for nomination outweighed his fear of the possibility of losing the primary contest.[23] The man who is ahead needs more certain information about how primaries are likely to turn out because he takes the greater risk.

The man who is behind in securing convention support or whose ability to win is in doubt engages in strategies of enticement in which he issues siren calls inviting the leading contenders into a primary. He suggests that they are cowardly, lacking in fighting spirit, afraid to face the public. By luring them into a primary, he hopes to deal a severe blow to their chances and thereby boost his own. In order to avoid this trap, it may be necessary for candidates to publicize their disdain for primaries, to specify in advance all the reasons why such a contest would be unnecessary, unfair, and a waste of time. The candidate who finds himself in a primary (and wishes to live and fight again another day) does well to have alibis ready to explain away seemingly disadvantageous results.

In a primary in which there are many contenders a defeated candidate may attempt to gain advantage from what may be regarded as an ambiguous result by claiming that the man who actually won was allied to him ideologically. The results may then be viewed as a victory for the ideology rather than defeat for the candidate. After La Follette had won an overwhelming victory in the 1912 Republican primary in North Dakota, Theodore Roosevelt issued a statement "claiming an immense progressive victory." He even went beyond this to count the La Follette delegation as part of the Roosevelt camp once it had cast "a complimentary vote for La Follette." [24] In the same way, Rockefeller supporters in 1964 hailed the New Hampshire Republican primary, which was won by Henry Cabot Lodge, as a defeat for Goldwater and a victory for the moderate wing of the Republican party.

One strategy for primaries, the write-in, offers the maximum possibility of gain with the minimum possibility of loss. If a candidate gets virtually no votes, he can easily explain this by saying that he did not campaign and that it is difficult for people to write in names. If he receives over 10 per cent of the vote, he can hail this as a tremendous victory under the circumstances. In Nebraska in 1964 Nixon received 35% of the vote as a write-in in the primary and it was "claimed that 'Nebraskans have nominated the next Republican candidate for President . . .' a claim that was forgotten after the Nixon debacle in Oregon just three days later." [25]

If a candidate should win, he can build it up to the sky, stressing the extraordinary popularity required to get people to go to all the trouble of writing in a name.[26] But the man who is behind cannot rest content with being able to explain away a poor showing; he must win to establish himself as a contender. The strategy of the write-in, consequently, is most accessible to the man who is ahead and hopes to solidify his position while minimizing his risks.

The foregoing discussion should help us to understand why those who win primaries sometimes do not win the nomination. Part of the reason is that there are not many primaries and not all of those actually commit delegates to vote for a candidate. Of greater significance, however, is the fact that primary activity is often (though by no means always) a sign that a candidate has great obstacles to overcome and must win many primaries in order to be considered for the nomination at all. The image communicated to political professionals by a few primary victories, unless they are overwhelming, may be less that of the conquering hero than that of the drowning man clutching at the last straw.

Thus, entering and winning primaries may be of little value unless the results are widely interpreted in such a way as to improve a candidate's chances. The contestant who "loses" but does better than expected may reap greater advantage from a primary than the one who wins but falls below expectations. It is, therefore, manifestly to the advantage of a candidate to hold his claims down to minimum proportions. Kennedy tried in 1960 to follow this advice in Wisconsin—he claimed Humphrey had been Wisconsin's third Senator—but the press, radio, and TV took note of his extensive organization and of favorable polls, and in advance pinned the winner-by-a-landslide label on the Senator from Massachusetts.[27] The public media have taken some of the control over "expectations" from the candidates.

Yet there is more to the strategy of primaries than mere calculation of chances on the candidate's part. The desires of the existing state organizations may also have to be taken into account. The state organization may be sponsoring a favorite son who, it hopes, may be nominated in case of deadlock. It may wish to remain uncommitted in order to increase its bargaining power by making a claim on the winner in return for throwing last minute support to him. The party may be divided and fear internecine warfare over rival candidates which would leave it in a shattered condition. For all of these reasons, the state leadership may request candidates to stay out and may threaten to work against them in the primary and at the convention if they disobey. Presidential aspirants may have to rest content with second or third choice support unless their position is so desperate that they have little to lose by antagonizing the state party.

Paradoxically, the candidate who can show that he has no choice but to enter a primary may gain a bargaining advantage.[28] The state leaders may then decide that it is worth making concessions to him to avoid the internal strife that would be caused by a primary contest. This is more or less what happened in 1960, when John Kennedy, fortified by a poll claiming that he would win, insisted that he absolutely had to have Ohio's votes to have a chance at the national convention. Ohio Governor Michael DiSalle, who wanted to run as a favorite son, had to back down in order to avoid a primary fight that could have been extremely embarrassing to him and ran on a slate pledged to Kennedy. The Governor's decision was prompted by the knowledge that the Cuyahoga County (Cleveland) party faction, which was hostile to him, would run a slate pledged to Kennedy and use this as a weapon to reduce the Governor's stature within the state. The struggle for power within a state may have much to do with its action at the convention.[29]

State and District Conventions

Most of the delegates are still chosen, not by primaries, but by state and district conventions. This process provides relatively few contests over the selection of delegates, although these may be important. Most attempts to influence delegates chosen in this way are made after they are chosen. The first strategic requirement for the candidate seeking to influence these delegations is an intelligence service, a network of informants who will tell the candidates which delegations are firmly committed, which are wavering, and which may be persuaded to provide second or third choice support. Advance reports on the opportunities offered by internal divisions in the state parties, the type of appeal likely to be effective in each state, and the kinds of bargains to which leaders are most susceptible, may also be helpful. The costs of this information may come high in terms of time, money, and effort, but it will be worth it to the serious candidate who needs to know where to move to increase his support and block his opponents.

Aspirants for nomination vary greatly in the degree to which they know other politicians throughout the country. Men like former Vice-President Richard Nixon and former Senator Barry Goldwater, who have travelled extensively and extended assistance to members of their party, may simply need to keep their files up to date in order to have a nationwide list of contacts. When the time comes, they know whom they can call upon for assistance in gathering information, persuading delegates, and generally furthering their cause. Candidates who lack this advantage, however, have to take special steps in order to build up their political apparatus. In paving the way for Franklin D. Roosevelt's nomination in 1932, James A. Farley began early by sending invitations to Roosevelt's inauguration as Governor of New York to party leaders throughout the country. Most invitations were refused but a valuable correspondence grew out of this approach. Farley next sent a small manual containing a few facts about the New York Democratic party organization to people throughout the country. The response encouraged a follow-up pamphlet which presented, without comment, the New York gubernatorial vote in every county since 1916. It was intended to be impressive testimony of FDR's vote-getting ability. When many people wrote back expressing an interest in FDR's candidacy, offering suggestions, or just saying "thanks," Farley replied with a personal message and endeavored to keep up the contact through further letters, phone calls, and even a phonograph record. Later, in 1931, Farley took a trip through the West, ostensibly to visit the Elks Convention in Seattle, but actually to contact over 1,000 party leaders in all but three states west of the Mississippi. Upon his return, every one of Farley's contacts received a personal letter.[30]

The well-organized candidates contact the delegates personally or through close associates. They may show a winning personality, make implied promises of good things to come, discuss or avoid controversial issues of special importance to the locality, as seems best calculated to increase their support. If a favorable public opinion poll is handy or can be arranged, this will often be cited to substantiate the claims of victory which must be made to convey the impression that it would be a good idea to climb on the bandwagon. More than one can play at this game, however, and "pollsmanship" is becoming a common art whose practitioners know how to secure the desired impression and blunt harmful ones. There are good reasons to suppose that the number of polls taken exceeds the number made public since sometimes the news they disclose disappoints the candidate who paid for them.

AT THE CONVENTION

The national convention is a mass meeting in which the participants necessarily play widely varying and unequal roles. The candidates and their chief supporters are busily, perhaps frantically, perfecting their organization and trying to influence as many delegates as they can. The leaders of "bossed" or "pledged" delegations are either actively supporting their candidate or negotiating for the disposal of the votes they command within the limits of discretion which their delegation places on them. These are the men who conduct negotiations among the delegations when an impasse develops. There are also factional leaders and independent delegates within state delegations who play an important part in determining what their delegation or a part of their delegation will do. They bargain *within* their delegation rather than *among* the various state delegations. The ordinary delegate, however, whose vote may have been pledged in a primary or who is controlled by others may have little to do. He stands and waits, important only if the nomination becomes closely contested and circumstances operate to release him from prior commitments and the control of his state party organization. Only then will he be assiduously wooed, occupying a place in the scheme of things much like the independent delegates. In setting the stage for the balloting, therefore, we will deal first with the convention activists—candidates and their organizations, party "bosses" and leaders of large delegations, independent delegates, and state factional leaders—and then with the rank-and-file delegates.

Candidates and Their Organizations

There is an extraordinarily wide divergence among candidate organizations. They range from the comprehensive, integrated, and superbly effective to the fragmented, uncoordinated, and virtually nonexistent. We can only suggest the range of organizational accomplishment through some general comment and a few examples.

In 1960, Senator John F. Kennedy wanted a communications network which would provide him with a continuing and accurate stream of vital information.[31] He wanted detailed personal information about as many delegates as possible in order to know how they were likely to vote and how they might best be persuaded to stay in line or to change their minds. More than a year before the convention the Kennedy-for-President organization started a card file containing information on people throughout the nation who might be delegates and who might influence delegates. Included on each card was the prospective delegate's name, occupation, religion, party position, relation (if any) to the Kennedy family or its leading supporters, ambition, policy preferences if strongly held, and likely vote. This was brought up-to-date prior to convention time and entries were made in a central register as new information developed. Thus when it appeared that a delegate needed to be reinforced or might not vote for Kennedy, his card was pulled, and the information was used in order to determine the best way to convince him.

At the national convention, before the balloting for the Presidential nomination starts, one or more days are consumed in a variety of party rituals: speech-making, the seating of delegates, the presentation of the platform, "ladies day," and so on. During that time delegates and their leaders mill about, exchange greetings and gossip. It is this set of circumstances that challenges even the most efficient candidate organization.

In order to keep an up-to-date, and when necessary, an hour-by-hour watch on developments within the state delegations, the Kennedy organization assigned an individual to each state. This person might be a delegate or an observer such as a Senator or a member of the candidate's staff. When it was deemed inadvisable to choose a delegate for fear that any choice would alienate one faction or another, a person outside the state was chosen. These liaison men kept tabs on individual delegates and maintained a running record of the likely distribution of votes. When necessary, the liaison men sent messages to the candidate's headquarters and reinforcements were sent to bolster the situation. At the Kennedy headquarters, the seriousness of the report would be judged and a decision made on how to deal with it. Senator Kennedy himself might call the wavering delegate, one of his brothers might be dispatched, a state party leader might intervene, or some other such remedy applied.

In the hurly-burly, crush, and confusion of convention activity, it cannot be assumed that any messages which are sent are necessarily received, or that decisions which are made are communicated to those who must carry them out. The Kennedy organization took great care to prepare a message center which would receive messages and locate the people they were aimed at and which could send out instructions and receive feedback on the results. Each key staff person was required to phone his whereabouts to a central switchboard. This made it possible for the Kennedy forces at the convention to deploy and reassign their people on a minute-by-minute basis, as developments seemed to require.

A system set up only to deal with emergencies would have limited usefulness to a candidate who wanted regular reports so that he could appraise them in a consistent way. Every morning every liaison man assigned to the Kennedy headquarters attended a staff meeting at which he deposited with the secretary a report on his activities for the previous day. These reports were sent to what was called the "secret room" and the information was transferred to state briefing files. From these files, a daily secret report of delegate strength was written and given to the candidate and his top advisers.

At the morning staff meetings, Robert Kennedy would ask each liaison man for his estimate of the number of Kennedy votes. Keenly aware of the dangers of communicating an attitude which suggested that he wanted high estimates, Robert Kennedy challenged the liaison men if he felt that their estimates were too high, but not if they appeared too low. On occasion he would reprimand a liaison man for including a delegate as a certain Kennedy supporter when other information indicated that this was not true. The success of this procedure was indicated by the fact that by the time the alphabetical order of balloting had reached Wyoming on the first (and last) ballot, the Kennedy organization's estimate of their delegate strength was proven correct within a one vote margin.[32]

The danger of confusion and mishap is multiplied during the balloting because the convention floor is filled and it is difficult to move about freely. The Kennedy organization arranged for telephones on the convention floor. Six telephones were set up beneath the seats of chairmen of friendly delegations who were seated around the gigantic convention hall. These phones were connected to the Kennedy headquarters outside the hall. Inside the headquarters, staff members sat near the telephone and simultaneously scanned several television sets to look for possible defections. Had the telephones failed to work (they were pre-tested), walkie-talkie radios were available to take their place.[33]

By comparison with the Kennedy efforts, most of the organizations which have successfully nominated Presidential candidates in American history have been uncoordinated, diffuse affairs. For example in 1952 none of the various factions in the Democratic party that favored the nomination of Adlai Stevenson had the wholehearted cooperation of their candidate; information gathering was casual; tactical maneuvers were in some cases hit upon accidentally or as afterthoughts. The factions working for the Stevenson nomination did not cooperate with one another to a significant degree and in fact squabbled among themselves on occasion. Yet Stevenson was nominated; his success came about because he was the second choice of an overwhelming number of delegates who could not agree on any of their first choices, and the first choice of a significant number of leaders in spite of his disinclination to pursue the nomination in an organized fashion.[34]

Delegates

We can identify two categories of delegation activists: (1) party bosses and state leaders who control many votes other than their own and who participate in high level negotiations on the disposition of these votes and (2) delegates of independent standing who may control only their own votes or those of a faction within their home state, but who, because of their special skills at negotiation and maneuver, or because of their high personal prestige, or simply because of the open and unbossed character of their state delegation, play significant roles at the convention. From this latter group are drawn the delegates who man the key subcommittees and committees on the platform and on credentials, and they often have a real voice in determining the vote of their delegation.

The roles of these activists may be contrasted with the activities of rank-and-file members of bossed delegations—delegations pledged by primary law, or in the hands of local and state party leaders. It is not uncommon for large state delegations to split their votes into halves or thirds, so as to enable a large number of the party faithful to make the trip to the convention city, but these votes are not often independently cast. Essentially, party leaders of the large delegations determine the disposition of these votes. The delegates who, in a formal sense, hold the votes are thus left with little or no political decision-making to participate in. They spend their time milling around and conversing with one another. Some delegates may sample the recreational facilities of the convention city. Others may visit the campaign headquarters of the candidates. The more fortunate ones return home at least with something to talk about and perhaps a word from a famous television newscaster who could be counted a celebrity. But for the most part these delegates find themselves crushed by the masses of people, uncertain of whom to speak to (especially before delegates' badges are issued as identification), and subject to rebuff. Many of these delegates are important people back home, but at the convention they often feel like "a little fish in a big pond" and worry about their status in the new environment.

As the convention provides an environment conducive to anxiety, so it also provides opportunities for adjustment. Anxiety induced by strangeness of place can be mitigated but not erased by familiarizing oneself with the surroundings. There is not enough time for that. Instead, the delegates immediately seek out familiar connections with the past. The cry goes out: "Are there Rotarians to make up a meeting?" and soon a quorum is found and a convivial group goes through the old ritual. Mayors breakfast together; Negro delegates converse and go off to a convention-wide meeting of their fellows; Congressmen meet their associates from the Capitol; union members converse about their special policy interests; and delegates from the large counties seek each other's company. Still, some are left out.

In view of the preceding comments, the functions which personal attentions like handshakes from the leading candidates and pictures taken with prominent persons perform for delegates should be evident. Richard Nixon's practice in 1960 of having a separate photograph taken of himself with every delegate, however exhausting and perfunctory this may appear, demonstrates a real appreciation of what this gesture means to many delegates.

Straws in the Wind

When an incumbent President desires renomination, his influence is normally great, his party can hardly hope to win by repudiating him, and his nomination is virtually assured.[35] Sometimes, the titular leader of the party or some other candidate is so far ahead, as Nixon was in 1960, that there is nothing left for the delegates to do but ratify the decision that has already been negotiated by leaders of the state parties.

But we are mainly concerned with those nominating conventions where there is uncertainty at the time of the convention about who will be the nominee. In an uncertain convention, delegates crave information on what is going to happen and when. For most of them, of course, the convention is a spectator sport, since they will be acting under instructions from the voters in their state primary or from their state party leaders. But even so, they want to know who is ahead and who is behind and what the chances are of majority agreement on one of the leading candidates. Rumors are rife because no one has been able to establish an unshakable claim of victory, because it is to the advantage of more than one aspirant to be thought to be winning, and because people like to speculate. In the grip of uncertainty, the delegates grasp for any objective information that may be gleaned from the events of the convention itself.[36]

Before the balloting on the candidates begins at the convention, there often are votes on contested delegations, on a plank in the platform, on some rule governing convention life such as a loyalty pledge, or on the person who is to be permanent chairman. If some of the candidates become identified with one or the other side on these preliminary votes, the results may be considered a test of who is likely to win the nomination. Thus, candidates who identify themselves with one side or another may prejudice their chances of nomination. They must calculate the effects of the loss of such a vote. In 1932, Franklin Roosevelt nearly lost his bid for the nomination by coming out against the two-thirds rule then required for nomination. Fortunately for his chances, FDR's supporters at the convention discovered that the opposition to the change in rules was greater than the opposition to him and he beat a hasty retreat from his previous position.[37]

Many of the same strategic considerations hold in relation to any conflict that may develop over the permanent chairman. This struggle may be important because the chairman has significant procedural powers at the convention. He can speed up adjournment to give a particular candidate time to make bargains, or he can harm another's chances by refusing to recognize a state delegation about to go over to that candidate at a crucial moment. The importance of being chairman was demonstrated at the 1920 Republican Convention when Senator Henry Cabot Lodge wanted to permit the party leaders to find a way out of an impasse that had developed. Shortly after the fourth ballot, Senator Reed Smoot of Utah moved to adjourn the proceedings. A resounding "no" echoed throughout the auditorium as Lodge put the motion to a vote and immediately declared the convention adjourned.[38] Twenty years later, at another Republican Convention, Senator Bricker of Ohio asked Chairman Joseph Martin for a recess before the sixth ballot. This would have given the Taft and Dewey forces time to make a deal. Partial to the Willkie cause, however, Martin refused the request and the balloting continued, to be ended by victory for Willkie.[39]

Unless victory appears assured it may be unwise for a candidate to challenge a popular chairman. An alternate strategy is to accept an unfavorable chairman but to put forth a stream of publicity stressing the chairman's partiality, so that he feels under continuous scrutiny and may bend over backward to avoid charges of favoritism. Nowadays, however, the usual practice is for representatives of the leading candidates to agree upon major personnel of the convention—keynoter, permanent chairman, platform committee chairman—by negotiation well ahead of the convention itself.

Virtually any action can take on added significance if it reveals information hitherto unavailable to all. In the 1932 Democratic Convention a vote on seating a contested delegation was taken under conditions which freed many of the delegates from the unit rule. This showed observers which delegations were closely divided, information which imposition of the unit rule had helped to hide.[40]

Such apparently trivial matters as the date or the place in which the convention meets may take on special meaning if those decisions are believed to affect the fortunes of candidates. The fact that the 1844 Democratic Convention was delayed while Van Buren's letter opposing the annexation of Texas was having its effects was known at that time to be prejudicial to his chances. Locating the 1928 Democratic Convention in Houston, Texas, was widely interpreted as a move to mollify people in the South and led to the conclusion that this was necessary because party leaders intended to nominate Al Smith.

While candidates are being nominated, and during the balloting, demonstrations—partly spontaneous, largely prearranged—

take place on the floor. This raucous display is meant to let everyone know that a candidate has many loyal supporters. Hopefully, a demonstration at a crucial moment might succeed in igniting the spark of enthusiasm among the multitude of uncertain delegates. But, as supporters of Adlai Stevenson learned in 1960, this has the possibility of working only when delegates are really uncertain and uncommitted.

Despite the fact that everyone seems aware of what is going on, the same old tricks are played at every convention. Part of the reason is that once this practice has begun, unanimous consent is necessary to eliminate it; otherwise, the candidate who received no ovation would be deemed to have no support or not enough sense to stimulate it artificially. Another part of the rationale behind demonstrations should be clear from our argument: Reliable information may be so scarce that, despite all warnings, delegates may be swayed (as was the Republican Convention of 1940 that nominated Wendell Willkie) by the most immediate, tangible evidence before them—the roar of the crowd.[41]

The Balloting

The one route to political power open to all delegates in the convention is to contribute to the majority essential for the nomination of the man they believe will be the winner. This explains the so-called "bandwagon" behavior which can be seen in operation at many conventions. When delegates believe that one Presidential aspirant is certain of nomination, they will attempt to record themselves as voting for that aspirant as quickly as possible. Delegates committed to a favorite son candidate will trade their votes for access (or what they hope will be access) to the candidate they think most likely to win nomination. Note the differences in these two statements. In the first, delegates know which candidate will win, and hope to earn his gratitude by voting for him. In the corollary, delegates are less certain of the outcome, hence their commitment to an aspirant is more costly for him. The prospective candidate, in these circumstances, often makes promises of access to delegates in return for their support.

An aspirant who leads in votes for the nomination must actually win the nomination by a certain point in time, or else his chances of eventually winning decline precipitously, even though he remains in the lead temporarily. This is true when delegate support is given candidates because of the expectation of victory. When this victory falls short of quick materialization, delegates may question their initial judgment. Thus, the longer a candidate remains in the lead without starting a bandwagon, the greater the chance that his supporters will reassess his chances of victory and vote for someone else. In order to maximize access, delegates prefer to support the eventual winner before he achieves a majority. They are therefore guided by what they expect other delegates to do, and are constantly on the alert to change their expectations to conform to the latest information. This information may be nothing more substantial than a rumor, which quickly takes on the status of a self-fulfilling prophecy, as delegates stampede in response to expectations, quickly realized, about how other delegates will respond. The strategies which a candidate adopts depend, therefore, not only on showing that he can win but also on his position in the convention. The front-runner must score an early victory or resign himself to defeat. So long as he keeps gaining support, no matter how slightly, he is still in contention because it is assumed that he may have more strength in reserve. But the front-runner who begins to manifest any decline, or even in some cases a leveling-off in votes on successive ballots, can expect to see uncommitted delegates conclude that he has shot his bolt and begin to shift their support to more hopeful prospects.

Considered as a source of information, the balloting may be viewed as indicating not merely each candidate's vote but also whether he is moving up toward hope or down to despair. One strategy sometimes used in this connection is to "hide" a few votes on early ballots by giving them to others and reclaiming them little by little so as to show a steady increase.[42] Or a candidate may decide to bide his time and delay making his bid. In that case a weak initial total of votes is not likely to be commented upon because the front-runner occupies the center of attention. Later, a dark horse may occasion surprise by his rapid climb and hope that most delegates will decide to hitch their wagons to a rising star.

Aspirants sometimes combine their voting strength in the convention in order to prevent a front-running candidate from gaining a majority. They will then negotiate the nomination among themselves. If the front-runner's victory promises other aspirants insufficient access, they may defeat him by preventing a bandwagon in his favor. An apparently successful case of combining against the front-runner occurred in 1920 when Harry Daugherty, Harding's manager, realizing that General Leonard Wood had to be defeated to give Harding a chance, offered to lend Governor Lowden every vote he could spare until the Governor passed Wood in the balloting. Then the alliance would be terminated. "Certainly you couldn't make a fairer proposition," Lowden responded, and the agreement was consummated.[43]

The rational aspirant who leads but lacks a majority will therefore promise access to leaders representing the requisite number of votes, if he believes that no bandwagon will appear unstimulated. The front-runner may reasonably expect to win without cost (that is, without making such promises) unless leaders of opposing factions reach agreement on a ticket, and appear likely to combine against him. Early front-runners often win nominations precisely because they face a divided opposition.

The case of the Democrats in 1960 is a perfect example of this. In the pre-convention maneuvering, Adlai Stevenson might have cut into John Kennedy's liberal and labor support, had he made himself available as a candidate. Many party regulars from the urban political machines, and, in particular, ex-President Truman, had no special liking for Kennedy, and Senator Johnson could draw on a rather substantial reservoir of strength from

Southern delegations determined not to walk out even though they knew they would not approve of the civil rights plank of the platform.

These groups could not get together and settle on a candidate who was more satisfactory to *all* of them than the front-runner, Senator Kennedy. Labor clearly would accept no one to the right of Kennedy; the Southerners could abide nobody to the left of him. Adlai Stevenson was perhaps the leading candidate whose ideological location, prominence in the party, and public record could pass muster with these groups, but he had alienated Truman and in any case refused to go to work on his own behalf. And so, Kennedy's opposition stayed divided.

The time may come when a front-runner finds that he cannot win with his existing support. Then he bargains. He may offer the Vice-Presidential nomination to one or more leaders of important states; he may hint at cabinet posts, patronage, or preferred treatment; he may explore concessions on policy. But this account is too simple. Before he can bargain, the candidate must know with whom to bargain. And among those delegations which might be swayed must be found the ones amenable to what the candidate can offer. The necessity of maintaining an apparatus for obtaining this information is evident.

If a candidate thinks he can win on his own, he may be reluctant to risk sacrificing his ambition by "making a deal" to combine against a front-runner. Yet if he hesitates too long, he may lose all. This is apparently what happened to Thomas E. Dewey in the 1940 Republican Convention. As Senator Arthur Vandenberg recorded it in his diary, "I offered to flip a coin with Dewey to see which side of the ticket each would take. Dewey never saw me again until the final voting. But it was too late. He missed the boat when he clung to his own first place ambitions. Between us we could have controlled the convention if it had been done in the first instance." [44]

The candidate who wishes to get support must show that he already has some to begin with. This is particularly the case when one contender is considering throwing his support to another in order to assure the latter's nomination. There would be no point in sacrificing one's chances in favor of another candidate who would then not have enough votes to win. This kind of situation occurred around the time of the fiftieth ballot at the 1924 Democratic Convention. Al Smith informed Senator Oscar Underwood of Alabama that if two more Southern states would give Underwood their support, Smith would also give the Senator his support. The Underwood forces accepted the offer but they were unable to find other Southern states who would support their candidate, and so the scheme fell through.[45]

The bargaining process itself may be an excellent source of information on what important delegates are likely to do under a variety of circumstances. A series of probing actions may be carried out to discover what these delegates want, what they will take, what they will give in return. Out of the negotiations which are being carried on among leaders may emerge the beginnings of a commonly held picture of the shape of events to come.

Bargains may be tacit rather than explicit, made through intermediaries rather than by principals. Exactly what was promised may not be entirely clear or may be distorted later on, if this is deemed advantageous. The man who wishes to collect what he believes to be his due may have trouble securing effective guarantees. Thomas Dewey never quite manifested the same understanding that Charles Halleck did about an offer of the Vice-Presidency in return for support in the Republican Convention of 1948.[46] One delegate to the 1960 Democratic Convention told reporters that he was the nineteenth person to be offered the Vice-Presidency by the Kennedy forces. Under the circumstances, he allowed as how he would take cash.

It is possible that much less comes out of the convention in terms of reward for support than is commonly supposed. An incoming President, for example, may well decide to handle patronage through the dominant party faction in a state rather than suffer the disabilities of supporting a weak dissident faction that helped him at a convention. Nevertheless, if delegates believe that rewards are likely to follow support, as many apparently do, their actions will conform to this belief.

One by one the leading candidates try their luck. Timing is of the essence. Each candidate seeks the strategic moment to push his candidacy. A miscalculation, a decision, perhaps, to move ahead before sufficient support is available for the final push, may prove fatal to a candidate's chances. In a closely contested convention the prize may go to the candidate who possesses sufficient information about the intentions of others to make the successful move.

Whispering campaigns are begun, saying "Candidate X is certain to win; get on the bandwagon while you still have a chance." Rumors appear that a crucial delegation will swing to a particular candidate. The balloting may remain substantially unchanged and reveal no secrets. It is difficult to know what to believe. No mass meeting of thousands of delegates can hope to find out who is acceptable to most of them. It is up to the leaders to take over.

In the absence of quick agreement at the convention, the demonstrations and adjournments give party leaders time to meet and see if a candidate can be found who can receive a majority of votes. Generally, the most important leaders are Governors who exercise considerable influence in their state and may be able to control the votes of its delegates. National committeemen, state chairmen, elder statesmen, and Congressmen may be among those who attend. This is the "smoke-filled room" of convention lore. Its participants try to work out an agreement which will meet their desires. But they are severely limited in their choice by their estimate of what the people will accept at the polls and what the other delegates will stand for. The leaders are men of independent influence and differing interests and there may be only a limited range of agreement among them.

Little is known about negotiations among party leaders at conventions. But what we do know suggests that the essential trick is to convince others that one's preferred view of what will happen, or must happen, is the correct one. This is apparently what took place in the 1920 Republican Convention when Harry Daugherty succeeded in convincing party leaders that a deadlock was inevitable and that only Harding could break it. Much the same kind of thing occurred in 1844 when Gideon Pillow and George Bancroft spread the word that Cass, Calhoun, or Van Buren could not possibly win but that Polk would carry the day.[47]

In order to break a deadlock, it is necessary to convince some delegates that the candidate they prefer cannot win and that they would be well advised to switch to a man who can. The leaders at the 1920 Republican Convention decided to communicate this point convincingly by calling for several additional ballots during which nothing changed.[48] This also helped to assure losing party factions that their candidates had had a fair chance. At the 1924 Democratic Convention, however, which went to 103 ballots, the lengthy voting apparently did not communicate the hopelessness of their cause to the leading candidates. Not only did incompatability and intransigence block bargaining, but short-lived booms kept arising, an indication that the delegates shared no common view of future events.[49] The shock to loyal party members was so great that John Nance Garner chose to submerge his own chances and throw the 1932 convention to Franklin Roosevelt, rather than risk another agonizing stalemate.[50]

The Vice-Presidential Nominee

When the convention finally selects its Presidential candidate, it turns to the anticlimactic task of finding a running mate. Vice-Presidential nominees are chosen to help the party achieve the Presidency. Party nominees for President and Vice-President always appear on the ballot together and are elected together. Since 1804, a vote for one has always been a vote for the other.

The Vice-President occupies a post in the legislative branch of the government which is mostly honorific, and his powers and activities in the executive branch are determined by the President.[51] The electoral interdependence of the two offices gives politicians an opportunity to gather votes for the Presidency. Therefore, the prescription for an "ideal" Vice-Presidential nominee is the same as for a Presidential nominee, with two additions: He must possess those desirable qualities the Presidential nominee lacks, and he must be acceptable to the Presidential nominee.

The Vice-Presidency is the most important position from which Presidents of the United States are drawn. Just a third of our thirty-six Presidents have been Vice-Presidents. (Three were elected in their own right; eight first took office upon the death of a President.) American history has given us eleven good reasons—one for each man who succeeded to the Presidency—for inquiring into the qualifications of Vice-Presidents and for examining the criteria by which they are chosen.

The Presidential candidate who has firm control over his nomination is in a position to use the Vice-Presidential slot to help win the election. This is what Abraham Lincoln did in 1864 when he chose a "War Democrat," Andrew Johnson, who he hoped would add strength to the ticket. In the same way, John F. Kennedy chose Lyndon Johnson to help gather Southern votes, especially in Texas, and Richard Nixon chose Henry Cabot Lodge to help offset the Democratic party advantage in the Northeast. These two Vice-Presidential candidates were distinguished men who had a great deal to recommend them. But the help they could offer their parties was undoubtedly an important consideration.

Sometimes a Presidential candidate will try to help heal a breach in the party by offering the Vice-Presidential nomination to a defeated party faction. Or the Presidential candidate may try to improve his relationships with Congress by finding a running mate who has friends there. Harry Truman was chosen by Franklin Roosevelt for both these reasons.

There have been times when a President has insisted on having his personal choice selected as Vice-President. Andrew Jackson was adamant about running with Martin Van Buren, and Franklin Roosevelt went so far as to write out a refusal to accept the Democratic nomination in 1940 when party leaders balked at the thought of Henry Wallace.

The Presidential nominee clearly is expected to have a lot to say about whom he will run with on the party ticket. More and more in recent years the expectation has been that the Presidential candidate would make the choice himself after due consultation with party leaders. Indeed, failure to act decisively may well be regarded now as a sign of weakness. Yet there have been times when Presidential candidates have not wished to become involved in internal party battles and have let the convention decide. William Jennings Bryan would not even allow his own Nebraska delegation to vote on the Vice-Presidential nomination at the 1896 Democratic Convention, and Adlai Stevenson preferred to let Estes Kefauver and John F. Kennedy fight it out for the prize in 1956.

As the world has become a more dangerous place to live in, the need to have a capable Vice-President has become more evident, and the parties have apparently decided to restrict their choices to men of ability who, whatever electoral assets they may have, give promise of measuring up to the highest office in the land. Since World War II both parties, Republican and Democratic, have generally nominated men of experience and distinction with some notable qualities for high office. Presidents and party leaders have chosen among qualified men to find those who met their requirements. But while Vice-Presidents may be talented, they have not historically been chosen mainly for their talents.

When especially able men have appeared in the office from time to time, this may have been due more to the blessings of Providence than to wise actions on our part. If good results require noble intentions, then the criteria for choosing Vice-

Presidents may leave much to be desired. Why should the great parties, we might ask, not set out deliberately to choose the man best able to act as President in case of need? Should ticket balancing and similar considerations be condemned as political chicanery?

In a speech to the Harvard Law School Forum in 1956, former Vice-President Henry A. Wallace declared: "The greatest danger is that the man just nominated for President will try desperately to heal the wounds and placate the dissidents in his party. . . . My battle cry would be—no more deals—no more balancing of the ticket." In 1964, the Republican party evidently also endorsed this view. The selection of the 1964 Republican nominee, William Miller, was intended to violate criteria used in the past for balancing the ticket. Although he came from a region different from Barry Goldwater and is a Catholic, he was chosen primarily because of his ideological affinity with the Presidential candidate. The special style of Goldwater and his supporters required that consistency of views, opposition to the other party on as many issues as possible, and refusal to bargain prevail over the traditional political demands for compromise, flexibility, and popularity; and most of the one hundred and thirty-odd Goldwater delegates we interviewed at the Republican Convention were prepared to sacrifice victory if victory meant becoming a "me-too" party or "going against principle" by adopting what they termed the "devious and corrupt" balanced tickets of the past.

On the Democratic side, and in line with conventional practice of recent years, President Johnson chose a man of more evident Presidential calibre who was not a threat to him within the Democratic party but rather was helpful in unifying the party and maintaining its good electoral prospects. Johnson's own credentials as a liberal Democrat down through the years have not been strong; his choice as Vice-President in 1960 was opposed on these grounds by many labor leaders and by leaders from several of the most important urban Democratic strongholds.

Thus the 1964 choice of Senator Humphrey, a long-time liberal leader, did much to cement relations within the party and to unify Democrats of many shades of political preference solidly behind the national ticket. In choosing Humphrey, President Johnson adhered to a familiar strategy of "ticket balancing."

Thus, a Republican Presidential candidate from the East will try to pick a Vice-President from the Mid or Far West, though both will probably reside in large, two-party "swing" states. A liberal Democrat running for President will try to find a more conservative running mate. And so on. If it is impossible to find one man who combines within his heritage, personality, and experience all the virtues allegedly cherished by American voters, the parties console themselves by attempting to confect out of two running mates a composite father-son image of forward-looking—conservative, rural—urban, energetic—wise leadership which evokes hometown, ethnic, and party loyalties among a maximum number of voters. That, at least, is the theory behind the balanced ticket.

What can we say in general evaluation of these alternative strategies? From the standpoint of the electoral success of candidates, balancing the ticket seems only prudent. But there are reasons as well for ordinary citizens to prefer that candidates make an effort in this direction. One of the chief assets of the American party system in the past has been its ability (with the exception of the Civil War period) to reduce conflict by enforcing compromise within the major factions of each party. A refusal to heal the wounds and placate dissidents is nothing less than a declaration of internal war. It can only lead to increased conflict within the party. Willingness to bargain and make concessions to opponents is part of the price for maintaining unity in a party sufficiently large and varied to be able to appeal successfully to a population divided on economic, sectional, racial, religious, and ethnic grounds. To refuse entirely to balance the ticket would be to risk changing our large, heterogeneous parties into a multiplicity of small sects of "true believers" who care more about maintaining their internal purity than about winning public office.

This is not to suggest that the President and Vice-President must be worlds apart in their policy preferences in order to please everyone (or no one). There is obvious good sense in providing for a basic continuity in policy in case a President should die or be disabled. But this need not mean that the two men should be identical in every respect, even were that possible. Within the broad outlines of agreement on the basic principles of the nation's foreign policy and of the government's role in the economy, for example, a President would have no great difficulty in finding a variety of men who were somewhat more or less liberal than himself, who appealed to somewhat different groups, or who differed in other salient ways. To go this far in favor of party unity, factional conciliation, and popular preference should not discomfort anyone who realizes the costs of failing to balance the ticket in some important way.

Actually there is no evidence whatsoever to suggest that Vice-Presidents add or detract from the popularity of Presidential candidates with the voters. By helping unite the party, however, and by giving diverse party leaders another focus of identification with the ticket, a Vice-Presidential nominee with the right characteristics can help assure greater effort by party workers which may bring results at election time.

Even if balancing the ticket does not help the party at the polls, it may indirectly help the people. The act of balancing the ticket may aid our political parties in maintaining unity within diversity and thereby in performing their historic function of bringing our varied population closer together rather than pulling it further apart.

THE FUTURE OF NATIONAL CONVENTIONS

It may be that one of the lessons of recent Presidential elections is that national conventions are declining in importance as decision-making bodies.[52] They are not now taken seriously as decision-making instruments of the party of an incumbent President. The turnover of delegates from convention to convention is very high, averaging about 60%. This suggests the introduction of large numbers of delegates who are recruited by national candidates rather than by local parties. The success of both Senator Kennedy in 1960 and Senator Goldwater in 1964 make it plausible to argue that increasingly commitments are being made earlier and earlier in the nomination process, even when the nomination of the out-party is being contested among several factions.

Number of Presidential Ballots in National Party Conventions *

Year	Democrats	Republicans
1928	1	1
1932	4	1
1936	1	1
1940	1	6
1944	1	1
1948	1	3
1952	3	1
1956	1	1
1960	1	1
1964	1	1
First Ballot Total	8/10 (5 incumbents)	8/10 (2 incumbents)

Combined (Democrats and Republicans) First Ballot Nominations:
   Nonincumbents: 9/13
   Incumbents: 7/7

* Nominations won by incumbents are in italics.

The large number of first-ballot nominations (see the preceding table) in recent years suggests that important things are happening even in the out-party before the convention meets.

Nationwide television coverage of the primaries gives early-bird candidates a head start on the free publicity of the election year. Private polls (as well as those published in the newspapers) put more information about the comparative popularity of candidates in the hands of party leaders earlier than before. Thus the pressures upon state party leaders to decide what they want to do seem to be urging them to make decisions earlier in the election year—before national publicity creates a rush of sentiment in one direction or another that takes matters wholly out of their hands. When one or a few party leaders come to feel the need for early decisions, soon the others must follow suit, or lose their own room for maneuvering. These early decisions must, perforce, take place at widely separated places on the map, thus enhancing the bargaining power of candidates, who can deal with party leaders piecemeal under these circumstances, rather than having to face them *en masse* at a convention, where they can wheel and deal with one another.

If this tendency is correctly identified—and we should argue that it is a tendency for which only scattered and inconclusive evidence can presently be assembled—it leads to the further conclusion that over the long run, as mass communications media continue or possibly increase their saturation coverage of early events in the election year, successful candidates (at least of the out-party) increasingly will have to have access to large sums of money apart from the resources generally available to the party, a large personal organization, and an extra measure of skill and attractiveness on the hustings and over television. In these circumstances, other resources—such as the high regard of party leaders —would come to be less important. Thus, early candidacy, opulent private financing, and strong personal organizations such as characterized both the Kennedy and Goldwater preconvention campaigns can overcome strong misgivings on the part of party leaders whose main concern is winning elections. If out-party candidates in the future follow similar strategies, the national convention as a decision-making body may go into eclipse.

APPENDIX: SELECTION OF DELEGATES TO
NATIONAL CONVENTIONS

Not all states have primary elections, and different primaries
provide for the expression of different kinds of preferences. These
differences have rather substantial consequences for the behavior
of state delegations at the national conventions. Primaries can vary
in the following ways:

1) with regard to voters. In some states in order to vote in a primary,
one must have been registered as a voter with the party whose
primary one votes in. This is the "closed" primary. In the "open"
primary, the voter is allowed to appear at the polls and ask for
the primary ballot of the party whose delegates he wishes to
help choose, and no questions are asked.
2) with regard to the way in which alternatives are presented. In
some states, delegates run under their own names. In others,
they run as pledged to one Presidential aspirant or another. In
still others, delegates are run on a candidate's slate, and are identified only in terms of the Presidential hopeful they support.
3) with regard to the number of alternatives. Some states provide
for the entering of Presidential candidates on the ballot without
their consent; in others, the candidate himself must take the
initiative in placing his name on the ballot.
4) with regard to the existence of a preference primary. In some
states, in addition to the election of delegates, voters are given the
opportunity to express a direct Presidential preference. Furthermore, in some states there is a preference primary without election of delegates to the national convention—the delegates being
chosen by state party conventions. And in some states the delegates to *state* conventions are chosen by means of the preference
primary.

SOURCES: a. *Nomination and Election of the President and Vice-President of
the United States,* 86th Congress, 2nd Session, House Document No. 332
(Washington, 1960). b. *Compilation of the 48 Direct Primary Systems,* 2nd
ed., comp. League of Women Voters of New York (National Municipal
League, N.Y.: March 1957). c. *Preferential Presidential Primaries,* Library
of Congress, Legislative Reference Service (Washington 1961).

States	Method of Selecting Delegates to National Conventions	Candidate's Consent Needed to be on Ballot	Preferential Primary— Advisory or Binding	Open or Closed Primary
Alabama	primary, if contest[1]	no	optional[2]	closed
Alaska	state conventions	no	no	
Arizona	state executive committees	no	no	
Arkansas	state committee	yes	optional[3]	closed
California	primary	yes	yes—advisory	closed
Colorado	district delegates by district conventions; delegates-at-large by state convention	no	no	
Connecticut	state conventions	no	no	
Delaware	state conventions	no	no	
District of Columbia	primary	no	yes—binding	closed
Florida	primary	no	yes—advisory	closed
Georgia	Republicans—state convention; Democrats—state committee	no	no	
Hawaii	state conventions	no	no	
Idaho	state conventions	no	no	
Illinois	district delegates by primary; delegates-at-large by state convention	yes	yes—advisory	closed
Indiana	state conventions	yes	yes—binding	closed
Iowa	state conventions	no	no	
Kansas	state conventions	no	no	
Kentucky	state conventions	no	no	

[1] In practice, this means that Democrats use primaries; Republicans use state and district conventions.

[2] If held, advisory.

[3] A preferential primary must be held by a Presidential candidate's party if such candidate so petitions the state committee six months prior to the national conventions. If a preferential primary is held, it is binding on delegates.

States	Method of Selecting Delegates to National Conventions	Candidate's Consent Needed to be on Ballot	Preferential Primary— Advisory or Binding	Open or Closed Primary
Louisiana	district delegates by district conventions; delegates-at-large by state convention	no	no	
Maine	Republicans—district conventions; Democrats —state convention	no	no	
Maryland	state conventions	yes[4]	yes—binding	closed
Massachusetts	primary	yes	yes—binding	closed
Michigan	state delegate convention	no	no	
Minnesota	district delegates by district conventions; delegates-at-large by state convention	no	no	
Mississippi	state conventions	no	no	
Missouri	state conventions	no	no	
Montana	state conventions	no	no	
Nebraska	primary	no	yes—advisory	closed
Nevada	state conventions	no	no	
New Hampshire	primary	no	yes—advisory[5]	closed
New Jersey	primary	no	yes—advisory	closed[6]
New Mexico	state conventions	no	no	
New York	delegates-at-large by state convention; others —primary	no	no	closed
North Carolina	Republicans—district & state conventions; Democrats—state convention	no	no	
North Dakota	state conventions	no	no	

[4] Only if a delegate's statement of Presidential preference appears on the ballot.
[5] Binding if, and only if, the delegate has pledged himself to a Presidential candidate on the ballot.
[6] Voters must be registered with a party, but can ask for either party's ballot.

States	Method of Selecting Delegates to National Conventions	Candidate's Consent Needed to be on Ballot	Preferential Primary— Advisory or Binding	Open or Closed Primary
Ohio	primary	yes	yes—advisory[5]	closed
Oklahoma	state conventions	no	no	
Oregon	primary	no	yes—binding	closed
Pennsylvania	primary	no	yes—advisory[5]	closed
Rhode Island	state conventions	no	no	closed
South Carolina	state conventions	no	no	
South Dakota	primary	no	yes—advisory	closed
Tennessee	state conventions	no	no	
Texas	state conventions	no	no	
Utah	Republican—district & state conventions; Democrats—state convention	no	no	
Vermont	state conventions	no	no	
Virginia	state conventions	no	no	
Washington	state conventions	no	no	
West Virginia	primary	yes	yes—advisory	closed
Wisconsin	primary	yes	yes—advisory[5]	open
Wyoming	state conventions	no	no	

5) with regard to the legal standing of the preferences expressed in the primary. In some states, the Presidential preferences of voters in the primary are regarded as advisory on the state delegation. In others, the delegation is legally bound to support the candidate designated until released, or as long as the candidate has a chance to win.

NOTES

1. Much of the discussion in this chapter is drawn from our own observations of the nomination process over the mass media, for one of us in person at the Democratic National Convention of 1960 and the Republican National Convention of 1964, and from a set of basic

texts on American parties and elections, including Moisei Ostrogorski, *Democracy and the Party System in the United States* (New York, 1910); C. E. Merriam and H. Gosnell, *The American Party System* (New York, 1929); Peter H. Odegard and E. A. Helms, *American Politics* (New York, 1938); Pendleton Herring, *The Politics of Democracy* (New York, 1940); E. E. Schattschneider, *Party Government* (New York, 1942); D. D. McKean, *Party and Pressure Politics* (Boston, 1949); V. O. Key, Jr., *Politics, Parties and Pressure Groups*, 4th ed. (New York, 1958); H. R. Penniman, *Sait's Parties and Elections* (New York, 1952); Hugh A. Bone, *American Politics and the Party System* (New York, 1955); Austin Ranney and Willmoore Kendall, *Democracy and the American Party System* (New York, 1956); and William Goodman, *The Two-Party System in the United States* (Princeton, 1960); and Gerald Pomper, *Nominating the President: The Politics of Convention Choice*, 2nd ed. (New York, 1966).

We also found quite useful a more specialized literature on nominations, including Paul T. David, Malcolm C. Moos, and Ralph M. Goldman, *Presidential Nominating Politics in 1952*, Vols. I-V (Baltimore, 1954); Paul T. David, Ralph M. Goldman, and Richard C. Bain, *The Politics of National Party Conventions* (Washington, 1960); and Richard C. Bain, *Convention Decisions and Voting Records* (Washington, 1960).

2. See *Nomination and Election of the President and Vice-President of the United States including the Manner of Selecting Delegates to National Political Conventions*, 86th Congress, 2nd Session, House Document No. 332 (February 15, 1960) for an exhaustive description of the selection process, state by state, summarized in the table on pp. 112–114. See also *Nomination and Election of the President and Vice-President of the United States including the Manner of Selecting Delegates to National Political Conventions* compiled under the direction of Felton M. Johnson by Richard D. Hupman and Eiler C. Ravnholt with Robert L. Tienken, Senate Item 998 (January 1964), 43–46.

3. Frank Munger and James Blackhurst, "Factionalism in the National Conventions, 1940–1964: An Analysis of Ideological Consistency in State Delegation Voting," *The Journal of Politics* 27 (May 1965), 384. This article is a welcome corrective to the older view that delegates held no strong personal views and fits in well with recent research on party activists.

4. *Ibid.*, 378–379.

5. See, for example, Donald S. Strong, *Urban Republicanism in the South* (University, Ala., 1960); E. E. Schattschneider, *The Semisovereign People* (New York, 1960), Chapter V, "The Nationalization of Politics"; John C. Donovan, *Congressional Campaign: Maine Elects a Democrat*, Eagleton Series, Number 16 (New York, 1958); and Research Division, Republican National Committee, *The 1962 Elections* (mimeo., Washington, 1963).

6. See Paul Tillett, ed., *Inside Politics: The National Conventions, 1960* (Dobbs Ferry, N.Y., 1962) and Aaron B. Wildavsky, "The Intelligent Citizen's Guide to the Abuses of Statistics," in *Politics and Social Life*, eds. Nelson W. Polsby, Robert A. Dentler, and Paul A. Smith (Boston, 1963), pp. 825–844.

7. Key in *Politics, Parties and Pressure Groups*, p. 443, states succinctly the qualities of the ideally "available" Presidential candidate. He includes such factors as residence in a large politically uncertain state. He also says ". . . a man must be a Protestant [This was published in 1958] of good American stock and name to be 'available.' He should not be too closely affiliated with any particular interest or group nor should he have committed himself on a great and contentious issue before the time is ripe. Yet he must stand for something or a complex of things—a general point of view—in public life." Other factors listed are appearance, personal vigor, the possession of an attractive wife and children, and the luck to be in the right place, age group and so on, at the right time.

8. See Herring, *The Politics of Democracy*, pp. 203–224; Edward F. Cooke, "Drafting the 1952 Platforms," *Western Political Quarterly* 8 (September 1955), 465–480, and Part III of Tillett, *Inside Politics: The National Conventions, 1960*.

9. This is a point made by David, Goldman, and Bain, *The Politics of National Party Conventions*, pp. 398–404.

10. Richard M. Nixon, *Six Crises* (New York, 1962), pp. 313–314.

11. Karl A. Lamb, "Civil Rights and the Republican Platform: Nixon Achieves Control," in *Inside Politics: The National Conventions, 1960*, ed. Paul Tillett, pp. 55–84. Nixon was also concerned to see

that his party made a good impression on television. Nixon, *Six Crises*, pp. 313–320.

12. See Theodore H. White, *The Making of the President, 1964* (New York, 1965), Chapter 9.

13. See Harry W. Ernst, *The Primary That Made a President: West Virginia, 1960* (New York, 1962), p. 5 and Theodore H. White, *The Making of the President, 1960* (New York, 1961), pp. 94–95 for indications that participants were not at all clear at the time how to interpret these results.

14. Jack Arvey, as told to John Madigan, "The Reluctant Candidate," *The Reporter* (November 24, 1953).

15. In 1960, for example, Minnesota Democrats split among delegates friendly to Senator Humphrey and Governor Freeman—and to both of them. Freeman nominated John F. Kennedy for President. Senator Eugene McCarthy nominated Adlai Stevenson. And most of the delegation ended up voting for Humphrey.

16. David, Moos, and Goldman, *Presidential Nominating Politics in 1952*, II, 155–166.

17. Harry S. Truman, *Years of Trial and Hope* (Garden City, 1956), pp. 499–503 and Alben Barkley, *That Reminds Me* (Garden City, 1954), pp. 225–232.

18. For a general discussion of bargaining, see Robert A. Dahl and Charles E. Lindblom, *Politics, Economics and Welfare* (New York, 1953) *passim* and several works by Charles E. Lindblom that have been written since then, especially his *Bargaining: The Hidden Hand in Government* (Santa Monica, 1955) and *The Intelligence of Democracy* (New York, 1965).

19. One famous example has already been cited: The seating of Virginia in the 1952 Democratic Convention. See Allan P. Sindler, "The Unsolid South," in *The Uses of Power*, ed. Alan Westin (New York, 1962), pp. 230–283. See also Abraham Holtzman, *The Loyalty Pledge Controversy in the Democratic Party*, Eagleton Series, Number 21 (New York, 1960). Another example is, of course, the seating of Texas delegates at the 1952 Republican Convention. See Malcolm C. Moos, *The Republicans* (New York, 1956), pp. 468–479; William S. White, *The Taft Story* (New York, 1954), pp. 176–183; and

David, Moos, and Goldman, *Presidential Nominating Politics in 1952,* pp. 69–85.

20. See the articles on Symington in Eric Sevareid, ed., *Candidates, 1960* (New York, 1959) and Ralph G. Martin and Edward Plaut, *Front Runner, Dark Horse* (Garden City, 1960). See also Nixon, *Six Crises.*

21. Carl Sandburg, *Abraham Lincoln: The Prairie Years* (New York, 1926), II, 330. To an Indiana leader, Lincoln wrote that Republicans should "Look beyond our noses and say nothing on points where we should disagree."

22. See Ernst, *The Primary That Made a President;* White, *The Making of the President, 1960.*

23. James Reston, New York *Times,* June 3, 1964, p. 30.

24. Elting E. Morison, *The Letters of Theodore Roosevelt* (Cambridge, Mass., 1954), p. 525. See also George E. Mowry, *Theodore Roosevelt and the Progressive Movement* (Madison, 1946).

25. Robert D. Novak, *The Agony of the G.O.P. 1964* (New York, 1965), p. 368. In the 1964 Nebraska Republican primary the results were:

Goldwater	67,369	49%
Nixon (write-in)	42,811	35%
Lodge (write-in)	22,113	16%

26. General Eisenhower's write-in vote of over 100,000 in Minnesota in 1952 is, of course, the example we have in mind. See David, Moos, and Goldman, *Presidential Nominating Politics in 1952,* I, 32.

27. Ernst, *The Primary That Made a President;* White, *The Making of the President, 1960.*

28. Cf. Thomas Schelling, *The Strategy of Conflict* (Cambridge, Mass., 1960).

29. See Aaron B. Wildavsky, "What Can I Do? Ohio Delegates View The Democratic Convention," in *Inside Politics: The National Conventions, 1960,* ed. Paul Tillett, pp. 112–130.

30. James A. Farley, *Jim Farley's Story* (New York, 1948), pp. 11–13 and his *Behind the Ballots* (New York, 1938), p. 70; see also John F. Carter, *The New Dealers* (New York, 1934), p. 34.

31. Material on the Kennedy organization in 1960 is drawn from

Fred G. Burke, "Senator Kennedy's Convention Organization," in *Inside Politics: The National Conventions, 1960,* ed. Paul Tillett, pp. 25–39.

32. *Ibid.,* p. 39.

33. Recognizing the importance of communication at the Republican Convention of 1860, a supporter of Abraham Lincoln carefully seated all the solid Seward states close together and as far as possible from the states whose delegates were in some doubt about whom to support. Glyndon G. Van Deusen, *Thurlow Weed: Wizard of the Lobby* (Boston, 1947), p. 253.

34. See David, Moos, and Goldman, *Presidential Nominating Politics in 1952,* I; Robert Elson, "A Question for Democrats: If Not Truman, Who?" *Life* (March 24, 1952); Albert Votaw, "The Pros Put Adlai Over," *New Leader* (August 4, 1952); Douglass Cater, "How the Democrats Got Together," *The Reporter* (August 19, 1952); Arvey and Madigan, "The Reluctant Candidate: An Inside Story;" and Walter Johnson, *How We Drafted Adlai Stevenson* (New York, 1955).

35. Presidents Andrew Johnson and Arthur are the only clear exceptions since the Civil War. Coolidge and Wilson may also have had vague hopes of renomination.

36. See Ostrogorski, *Democracy and the Party System in the United States,* pp. 145–160, for excellent descriptions of convention confusion. Tillett, *Inside Politics: The National Conventions, 1960* contains up-to-date material in the same vein. White, *The Making of the President, 1964,* in contrast, describes the order and efficiency of conventions, like those in 1964, when there was no real contest for the nomination (see especially pp. 201–202). See also Ralph G. Martin, *Ballots and Bandwagons* (Chicago, 1964).

37. See Roy V. Peel and Thomas C. Donnelly, *The 1932 Campaign: An Analysis* (New York, 1935), pp. 92–93. Arthur Schlesinger, Jr., writes that strategist James Farley opposed the attempt to attack the two-thirds rule, "knowing well that not all delegates who were for Roosevelt were against the rule, and fearing that a defeat on this issue might set back the whole Roosevelt drive." Roosevelt backed down just in time. *The Crisis of the Old Order, 1919–1933* (Boston, 1957), pp. 299–300. See also Robert Morss Lovett, "Big Wind at Chicago," *The New Republic* (July 13, 1932), p. 228.

38. Wesley Bagby, "The 'Smoke-Filled Room' and the Nomination of Warren G. Harding," *Mississippi Valley Historical Review* 41 (March 1955), 657–674; the New York *Times,* June 12, 1960, p. 13.

39. Caroline T. Harnsberger, *A Man of Courage—Robert A. Taft* (Chicago, 1952), p. 146. See also Joseph Martin's memoirs, *My First 50 Years in Politics* (New York, 1960).

40. Peel and Donnelly, *The 1932 Campaign: An Analysis,* pp. 95–96. One thing which television viewers of the national conventions can observe at the stage when balloting takes place is the extent to which the various state delegations impose the unit rule on their members. When this rule is employed, as it is only at Democratic Conventions, the vote of the entire delegation is cast according to the decision of a majority within the delegation. Since having their delegation vote as a unit enhances the bargaining resources of state leaders, one would naturally assume that the unit rule is universally employed. But, in fact, this is not the case. On the contrary, the decision to adopt the unit rule is a ticklish one. Some state political leaders are faced with an intense, dissident minority within their delegations. Others may fear infringement upon the independence of their allies within the state party. While the adoption of unit voting assures leaders of a solid bloc of votes with which they can bargain, hard feelings may linger on within the state. When a minority element within a state is strong enough to gain representation on a convention delegation, muzzling it by imposing the unit rule is seldom wise. The unit rule is used to best advantage by those delegations whose members generally feel more strongly about preserving the bargaining advantages of a bloc vote than they do about any particular candidate. In a delegation firmly committed to a particular aspirant, the unit rule is superfluous, although it may still be used. But it is sometimes avoided by a leader who wants to reward delegates who stick together on the delegation's first choice. He releases them to vote as they individually please on their second choice, if the first choice is removed from contention. Hence, state delegations governed by the unit rule may well be relatively uncommitted in their Presidential preferences, and comparatively homogeneous in their political outlooks and allegiances.

41. Crowd sentiments, of course, are largely determined by the distribution of the tickets. Normally, these are apportioned by the

national committee among state party organizations, big financial contributors, and supporters of the various prominent candidates for President on as equitable and neutral a basis as party leaders can arrange. Thus, a gallery overwhelmingly in favor of a particular candidate is a rare phenomenon and suggests a rather more organized behind-the-scenes movement than meets the eye.

42. For instance, on the Roosevelt election of 1932: "Farley had held a few votes in reserve for the second ballot, knowing the importance of showing an increase each time round." Schlesinger, *The Crisis of the Old Order, 1919–1933*, p. 306.

43. Harry Daugherty, *The Inside Story of the Harding Tragedy*, (New York, 1932), pp. 36, 46; and Mark Sullivan, *Our Times* (New York, 1926–1935), II, 54. See also, Wesley Bagby, "The 'Smoke-Filled Room' and the Nomination of Warren G. Harding," pp. 657–674.

44. Arthur Vandenberg, Jr., ed., *The Private Papers of Senator Vandenberg* (Boston, 1952), p. 6.

45. Frank R. Kent, *The Democratic Party* (New York, 1928), p. 493.

46. See Jules Abels, *Out of the Jaws of Victory* (New York, 1959), pp. 65–68.

47. See Edward Stanwood, *A History of the Presidency from 1788 to 1897* (Boston, 1898), pp. 206–225.

48. Mark Sullivan, *Our Times*, VI, 35–67. See also Daugherty, *The Inside Story of the Harding Tragedy*, pp. 41–55.

49. See Kent, *The Democratic Party*, pp. 483–505.

50. Ferdinand Lundberg, *Imperial Hearst* (New York, 1936), pp. 273–275 and Schlesinger, *The Crisis of the Old Order, 1919–1933*, pp. 304–308.

51. See Irving G. Williams, *The American Vice-Presidency: New Look* (New York, 1954).

52. William Carleton, "The Revolution in the Presidential Nominating Convention," *Political Science Quarterly* 72 (June 1957), 224–240.

Chapter 3

The Campaign

Oɴᴄᴇ the conventions are over, the two Presidential candidates "relax" for a few weeks. On Labor Day they ordinarily begin their official campaigning. From that date onward they confront the voters directly, each carrying the banner of his political party. How do the candidates behave? Why do they act the way they do? And what kind of impact do their activities have on the electorate?

For the small minority of party workers, campaigns serve as a signal to get to work. How hard they work depends in part on whether the candidates' slogans, personalities, and visits spark their enthusiasm. The workers may "sit on their hands," or may pursue their generally unrewarding jobs—checking voting lists, mailing campaign flyers, ringing doorbells—with something approaching fervor. They cannot be taken for granted; activating them and imbuing them with purpose and ardor is perhaps the first task of the candidate.

For the population at large, much of which is normally uninterested in politics, campaigns call attention to the advent of an election. Some excitement may be generated and some diversion provided for those who were not aware, until they turned on the TV, that their favorite program had been preempted by a political speech. The campaign is a great spectacle. Talk about politics increases, and a small percentage of citizens may even become intensely involved as they get caught up in campaign oratory.

For the vast majority of citizens in America, campaigns do not function so much to change their minds as to reinforce their previous convictions. As the campaign wears on, the underlying party identification of most people rises ever more powerfully to the surface. Republican and Democratic identifiers are split further apart (polarized) as their increased awareness of party strife emphasizes the things that divide them.[1]

Three-quarters of American adults identify with a party. Among these, the Democrats enjoy a 3 to 2 advantage.[2] But Democrats tend to turn out less often. Given these facts, the outstanding strategic problem for Democratic politicians is to get their adherents to turn out and to vote for Democratic candidates. No need to worry about Republicans or Independents if Democrats can do their basic job. Democrats stress appeals to the faithful. They try to raise in their supporters the old party spirit. One of their major problems as we have seen is that most citizens who identify with them are found at the lower end of the socio-economic scale and are less likely to turn out to vote than are those with Republican leanings. So the Democrats put on mobilization drives and seek in every way to get as large a turn-out as possible. If they are well-organized, they scour the lower income areas. They try to provide cars for the elderly and infirm, baby sitters for mothers, and, occasionally, inducements of a less savory kind to reinforce the party loyalty of the faithful. The seemingly neutral campaigns put on by radio, TV, and newspapers to stress the civic obligation to vote, if they have any effect at all, probably help the Democrats more than the Republicans.[3]

The Republicans face a different strategic problem. They must, to be sure, try to get out their party adherents. But even if they do this well, it will not be enough. They must not only encourage people with Republican leanings to register and vote, they must also attract more than their share of the uncommitted, and they must persuade at least some of the Democratically inclined to forego their usual preference. This means playing down partisan appeals. Republicans ask voters to vote for the man and not for the party, since this gives the party its best chance of winning.

For Republicans involved in Presidential nominating politics, the most important fact of life is that their party is without question the minority party in the United States. What is more, the Republicans can claim the allegiance of what seems to be a minority of citizens that has shrunk steadily over the last twenty-five years.

Percentage of adults identifying themselves as:

	Republican	Democratic	Other
1940	38	42	20
1950	33	45	22
1960	30	47	23
1964	25	53	22

SOURCE: AIPO News Release, November 8, 1964.

The Survey Research Center at the University of Michigan has found repeatedly that about three-quarters of those in its samples eligible to vote claimed a party identification; of these, three-fifths were Democrats.[4] In Presidential elections in which considerations of party are foremost and allowing for the greater propensity of Republicans to turn out and vote, it has been plausibly argued that the Democrats could expect to win with around 53% or 54% of the vote.[5]

This is close enough to kindle hope justifiably in Republican breasts; despite the clear Democratic majority in this country, it must be assumed that either major party can win a Presidential election. But over the last thirty years it has generally been necessary for the Republicans to devise a strategy that could not only win, but win from behind.

With the handwriting so plainly on the wall, the strategic alternatives available to Republicans can hardly be regarded as secret. They can be boiled down to three possibilities. First, Republicans can attempt to deemphasize the impact of party habit as a component of electoral choice by capitalizing upon a more compelling cue to action. The nomination of General Eisenhower, the most popular hero of the Second World War, overrode party considerations and is a clear example of the efficacy of this strategy.[6] Efforts to play upon popular dissatisfaction in a variety of issue areas also exemplify this strategy, but these dissatisfactions must preexist in the population and must be widespread and intense before they will produce the desired effect. When issues do come to the fore in a compelling way, the payoff to the advantaged party is sometimes enormous, because these are the circumstances under which new party loyalties can be created.

Another possible Republican strategy, similar in some ways to the first, also seeks to depress the saliency of party in the minds of voters by blurring the differences between the parties, by seeking to efface certain of the stigmata that have been attached to the party over the years as stereotypes having general currency (e.g., "party of the rich").[7] This strategy gives full recognition to the arithmetic of Democratic superiority and also to the unit rule of the Electoral College, which weighs disproportionately votes cast in the large states that so often contain the heaviest concentrations of traditional allies of the Democratic party.[8] Although it has been used often by Republican nominees such as Willkie, Dewey, and Nixon, with results that always fell short—sometimes barely short—of victory, this "me-too" strategy has over the years become increasingly controversial among Republicans. The fact that no Republican candidate has actually been able to win with it has created doubts about its efficacy.[9] The "me-too" strategy may entail the advocacy of policies generally favored by most American voters, but this approach apparently does not correctly mirror the political sentiments of Republican activists.[10] Critics of the "me-too" approach have argued that this strategy merely alienates potential Republican voters while failing to attract sufficient Democrats. Alienated Republicans, so goes this argument, seeing no difference between the policies espoused by the major parties, withdraw from politics into apathy.[11]

Thus, a third strategy, whose claim of victory is based upon the presupposition of a hidden Republican vote, can be identified. This was the strategy pursued by the Goldwater forces in 1964. It has as its main characteristic the attempt to sharpen rather than blur party lines on matters of substantive policy. We will analyze this strategy in Chapter 4.

THEORY AND ACTION

The contents of election campaigns appear to be largely opportunistic. The swiftly changing nature of events makes it unwise for candidates to lay down all-embracing rules for campaigning which cannot meet special situations as they arise. A candidate may prepare for battle on one front and discover that the movement of events forces him to fight on another. Yet on closer examination, it is evident that the political strategist has to rely on some sort of theory about the probable behavior of large groups of voters under a few likely conditions. For there are too many millions of voters and too many thousands of possible events to deal with each as a separate category. Keynes pointed out years ago, quite rightly, that those among us, including politicians, who most loudly proclaim their avoidance of theory are generally the victims of some long dead economist or philosopher whose assumptions they have unknowingly assimilated. The candidates must simplify their picture of the political world, or its full complexity will paralyze them; the only question is whether or not their theories, both explicit and implicit, will prove helpful to them.

What kind of organization shall they use or construct? How

shall they raise money? Where shall they campaign? How much time shall they allocate to the various regions and states? What kinds of appeals shall they make to what voting groups? What kind of personal impression shall they seek to create or reinforce? How far should they go in castigating the opposition? These are the kinds of strategic questions to which Presidential candidates need answers—answers which necessarily vary depending on their party affiliations, their personal attributes, whether they are in or out of office, and on targets of opportunity that come up in the course of current events. Let us take up each of these questions in turn, taking care to specify the different problems faced by "ins" and "outs" and by Democrats and Republicans. For purposes of illustration, we shall turn often to the 1960 contest between John Kennedy and Richard Nixon and the 1964 Barry Goldwater–Lyndon Johnson battle.

INS AND OUTS

In choosing a campaign strategy much depends on whether the candidate is an incumbent or is trying to dislodge a man who is already in office. The man in office has the advantage of having had huge amounts of publicity. For better or for worse, he is probably better known than any challenger can be. He is experienced, and people have learned to depend upon him. While he is in office, he may be in a position to take actions which will help him, such as acting decisively in foreign affairs, as Johnson did in the Bay of Tonkin incident, taking "nonpolitical" trips to drum up support, and little things like making sure that veterans' administration checks get mailed out promptly or even a little ahead of time.[12]

The incumbent also has to face a number of disadvantages inherent in his position. Inevitably, Presidents have to do things which dissatisfy some people. Resentments build up. Should economic or military conditions appear to change for the worse, the President seeking re-election may well be the victim of a protest vote. Herbert Hoover felt the sting of this phenomenon deeply when the people punished the "ins" for a depression which Hoover would have given much to avoid. Moreover, the incumbent has a record. He has or has not done things, and he may be held to account for his sins of omission or commission; not so the man out-of-office, who can criticize freely without always presenting viable alternatives or necessarily taking his own advice once he is elected. The "missile gap" turned out to be something of a chimera after Kennedy got into the White House and he never found it possible to act much differently toward the Matsu-Quemoy situation than did Dwight Eisenhower, despite their over-publicized "differences" about this question during the campaign. The incumbent is naturally cast in the role of the defender of his administration and the challenger as the attacker who promises better things to come. After all, we would hardly expect to hear the man in office say that the other fellow could probably do as well or to hear the challenger declare that he really could not do any better than the incumbent, although both statements may be close to the truth.

The challenger has his own problems. He may not be well known and may find that much of his effort must be devoted to publicizing himself. All the while, the President is getting reams of free publicity and is in a position to create major news by the things he does—an administrative action to help Negroes, a call to the summit, an announcement of a new advance in space research.

The candidate aspiring to office may find that he lacks information, which puts him at a disadvantage in discussing foreign policy and defense issues. On the other hand, he may deliberately forbear from finding out too much for fear that he be restrained in his criticism by an implied pledge not to use information the President has furnished to him. Perhaps the major advantage the challenger possesses is his ability to criticize policies freely and sometimes in exaggerated terms, whereas the incumbent is often restrained by his current official responsibilities from talking too much about them. Obligations to other nations, for example, may restrain a President from talking about changes in foreign policy or from tipping his hand in a case like Cuba.

One of the most difficult positions for a candidate is to try to succeed a President of his own party. He loses many advantages of incumbency—huge publicity resources, ability to make decisions, a going organization—while taking on many of the disadvantages. No matter how hard he tries to avoid it he is stuck with the record made by the President of his own party. If he tries to disavow portions of this record, as Adlai Stevenson did when he tried to follow Harry Truman, the results can easily be disappointing. He may lose some support the current President has without gaining much for himself. He may actually turn public attention to allegedly bad aspects of the incumbent's record through his attempts to disassociate himself. As it turned out, Stevenson was badly hurt by allegations of corruption and failure to end the war in Korea under the Truman Administration.[13] Richard Nixon faced an easier task in attempting to succeed the far more popular Dwight Eisenhower. Indeed, he attempted to wrap himself in Eisenhower's mantle whenever the opportunity presented itself. Yet Nixon increasingly found himself on the defensive as Kennedy talked about getting the nation moving again and acting more energetically. Nixon said we *were* moving, but he could hardly promise to do too much more and make things too much better, since that would have implied a disavowal of President Eisenhower.[14]

FRIENDS, VOLUNTEERS, AND PROFESSIONALS

While the incumbent has a going organization, molded and tested through years in office, the challenger has to build one piecemeal as he goes along in the frantic days of the campaign when there is never enough time to do everything that has to be done. Should he have a man of his own run the show without much of a nod to the professionals? They may resist, if not sabotage, his efforts. Should he enlist the cooperation of the old party men knowing that he may thereby lose some control over his campaign? Should there be two centers of campaigning with the inevitable duplication and problems of coordination? There is apparently no costless solution to this problem. There always seems to be grumbling from party professionals and the candidate's own men about their relationship.

All candidates seek special volunteer organizations to help attract voters who prefer not to associate themselves with the party organizations. The distaste with which some middle and upper class people regard the rather earthy and predominantly lower class party organizations is difficult to overcome. It is easier to construct new organizations in which they can feel ennobled by attachment to an Eisenhower or Stevenson rather than (as they may feel) associating with a group of vulgar politicians. The danger here is that the volunteer organizations will take on lives of their own and attempt to dictate strategy and policy to the candidates. A few of the volunteers may transfer to the regular party and this may lead to serious internal dissension as happened in the successful move to oust Carmine DeSapio of Tammany Hall in New York City. The candidates need the volunteers, but it is advisable for them to follow the lead set by Kennedy and Nixon in keeping tight reins on them to assure reasonable coordination of efforts and to avoid being captured.

The mechanics of electioneering are no simple matter; they cannot be entrusted wholly to amateurs. Not only must the candidate get to his various speaking engagements when he is supposed to, but he also needs to have some good idea of whom he is speaking to and what kind of approach to take. In the hurly-burly of the campaign, where issues and plans may change from day to day, where yesterday's ideas may have to end up in the wastebasket to make room for today's problems, where changes of schedule are made in response to the opportunities and dangers suggested by private and public polls, a poor organization can be severely damaging. The troubles of Adlai Stevenson present a case in point. His apparent distaste for the niceties of organization in 1956 hurt him badly. He was excessively rushed going from one place to another so that he lost the valuable assets of composure and thoughtfulness which should have been his stock in trade. If he continually made speeches which were inappropriate for his audiences, it may have been because he was badly informed about who his audience would be, not because he was talking "over people's heads." For instance, he once went to New Haven during the 1956 campaign, and made a speech redolent with allusions to Yale and Princeton, with punch lines depending on knowledge of what the "subjunctive" was, to an audience which happened to be composed largely of old-time Democratic party workers from around Connecticut.[15] To be sure, some mix-ups, if not a few outright fiascoes, are inevitable given the frantic pace and the pressure of time. Resilience is not the least qualification of a Presidential candidate.

WHERE TO CAMPAIGN?

In deciding where to campaign, the candidates are aided by distinctive features of the national political structure which go a long way toward giving them guidance. They know that it is not votes as such that matter but electoral votes which are counted on a state-by-state basis. The candidate who wins by a small plurality in a state gains all the electoral votes there are for that state. The candidates realize that a huge margin of victory in a state with a handful of electoral votes will not do them nearly as much good as a bare plurality in states like New York and California with large numbers of electoral votes. So their first guideline is evident: Campaign in states with large electoral votes. There is, however, not much point in campaigning in states where a candidate is bound to win or to lose. Thus, states which almost always go for one party receive only perfunctory attention. Hence, the original guideline may be modified to read: Campaign in states with large electoral votes which are doubtful. In practice, a "doubtful" state is one where there is a good chance for both parties to capture the state, and politicians usually gauge this chance by the extent to which the state has delivered victories to both parties at some time in recent memory. Republicans and Democrats thus spend more time in the large doubtful states, such as New York, Ohio, Texas, and California, than they do in the deep South which will probably go Democratic or upper New England which will probably go Republican. And even if one or two of these one-party states should change in one election, the likelihood of such an event is too slim and the payoff in terms of electoral votes too meager to justify extensive campaigning when time might better be spent elsewhere. As the campaign wears on, the candidates take soundings from the opinion polls and are likely to redouble their efforts in states where they believe a personal visit might turn the tide.

Here we once again come across the pervasive problem of uncertainty. No one really knows how much value in changed votes or turnout is gained by personal visits to a particular state. Most voters have made up their minds. Opponents of the candidate are unlikely to go to see him anyway and one wonders what a glimpse in a motorcade will do to influence a potential voter. Yet no one is certain that whistle-stop methods produce no useful result. Visiting localities may serve to increase publicity because many of the media of communication are geared to "local" events. It also provides an opportunity to stress issues like public power or race relations which may be of special significance to citizens in a given region. Party activists may be energized by a glimpse at, or a handshake with, the candidate. New alliances, such as the one that emerged in 1964 between Goldwater and many long-time Democratic sectors of the deep South, can be solidified. And so rather than let the opportunity pass, the candidates usually decide to take no chances and get out on the hustings. They hedge against uncertainty by doing all they can.

Consider the case of John Kennedy in Ohio. He traversed that pivotal state several times in the 1960 campaign and exerted great physical effort in getting himself seen traveling across the state. But when the votes were counted, he found himself at the short end. The future President professed to be annoyed and stumped at why this happened. An analysis of the voting returns showed that Kennedy's vote was correlated in a high and positive degree with the percentage of Catholic population in the various counties.[16] Kennedy made a considerable improvement over the Democratic showing in 1956, but that was not enough to win. Despite evidence of this kind, which suggests that personal appearances may well be overwhelmed by other factors, visits to localities will undoubtedly continue. Who can say, to take a contrary instance, that Kennedy's visit to Illinois did not provide the bare margin of a few thousand votes necessary for victory?

There was a time when Presidential nominees faced the serious choice of whether to conduct a front porch campaign or to get out and meet the people. A candidate like Warren Harding, who his sponsors felt would put his foot in his mouth every time he spoke, was well-advised to stay home. More hardy souls like William Jennings Bryan took off in all directions only to discover that to be seen was not necessarily to be loved. An underdog, like Harry Truman in 1948, went out to meet the people because he was so far behind. A favored candidate, like Thomas Dewey in 1948, went out to meet the people to avoid being accused of complacency. Everybody is doing it probably because it is the fashion, and the spectacle of seeing one's opponent run around the country at a furious pace without following suit is too nerve-wracking to contemplate. That no one knows whether all this does any good is beside the point. Some future candidate might want to consider running a different kind of campaign, taking account of the fact that radio and television make it possible to reach millions, without leaving the big metropolitan areas. Such a candidate might fix upon something like a half or a full dozen regional centers and make his appearances and speeches in these places. The added time for reflection and the additional reserves of energy he would gain over the previous method might do something to improve the quality of his campaign. And should he happen to be elected, he might become the only President-elect in recent history not to be utterly exhausted on Election Day.

PARTY IDENTIFICATION

We have seen that most votes are determined most of the time by party identification. The candidates are keenly aware that this is the case. Moreover, they know that a substantial majority of voters favor the Democratic party. Consequently, if an election is widely perceived as a straight contest between the parties, the Democratic candidate is likely to win. The strategic implications are clear. Democratic candidates go around invoking the name of their party over and over again. If they feel it inadvisable to criticize an opponent, like General Eisenhower, they know that they have a good target in the Republican party. The objective of the Democrats is to have as many voters as possible identify their candidate with the Democratic party label, since it is the preferred party of most of the population.[17]

A Republican strategy that faces up to this problem of party identification can be inferred from Nixon's tactics during the 1960 campaign. He refused to make the contest into a party fight and called for support from all men of good will. He played down his Republicanism and attempted to divide Kennedy from the Democratic party by saying that the old party greats—Jefferson, Jackson, and Wilson—would have had no truck with the alien, radical philosophy of this upstart. Kennedy, Nixon asserted, had grievously departed from the true principles of the Democratic party (whatever they were supposed to be) and no longer deserved the support of the members of that great organization. In fact, Nixon implied that he was a better "real" Democrat than Kennedy. So anxious was Nixon to bask in the warmth of the Democratic sun, that he talked of appointing good Democrats to office. If he could have had his way, no Democrat need have believed that Nixon's feelings about the party were so hostile as to necessarily justify a vote against him on these grounds.[18]

DOMESTIC ISSUES

On the broad range of domestic affairs and "pocketbook" issues, the Democrats are highly favored as the party most voters believe will best meet their needs. Statements like "The Democrats are best for the workingman" and "We have better times under the Democrats" abound when people are asked to state how they feel about the Democratic party. The Republicans, on the other hand, are viewed as the party of depression under which jobs are scarce and times are bad. A campaign in which the salient issues are domestic, therefore, is more likely to aid the Democrats than the Republicans.[19]

Domestic policy thus occasions little difficulty for the Democratic party. Its task is to be liberal in several senses of that word. It promises something for everyone. There are sizable extensions of social welfare programs financed by the Federal government, increased minimum wages for the underpaid, medical insurance for the aged, high price supports for the farmer, irrigation for arid areas, flood protection and power dams for the river basins, and so on. No one is left out, not even businessmen who are promised prosperity.

Republicans are clearly on the defensive in the realm of domestic policy, a situation stemming from the fact that they were in office when the Great Depression took place. They try to play down domestic issues. They do best when emphasizing foreign policy ("bring the boys back from Korea"); style issues ("mink coats and five percenters"); general management of government ("we can do it better"); or an outstanding personality ("I like Ike"). When domestic issues are debated, a Republican candidate like Richard Nixon takes care to stress that he is in favor of the New Deal's social reforms whatever else he may say about it.

And he adds that he is in favor of helping farmers, laborers, old people, pensioners, teachers, and other worthy folk extend their gains. That he will do this better and cheaper becomes his refrain and the major point of difference with his opponent. He is understandably upset at Democratic insinuations that he and his party have not become fully reconciled to Social Security. Over and over again in his television debates with Kennedy, Nixon insisted that he and his opponent agreed on goals of domestic policy, and that the only difference separating the two men was the minor matter of means.[20] For if the gulf between the parties was thought to be wide on "pocketbook" issues, a majority of voters would unhesitatingly choose the Democrats.

Both parties, of course, have some difficulty in reconciling their Presidential and Congressional wings, but in the realm of domestic policy the Democrats have an easier task. The crucial electoral votes come from large states where the labor union and minority group interests reinforce the Presidential aspirant's demand for liberal policies. Democratic conservatives, who are in any event in a minority even in Congress, can be and largely are ignored, except perhaps for lip service to the idea of a balanced budget. A strong civil rights stand risks loss of Southern support, but Negroes are strategically placed in states with the highest number of electoral votes. Since Franklin D. Roosevelt, all Democratic Presidential candidates have decided that they can win without the South but not without the large states in other sections of the country. Television and radio make the old practice of saying different things in different parts of the country rather more dangerous than it used to be. In fact, a kind of reversal has set in. Contemporary candidates are more likely to get favorable publicity if they attack segregation before Southern audiences. This not only comes immediately to the attention of admiring audiences in the Northern Negro strongholds, but also not incidentally demonstrates the courage and integrity of the candidate. Whether from conviction or calculation of advantage,

Democratic candidates have no trouble coming out strongly for civil rights.

The Republicans face much more difficult problems of internal dissension. Their Congressional contingent is cohesive and generally conservative. The result is that Republican Presidential candidates more often than not repudiate their Congressional brethren. Party conservatives do not like the "me-too" implications of the stands taken by their Presidential candidates like Nixon. They felt he ought to have hit harder at what they regard as Democratic statism and looseness with the public purse. But the numbers of strategically placed voters, or the groups from whom they take their cues, who disagree with this approach in domestic affairs is too great for a Republican candidate who wants to win to forget them. Though Nixon talked tough at times in remarks directed to selected Republican audiences, he understandably refused to alter the tenor of his remarks in general. Like all Republican candidates since 1936, with the exception of former Senator Goldwater, he apparently concluded that there were not enough conservatives to elect him, that they had no place to go, and that he would get their votes anyhow as, indeed, he did. Nixon continued to send conservatives out on the hustings to mollify the right-wing but he refused to commit political suicide by making wholesale attacks on the Democratic party and its domestic policies.

FOREIGN AFFAIRS

In the realm of foreign affairs, the Republicans have the advantage. The fact that the Democrats occupied the Presidency during World Wars I and II and the Korean War apparently convinced most voters that Democrats tend to lead the country to war. This belief may be reinforced by the war in Vietnam. Republicans have escaped this stigma and are known as the party of peace.[21] Whether this impression is any more useful or valid than that of Republicans as the party of depression is beside the point for present purposes.

We are after the strategic implications, which are important. For if foreign affairs issues can be made sufficiently important to enough voters, the Republicans stand a better chance of winning. Republicans do best by building up foreign affairs and playing on the fear that Democrats are not competent in this field. Democrats have the choice of deemphasizing foreign policy, something that has become increasingly difficult to do, or trying to show somehow that they are more peace-loving than Republicans, though also at least as tough on Communism. So President Johnson combines military action in Vietnam with "peace offensives." A Republican outcry against the United States involvement in Vietnam might regain them their reputation as the party of peace at the expense of demonstrating ideological inconsistency. However, a Republican stand supporting escalation in Vietnam could be interpreted by the voters either as the Republicans wanting more fighting (war party) or the Republicans wanting the boys home sooner (peace party).

How this used to work in practice can be seen in Richard Nixon's campaign, as the lamb of domestic controversy turned into the lion of foreign affairs. Nixon sought to differentiate himself as much as possible from Kennedy in the field of foreign affairs. He suggested that he was uniquely capable of securing peace without surrender, and that Kennedy was not. He tried to strengthen the prevailing impression of the Democratic party as the party of war. He implied alternatively that Kennedy would permit the Communists to make unwarranted advances (for example, in Matsu and Quemoy), and that the Democrats would make rash moves (Cuba). Even Nixon's espousal of an aggressive line, such as he took regarding Matsu and Quemoy, helped him because in foreign affairs voters trust the Republicans. On the other hand, Kennedy's equally aggressive stand toward Cuba in his speeches did not correspondingly help him.[22]

All this may appear paradoxical, but it is perfectly understandable in the light of our knowledge of voting behavior. Kennedy did not succeed in convincing most voters that issues of foreign policy were more important than domestic concerns. He won on his party affiliation, on domestic issues, and on his appeal to Catholics.[23] Had he accomplished his purpose of alerting voters to the importance of foreign affairs, there is every reason to believe he would have lost support, since voters, in line with their previous inclinations, would have decided that the perilous times called for a Republican in the White House.

The television debates reflected this. Those viewers of the debates who were especially attentive to foreign policy issues were more likely to be pro-Nixon than pro-Kennedy, just the reverse of the situation in domestic affairs. A summary of public opinion surveys on the debates concludes: "The evidence suggests that foreign affairs was the paramount issue during the entire campaign and . . . since Nixon was generally conceded to be the more expert and experienced in foreign affairs—he was far ahead of Kennedy in perceived ability at 'handling the Russians' and 'keeping the peace'—the focus on foreign affairs was clearly to Nixon's advantage." [24]

PRESENTATION OF SELF

Another set of strategic problems concerns the personal impression made by the candidates. A candidate is helped by being thought of as trustworthy, reliable, mature, kind but firm, a devoted family man and in every way normal and presentable. No amount of expostulation about the irrelevance of all this ordinariness as qualification for an extraordinary office wipes out the fact that candidates must try to conform to the public stereotype of goodness, a standard which is typically far more demanding of politicians than of ordinary mortals. It would be a rather excruciating process for a candidate to remodel his entire personality along the indicated lines. And, to be fair, the candidates are not so far from the mark as to make this drastic expedient necessary or they would not have been nominated in the first place. What the candidates actually try to do is to smooth off the rough edges, that is, to counter the most unfavorable impressions of specific aspects of their public image to which they believe they are susceptible. Kennedy, who was accused of being young and immature, hardly cracked a smile in his debates with Nixon, while the latter, who was said to be stiff and frightening, beamed with friendliness. Kennedy restyled his youthful shock of hair, and Nixon thinned his eyebrows to look less threatening.

The political folklore of previous campaigns provides candidates with helpful homilies about how to conduct themselves. Typical bits of advice include the following: always carry the attack to your opponent; the best defense is offense; separate the other candidate from his party; when in doubt as to the course which will produce the most votes, do what you believe is ethically or morally right; guard against acts that can hurt you because they are more significant than acts that can help you; avoid making personal attacks which may gain sympathy for the opposition. Unfortunately for the politicians in search of a guide, these bits of folk wisdom do not contain detailed instructions about the conditions under which they may be applied.

The case of Adlai Stevenson suggests a familiar dilemma for candidates. Shall they write (or have written) new speeches for most occasions or shall they rest content to hammer home a few themes, embroidering just a little here and there? No one really knows which is better. Stevenson is famous for the care which he devoted to his speeches and the originality he sought to impart to his efforts. Had he won office he might have established a trend. As it is, most candidates are likely to follow Kennedy, Nixon, Johnson, and Goldwater in using just a few set speeches. In view of the pervasive inattention to public affairs and political talk in our society, this approach may have the advantage of driving points home (as well as driving mad the newsmen who must listen to the same thing all the time).[25]

More important, perhaps, is the desirability of appearing comfortable in delivery. Televised speeches may establish the major opportunity for a candidate to be seen and evaluated by large numbers of people. Eisenhower's ability to project a radiant appearance helped him; Stevenson's obvious discomfort before the camera hurt him. On this point we have evidence that those who listened to Stevenson's delivery over radio were more favorably impressed with him than those who watched him on TV.[26] With television occupying an important place in American life, ability to make a good appearance is not a trivial matter. There is little reason to believe, however, that we are headed for a society in which TV performers can run for public office and expect to win—except, of course, in California, where party organizations traditionally have had little control over the selection of candidates to run for office.

The major difficulty with the strategic principles we have been discussing is not that they are too theoretical, but that they do not really tell the candidates what to do in case they are mutually incompatible. Like proverbs, one can often find principles to justify opposing courses of action. ("Look before you leap" but "he who hesitates is lost.") Nixon could not take full advantage of international affairs without hitting so hard as to reinforce the unfavorable impression of himself as being harsh and unprincipled. Kennedy could hardly capitalize on the Rooseveltian image of the vigorous leader without attacking the foreign policy of a popular President. The result is that the candidates must take calculated risks when existing knowledge about the consequences of alternative courses of action is inadequate. Here, hunch, intuition, and temperament necessarily play an important role in choosing among competing alternatives.

THE TELEVISION DEBATES

The famous TV debates between Nixon and Kennedy provide an excellent illustration of the difficulty of choosing between competing considerations in the absence of knowledge as to the most likely results. With the benefit of hindsight, many observers now suggest that Nixon was obviously foolish to engage in the debates.

Let us try to look at the situation from the perspective of each of the Presidential aspirants at the time. Kennedy issued a challenge to debate on television. The possible advantages from his point of view were many. He could use Nixon's refusal to debate to accuse him of running away and depriving the people of a unique opportunity to judge the candidates. Among Kennedy's greatest handicaps in the campaign were his youth and the inevitable charges of inexperience. Television debates could and did help to overcome these difficulties by showing the audience not so much that Kennedy was superior in knowledge but that there was not that much difference in the information, age, and general stature of the two men. Whatever administrative skills or inside information Nixon might have would not and did not show up on the screen as the candidates necessarily confined themselves to broad discussions of issues known to all politically literate people. Kennedy could only guess but he could not know that Nixon would not stump him in an embarrassing way in front of millions of viewers. But Kennedy was in a position to know that despite the reams of publicity he had received, he was unknown to many voters, much less known than the Vice-President. Here was a golden opportunity to increase his visibility in a sudden and dramatic way. And his good looks were not calculated to hurt him with those who like to judge the appearance of a man.[27]

Nixon was in a more difficult position. To say "no" would not have been a neutral decision; it would have subjected him to being called a man who was afraid to face his opposition. Saying "yes" had a number of possible advantages. One stemmed from the fact that the Republicans are the minority party in terms of adherents in the United States. Normally, most people do not pay very much attention to the opposition candidate, making it difficult to win them over. They avoid contact with his statements and screen out his messages. Televised debates would provide a unique instance in which huge numbers of people attracted to both parties could be expected to tune in attentively. Nixon had good reason for believing that if he made a favorable impression he would be in a position to convince more of the people (the Democratic identifiers) he needed to convince than would Kennedy. The risk that Kennedy might use the opportunity to solidify the support of those attracted to a Democrat simply had to be taken. Another potential advantage which might have accrued to Nixon arose from the heritage of his previous political life. He had been labeled by some people as "tricky Dick," an immoral and vindictive man. This picture might have been supplanted on television by the new Nixon of smiling visage and magnanimous gesture who had it all over his opponent in knowledge of public affairs. Nixon had to judge whether his handicap was serious or whether it was confined to convinced liberals whose numbers were insignificant and who would never have voted for him in any event. He also had to guess whether it would be worthwhile to overcome this handicap, even if it also meant giving Kennedy an opportunity to overcome his own disabilities.[28] Perhaps a record of success in debate situations going back to high school was not irrelevant in guiding Nixon to his eventual decision to go on television with his opponent.[29] Surveys taken after the event suggest that Nixon miscalculated.[30] But if he had won the election instead of losing it by a wafer-thin margin, he would hardly have been reminded of any error on his part, and there would probably have been discussions of what a brilliant move it was for him to go on TV.

The election of 1964 presented an entirely different set of circumstances. President Johnson, an incumbent enjoying enormous personal popularity at the head of the majority party, had nothing to gain and everything to lose by debating his rival. And so, despite strenuous efforts by Senator Goldwater and his allies to involve the President in debates, none were held.

GETTING A GOOD PRESS

Until 1964 most newspapers supported Republican candidates in their editorials and (to some extent) in their news columns; no doubt this predilection will reassert itself in future campaigns. Most reporters assigned to cover the candidates, on the other hand, are inclined to support Democrats, and this may show in their stories. Except for a few who may be on the fence, it usually does not pay for candidates to try to line up support from publishers who have already made up their minds, before the campaign has officially started. But the candidates can and do assiduously court the newspapermen assigned to them.[31]

The space a candidate gets and the slant of the story may depend to some extent on how the reporters regard him. If they find it difficult to get material, if they find the candidate suspicious and uncommunicative, this too may have its effect on how much and what gets published. Little things like phasing news to meet the requirements of afternoon papers or supplying reporters with human interest material is helpful to the candidate. Thus, the personality of the candidate, his ability to command the respect of the rather cynical men assigned to cover him may count heavily. Democratic candidates probably have to work a little harder at cultivating good relations in order to help counteract the editorial slant in most papers. They also must make the most of their opportunities in public appearances, radio and TV speeches to counteract the impression given in segments of the press. If what they say and do "makes news," and their press secretaries help promote the stories, they may get space through the desire of the newspapers to sell copies.

Thus far, we have spoken of the press as if it were a monolithic entity. So do the candidates for the most part. But they also recognize that there are all sorts of papers with differing biases, needs, and audiences. A great deal of a candidate's attention is devoted to stories destined for the Negro, religious, and ethnic interest group press. The circulations of these publications may not be huge but it is assumed that these papers have readers who are especially concerned with topics like race relations. A story on religion in a Protestant journal may do more to convince people than much greater coverage in the daily press.

MUD-SLINGING

In the closing days of what appears to be a close race, there may be a temptation for the parties, now thoroughly engrossed in the heat of battle, to unloose a stream of invective directly at the other side. How much of this they do and how often they do it is partially determined by the kind of people they are. In the long run, however, the standards of the voting population determine the standards of the candidates. Should it happen that vituperation is rewarded, we can expect to see it occur again. Should it prove to be the case, however, as in the Scandinavian countries, that departures from proper deportment are severely punished at the polls, candidates can be expected to take the hint.

In the United States we seem to be in a middle position in regard to mud-slinging. It is not everyday practice but neither is it a rarity. A history of Presidential campaigns suggests that vituperation is largely irrelevant to the outcomes of campaigns and that its benefits are problematical.

Thomas Jefferson was accused of seducing a highborn Virginia maiden, fathering a brood of mulattoes, and being an atheist. Andrew Jackson was called a murderer, gambler, and an adulterer. Lincoln was charged with being a vulgar village politician and fourth-rate lawyer. President Grover Cleveland was accused of fathering an illegitimate child and, though he was not certain of its paternity, he admitted responsibility. His opponents taunted him with the chant:

> *Ma, Ma, where's my Pa?*
> *Gone to the White House*
> *Ha! Ha! Ha!* [32]

The point is, however, that all these men won office as have many others who have been subject to similar aspersions.

Even more instructive is the case of William Henry Harrison whom Democratic politicians derogated with the remark that he would be content to spend the rest of his life in a log cabin drinking hard cider. His party seized on this to make him into a symbol of the common man and drowned out all attempts to discuss issues with cries about humble living in log cabins. Van Buren, the Democratic candidate, was crushed with doggerel like this:

> *Let Van from his coolers of silver drink wine*
> *And lounge on his cushioned settee*
> *Our man on his buckeye bench can recline*
> *Content with hard cider is he.*

The candidate faces the difficulty of deciding what kind of invective to ignore as potentially damaging and what kind to turn to his advantage. Franklin Roosevelt paid no attention to most accusations about him but seized on an attack involving his dog, Fala, to rib his opponents unmercifully for impugning a dog that could not reply.[33] If all else fails, it is always possible to take the advice attributed to a Chicago politician who said that in politics, as in poker, the way to meet scandalous charges was to "Call 'em and raise 'em. If you are denounced as a fool, call your opponent a damned fool; if he says you are a crook, call him a robber; if he intimates that you are careless with the truth, tell your audience that he is a pathological liar."

Why, we may wonder, are men supposed to behave in a more exalted fashion in politics and in the midst of a passionately fought contest than we would expect of them in other areas of life? Successful public officials, like successful businessmen and union leaders, deal with man as he is, not as they would wish him to be. Campaigning is concerned primarily with winning support; any secondary effects it may have, such as educating the public, are incidental. If we wonder at the level of appeals made to us in elections we need only look so far as our own qualities to get the answer. These are occasions when we might be thankful that our politicians do not fully reflect the ethical standards actually practiced (not preached) in society. Knowledge of our own character may explain the wish (and expose the fallacy) of expecting politicians to be better than we are.

FEEDBACK

As the campaign progresses, the candidates attempt to take soundings from various sources and to modify their behavior as seems best suited to make the most of opportunities as they arise. But this process presents tremendous problems in the chaotic atmosphere of a campaign. Even under conditions of comparative tranquility, who knows what the world is like? In our everyday lives we make assumptions that simplify reality tremendously in order to make decisions. Consider, then, the poor candidate who must try to take hold of a complicated universe in which the actions and the reactions of millions of voters, his own staff, his opponents, party workers, the press, and other relevant publics have to be taken into account under widely varying conditions. There is, of course, hardly any time to think about these matters. The strategies adopted by the candidates surely depend on some notions about what the consequences of these strategies will be. In turn, it is necessary to make assumptions about how people are going to act in response to one's own actions. Yet, no one can be certain that the simple picture of the world in his mind corresponds to the complex reality.

The candidate evolves an organization and a staff whose purpose in part is to inform him of the state of the political world. But he comes to know soon enough that it is unwise to trust completely his closest associates. Their fortunes are identified with his, their future prospects may depend on his, and their very battles for him may warp their judgment. Will they come to think that bad news should be withheld lest it sap his will to win? Will their hopes and fears color their judgment? Will the fact that they, in turn, depend upon other "loyalties" mean that those they trust are also unreliable? It is clear that the candidate has to place some sort of discount on the reports of his advisers. But it is not clear how much of a discount should be taken.

In trying to get a more objective estimate of the political situation, a candidate has a number of devices available—polls, the mass media, audience reaction—which are better than nothing but which are ambiguous and difficult to interpret. The first question about a poll is whether or not to believe it. Perhaps the apparent findings are more an artifact of the way the questions are phrased and the kind of people who administer them than of any objective reality. When in doubt candidates may have two polls taken, though this is terribly expensive and find that they do not correspond. Then the candidates, who have some reason to fancy themselves political experts, may cast the polls to the winds and rely on their own observations. Moreover, polls are static things and conditions may change more rapidly than a polling organization can find out. The questions asked may be the important ones in the mind of the pollster but not necessarily in that of the voter. And if the results seem intolerably pessimistic, the candidate may decide that there is no point in listening to the voice of doom anyhow. So he may turn next to the mass media. If newspapers happen to be on his side, he risks the distortions of favoritism; if they are against him, he risks the distortions of malice. If they are neutral he may wonder if they know any more about what is going on than he does. Yet he ignores what they say at his peril. The candidate cannot possibly read all the papers or listen to all the commentators; he requires summaries. Here again appears the risk of unconscious distortion by his eager staff.

Closest to the candidate's experience in the mad rush of the campaign are the audiences he addresses, and he may anxiously scan their response. At the beginning of the campaign, he is likely to try out different approaches on audiences composed of the party faithful. As a result, he may discover that what the "people" want are the kinds of traditional cries that rally those who are already disposed to vote for him; but this, at least for Republicans, may not reach the voters he needs to convince. The Republican candidate discovers that the people want an end to disastrous government spending, and the Democratic standard-bearer learns that they want more welfare programs. As the campaign progresses, candidates begin to believe that the crowds are no longer so one-sided, and their varying size and enthusiasm may be read as significant portents. There are, however, many different possible reasons to explain why crowds turn out: curiosity, desire to heckle, nothing else to do, a look at a glamorous figure, as well as the desire to support a particular candidate. A large crowd may mean many things. It may mean that the candidate's managers have picked their spot wisely (such as a market day at a farm distribution center) and have brought their man to a crowd rather than a crowd to him. Or a large crowd may mean that the candidate has succeeded in gaining intense support from the strongest party identifiers, but its enthusiasm may tell him nothing about his general prospects or the appeals he needs to make. The disparity between the roaring crowds and the vote in a state like Ohio may have brought home the reality of this kind of misperception to the Kennedy forces.[34]

While the candidate is making his assessment as best he can, others in his organization are doing the same. The party organizer for example may gauge the trend of the campaign by the number of people who show up at party headquarters willing to do some work. This may be as good an index as any. Like the mass meeting, however, attendance at headquarters may be an unreliable indicator of success. Party headquarters may be attracting an influx of a special, limited segment of the public attracted to a man like Adlai Stevenson or lonely people who find this a good way to meet others. The reports of workers in the various states may or may not be more useful. Although they may be wholly accurate, they are subject to the usual biases and may be representative only of narrow portions of the public rather than a good sample of the electorate.

After an election it may be amusing to note that an activity like Les Biffle's nationwide tour masquerading as a chicken farmer proved more reliable for Harry Truman than the polls;[35] during the campaign, however, this was just one among a number of cues. The candidates are always in the dark because they can never be sure which cues to believe or whether to believe any of them. If they had lots of time, they might pore over the various clues, signals, and hints and arrive at a composite estimate which might make sense. Time is in terribly short supply, however, and so the Presidential candidate is reduced to a haphazard savoring of some of the relevant signs. He may add some credence to one clue, subtract from another, and ultimately rely on his own intuition. The conduct of a campaign is far from being an established science; at best it is a shaky art.

One hears much about campaign blunders as if there really was objective assurance that another course of action would have turned out better for the unfortunate candidate. The most famous of these in recent years was Thomas E. Dewey's decision in 1948 to mute the issues, which was said to have snatched defeat from the jaws of victory.[36] A vigorous campaign on his part, it was said, would have motivated many Republican identifiers to turn out, would have taken steam out of Harry Truman's charges, and would thus have brought electoral victory to Dewey. Perhaps. What we know of the 1948 election suggests that it provoked a higher degree of voting on the basis of economic class than any of the elections which have succeeded it.[37] A slashing attack by Dewey, therefore, might have polarized the voters even further. This would have increased Truman's margin since there are many more people with low than with high incomes. Had the election gone the other way—and a handful of votes in a few states would have done it—we would have heard much less about Dewey's blunder and much more about how unpopular Truman was supposed to have been in 1948.

A whole series of "mistakes" have been attributed to Richard Nixon. Here are two, culled from a best-selling book on the 1960 campaign. On the civil rights plank of the Republican platform: "The original draft plank prepared by the Platform Committee was a moderate one. . . . This plank, as written, would almost certainly have carried the Southern states for Nixon and, it seems in retrospect, might have given him victory. . . . On Monday, July 25th, it is almost certain, it lay in Nixon's power to reorient the Republican Party toward an axis of Northern-Southern conservatives. His alone was the choice. . . . Nixon insisted that the Platform Committee substitute for the moderate position on civil rights (which probably would have won him the election) the advanced Rockefeller position on civil rights. . . ." [38] On Nixon's failure to protest the imprisonment of Martin Luther King during the campaign: "He had made the political decision at Chicago to court the Negro vote in the North; only now, apparently, he felt it quite possible that Texas, South Carolina, and Louisiana might all be won to him by the white vote and he did not wish to offend that vote. So he did not act—there was no whole philosophy of politics to instruct him." [39]

Apparently, there are times when hindsight converts every act of a losing candidate into a blunder. Nixon, as a recent loser in a Presidential race, is now in a position to enjoy the fruits of the wisdom gained by his experience. If he runs again, however, he may still find it difficult simultaneously to woo the Negro and the South. Since the piecemeal accidents of a long history have thrown both of these groups largely into the Democratic camp, it would, we suggest, take more than the siren call of a Republican candidate to lure them both, simultaneously and in public, to the Republican cause.

We have previously dealt with Nixon's decision to engage in television debates with Kennedy. Let us take a look at his decision on timing the campaign. Nixon calculated that the election was going to be very close because the Democrats were the majority party in the country, and the Republicans lacked a candidate with the special appeal of a national hero like Eisenhower. Nixon reasoned, therefore, that the candidate who closed his campaign with the strongest spurt would be the winner.[40] Consequently, he held his fire somewhat until the latter part of October, hoping thereby to peak his campaign while Kennedy's was falling off. This is precisely what he did, and Kennedy's supporters were worried that he had lost and Nixon had gained impetus in the last two weeks. Nevertheless, Kennedy won. What lesson might a future candidate derive from this experience? Nixon's strategy of timing has a common sense ring to it. Yet it is really difficult to say whether it had meaning. Would he have done better to come to a peak earlier? Might the general public not have gotten tired of a full-blast effort straight through? There is no way of knowing. It is possible that Nixon lost because of his strategy, that he gained though not enough, or that the strategy had no effect whatsoever. It would have been possible to use a successive survey of the same voters to check on whether votes were changed in his favor during the period he put on the steam, but other factors could also affect the outcome of such a study. Further, there is no way of measuring how well he might have done had he pursued a different strategy.

Should the candidate arrive at a coherent strategy which fits reasonably well with what is known of the political world, he still will find that the party organization has an inertia in favor of its accustomed ways of doing things. The party workers, upon whom he is to some extent dependent, have their own ways of interpreting the world, and he disregards their point of view at some risk. Should the candidate fail to appear in a particular locality as others have done, the party workers may feel slighted. More important, they may interpret this as a sign that the candidate has written off that area and they may slacken their own efforts. Suppose the candidate decides to divert funds from campaign buttons and stickers to polls and television or to campaign trains? He may be right in his belief that the campaign methods he prefers may bring more return from the funds that are spent.

But let the party faithful interpret this as a sign that he is losing —where, oh where, are those familiar signs of his popularity?— and their low morale may encourage a result which bears out this dire prophecy. An innovation in policy may shock the loyal followers of the party. It may seem to go against time-honored precepts which are not easily unlearned. Could a Republican convince his party that a balanced budget is not sacred? A selling job may have to be done on the rank-and-file, or otherwise they may sit on their hands during the campaign. It may make better political sense (if less intellectual sense) to phrase the new in old terms and make the departure seem less extreme than it might actually be. The value of the issue in the campaign may thus be blunted. The forces of inertia and tradition may be overcome by strong and persuasive candidates; the parties are greatly dependent on them and have little choice but to follow them even if haltingly. But in the absence of a special effort, in the presence of enormous uncertainties and the inevitable insecurities, the forces of tradition may do more to shape a campaign than the overt decisions of the candidates possibly can.

APPENDIX: PREDICTING ELECTIONS

As the time for voting draws closer, more and more interest focuses on attempts to forecast the shape of the outcome. This process of forecasting elections is not at all mysterious; it depends on well-settled findings about the behavior of American electorates, many of which have already been discussed. But it may be useful for citizens to understand how the "experts" go about picking the winner.

There are several ways to do it. One way, popularized by journalists Joseph Alsop and Samuel Lubell, is to go into neighborhoods where there are people who have in the past voted with great stability in one pattern or another and interview the residents. There are neighborhoods, for example, that always vote for the Republicans by a margin of 90% or better. Let us say that the interviewer finds that only 50% of the people he talks to tell him they are going to vote for the Republicans this time, but when he visits areas voting heavily Democratic, respondents continue to support the Democratic nominee heavily. A finding such as this permits the reporter to make a forecast, even though it is only based on a very small number of interviews, which may not at all represent the opinions of most voters.

Reporters who use this technique very rarely make firm predictions about election outcomes. Instead, they concentrate on telling about the clues they have picked up: what they learned in heavily Negro areas, what the people in Catholic areas said, what Midwest farmers say, what people from localities that always vote with the winner report, and so on.[41] This technique is impressive insofar as it digs into some of the dynamic properties of what goes into voting decisions. It reports what the issues are that seem to be on people's minds. It examines the different ways in which members of different sub-groups see the candidates and the campaign. It is also a technique which can be executed at relatively low cost. But it is unsystematic, in that people are not polled in proportions reflecting the distributions of their characteristics in the population (so many men, so many women, so many white, so many Negro and so forth) and thus the results of this technique would be regarded as unreliable in a scientific sense, even though they may enhance people's intuitive grasp of what is going on. The results are also unreliable in the sense that two different journalists using this method may come to drastically different conclusions, and there is no certain way of resolving the disagreement, nor any prescribed method for choosing between their conflicting interpretations.

A second technique has been used most extensively by the economist and statistician Louis Bean and does not rely on interviews at all.[42] Bean, it will be remembered, contradicted all the polls and predicted that President Truman would be re-elected in 1948. The Bean method relies principally upon assumptions about 1) the stability of voting habits, 2) the stability of the relationship between turnout and the two-party vote, 3) the stability of the relationship between the two-party distribution of the vote in one area and the two-party distribution of the vote in another, and 4) the continuation of trends in voting in whatever direction they may be heading. Some of these assumptions are quite dubious, as we shall see, and Bean customarily hedges his predictions by claiming that they will hold unless some issue or another intercedes to upset them. His method does not provide a way for the impact of issues to be examined, and, in fact, Bean does not demonstrate how the effects of issues have sustained or failed to sustain his predictions.

The basic material out of which Bean constructs his forecasts is a historical record of two-party voting. Let us suppose the Democratic percentage of the two-party vote has risen in each of the last five elections. The Bean technique continues the line on the graph in a simple extrapolation. Even when the percentage of the two-party vote does not describe a straight line on a graph, it is possible to make an extrapolation by assuming that the historical pattern of fluctuation will be followed in the future.

Another type of analysis done by Bean made use of the September election results in Maine. Recently, Maine moved its election day from September to November, thus bringing its election day into line with practice in the rest of the country. But for many years it was possible to make a forecast based on the Maine results. Maine's distribution of the two-party vote, Bean said, bore a historically consistent relation with the national two-party vote distribution, rising and falling at about the same rate (but always somewhat below the nation on the Democratic graph, and above the nation on the Republican graph). And so it was possible to forecast the outcome nationwide, or in any state, by noting the two-party ratio in the early Maine results and correcting it for two-party voting habits in the area whose result he wanted to predict.

The strength of forecasting from historical voting statistics arises out of the marvelous stability of American voting habits. But the weakness of such a technique is also manifest. Sometimes gross changes in populations, through immigration, or changes in the appeals of the parties to different voting groups, will throw the historical two-party vote ratios in the sample area out of joint. When a forecast made with this technique is wrong, it is usually quite difficult to tell whether transitory or lasting causes are at the root of it. This limits the usefulness of the forecast greatly, since, in the end, it rests on assumptions which have only partial validity in any one election, and nobody can say precisely how or where or to what extent they may be valid.

A third technique is a variant of the two foregoing types of analysis and is used by electronic computers at the radio and television networks on election night. The basic principle of these machines, for our purposes, can be described simply. They are given information about the past voting history of various locales. As these locales report their returns on election night, the machine compares this year's result with the information about previous years and arrives at a prediction of how this year's election will turn out, when all the votes are counted. The system is exactly the same as we have already described for Alsop and Lubell, only the machine can be loaded with historical information about many localities: precincts, wards, and so on, and then the machine compares this historical information, not with voting *intentions* as expressed by a few interviewees, but by voting *results* as expressed by the whole voting population of the area. The method the machine uses to predict the outcome early in the evening is roughly the same as Louis Bean's technique, only, once again, instead of the Maine election, the machine has results from a great many early reporting areas and can therefore correct discrepancies arising out of one or two purely local situations.

Interestingly enough, at least one of the network machines on election night in 1960 was not programmed in the way described above. The IBM system set up for CBS began election night in 1960 with the erroneous prediction that Richard Nixon would win the Presidency—a prediction that was later corrected as more and more returns came in.[43] It is useful to pause for a moment to look at this mistake, because it demonstrates clearly that these machines, like any other tools, are only as good as the people who use them.

The IBM computer was fed information based not on the geographic locale of the vote, but rather on the order in which the vote was reported to election headquarters. Thus, all the machine knew in 1960 was how many Democratic votes and how many Republican votes had been reported at 7 p.m. in previous elections, at 7:15, and so on. But it did not know *where* these votes had come from. The introduction of a faster method of vote-counting in Kansas between 1956 and 1960 was the reason for the IBM computer's early mistake. A flood of Kansas Republican votes arrived earlier than ever before. The computer, not knowing where they came from, compared them with the early returns in 1956, which were from the "swing" state of Connecticut and drew a false conclusion.

Since the order in which states report their vote varies quite a bit more than the voting habits of people living in specific early-reporting places, all the computers seem likely in the future to be working on geographic assumptions. It will, in all probability, be almost impossible to find out what assumptions the computers are using during election night coverage, however, because of the network reporters' dislike of imparting "complicated" information. It is so much friendlier to give the machine a nickname and ask it to "do tricks" and to bat one's eyelashes helplessly at the TV camera while the "mysterious" machine does its prosaic work.

The final method for predicting elections is the most powerful, the most controversial, and by all odds the most famous: polls. These are based on a few simple assumptions that have been found to be quite correct over the years. One is that people will generally tell you the truth if you ask them how they are going to vote. Another is that it is not necessary to ask everyone what he is going to do in order to get as accurate a forecast as if you had asked everyone.

The polls are commercial operations and, these days, they are big business. In addition to the publicly available polls, such as the Gallup newspaper reports, politicians commission private polls. They are expensive. They entail writing up a list of questions and asking them all, and all in the same way, to several thousand people, spread all over the country, collecting the answers, and figuring out what it all means. Each of these phases of the operation—question writing, selecting the sample of the total population to be interviewed, interviewing, organizing the answers, and interpreting the results—is a job requiring skill and training. It is this that commercial polling organizations provide.

Some of these organizations, regrettably, treat the technical aspects of their operation as trade secrets (which they are not) and persist in leaving the impression that their forecasts are the result of a particularly efficacious kind of witchcraft. Since the fiasco of 1948, when pollsters were so sure of the result that they became professionally careless, there has been less ballyhoo. But the general reader will do well to keep a sharp eye on the following points as the polls begin reporting early in the campaign.[44]

1) How big is the population which is reported to be "undecided"? There are some elections in which members of this group

cast the crucial ballots. Pollsters have a rule in reporting their results which goes this way: "If the undecided people were to cast their ballots in the same proportion as those who have made up their minds. . . ." But wait. If these people *were* like the decided, they too would have made up their minds. Sometimes they *do* vote like early deciders. But sometimes they don't. Unfortunately, not enough is known about when they do and when they don't; the best advice we can give is to pay close attention to what the pollster says he is doing about them, and if they are more than 10 to 15 per cent of the population sampled, then place little confidence in the poll report. Until these people make up their minds, it is too early to tell about the outcome.

2) What is the stability of general sentiment in the population? Very often, the polls will report wide swings of sentiment from week to week. In 1960, The Gallup organization began averaging one week's totals with the previous week's part-way through the campaign—without telling its readers.[45] This tended to depress the extent of an apparent shift of sympathy from Nixon to Kennedy, and it also tended to make the figures appear a great deal more stable and settled than they actually were. In general, wide swings of sentiment from week to week mean that opinions have not crystallized sufficiently for a reliable prediction to be made.

3) Remember that the polls are based on a gross, overall nationwide sample, but that Presidential elections are decided by the distribution of votes in the Electoral College. Thus a really reliable prediction would have to include a state-by-state breakdown. This is prohibitively expensive, and so it is not done. If it were done, it would be possible to detect situations like the following:

> Candidate A has 49% of the popular vote in polls taken in all the populous states and 75% of the popular vote in sparsely settled states. He loses badly to Candidate B in the Electoral College, although it looks like a close election.

Pollsters generally caution that they are trying only to forecast the percentage distributions in the popular vote. Here again, if the result is closely divided around 50%, then the poll may be quite close to being perfectly accurate, but still forecast the wrong winner.

4) Some people never show up to vote on Election Day; these

tend to be undecideds and Democrats (in that order) more often than Republicans, but in any event some sort of grain of salt has to be taken with results in order to account for the phenomenon of differential turnout. Most experienced polling organizations do build some sort of correction into their results based on assumptions about how many people in their sample will actually vote. It is important to know precisely what this assumption is and what the resulting corrections are.

5) Many people are plagued with the feeling that the samples used by pollsters—of two to five thousand people—are inadequate to represent the feelings of the millions of Americans whose voting they are supposed to represent. This, by and large, is a false issue. Experience has shown that very few of the errors one makes with a sample of 3,000 are correctable with a sample of 15 or 20 thousand, although the expense of polling such a population rises steeply.[46]

Generally, it is not a sampling error that is at fault nowadays when pollsters' predictions go awry, but illicit "cooking" of the data or incompetent interpretations of findings. There is one famous instance of a sampling error, when polling was in its most rudimentary stages. In 1936 the *Literary Digest* predicted a landslide victory for the Republican Alfred Landon.[47] When Franklin D. Roosevelt won in overwhelming fashion, the *Digest* became a laughingstock and soon thereafter went out of business. What had happened was simple enough. The magazine had sent out millions of postcards to telephone subscribers asking them how they intended to vote. The returns showed a huge Republican triumph. Surely, the *Digest* must have thought, we cannot possibly be wrong when our total response is so large, and so one-sided. But, of course, something was terribly wrong. And that stemmed from the fact that in the Depression years only the relatively wealthy had telephones. So the *Digest* got its returns from that group in the population most likely to vote Republican and completely ignored the much larger number of poorer people who were going to vote Democratic. Moreover, there is a much greater tendency for people of wealth and education to return mail questionnaires so that the bias in favor of people likely to vote Republican was further enhanced.[48]

In 1948, a whole series of errors were made, but none of them seem to have been connected with the size of the sample. In that year, the Gallup, Roper, and Crossley polls all predicted that Governor Dewey would unseat President Truman. Among the problems with the polls that year, the following were uncovered by a committee of social scientists after the event:[49]

a) The pollsters were so sure of the outcome that they stopped taking polls early in the campaign, assuming that the large population of undecideds would vote, if they voted, in the same way as those who had made up their minds early in the campaign.

b) The undecideds voted in just the reverse proportions.

c) Many instances were revealed where polling organization analysts, disbelieving pro-Truman results, arbitrarily "corrected" them in favor of Dewey. The methods of analysis employed were not traced in any systematic way, however, because they could not systematically be reconstructed from records of the polling organizations.

d) Sampling error occurred, not because of the size of the samples, but because respondents were selected by methods that gave interviewers too much leeway to introduce biases into the sample. The so-called "quota-control" method (which instructs interviewers, for example, out of 20 interviews to pick ten men, ten women, fifteen Protestants, four Catholics, one Jew, seventeen whites and three Negroes, and so on) has been replaced with "stratified random samples" in which geographic areas are picked randomly, and neighborhoods and houses within neighborhoods are selected randomly with controls so that areas representing a variety of economic levels are sure to be selected. This gives the people in charge of the poll greater control over who is going to be in their sample and prevents interviewers from asking only people who live near them, or who are conveniently accessible in some other way, and are likely to be similar to them in social standing and political outlook.

Predicting Presidential elections is largely a matter of satisfying curiosity. It is a great game to guess who will win, and we look to the polls for indications of the signs of the times. But the importance of this kind of prediction is not great. After all, we do get to know who has won very soon after Election Day with much greater detail and accuracy than the polls can supply. The bare prediction of the outcome, even if it is reasonably correct, tells us little about how the result came to occur. More may be learned if it is possible to break down the figures to see what kind of groups—ethnic, racial, economic, regional—voted to what degree for which candidates. Yet our enlightenment at this point is still not great. Suppose we know that in one election Catholics voted Democratic 60% of the time and in another election this percentage was reduced to 53. Surely this is interesting; but unless we have some good idea about why Catholics have switched their allegiance, our knowledge has hardly advanced. The polls often tell us "what" but seldom "why." There is, however, no reason why polling techniques in the future cannot be used to answer "why" questions.

The usual polling technique consists of talking to samples of the population at various points in time. The samples may be perfectly adequate but *different* people constitute each successive sample as the interviewers seek out people who meet their specifications. It is difficult to discover with any reliability why particular individuals or classes of people are changing their minds because interviewers ordinarily do not go back to the same people who gave their original preferences. A panel survey is used to overcome this difficulty.[50] In a panel survey, a sample of the voting population is obtained and the very same people are interviewed at various intervals before Election Day and perhaps afterwards. This technique makes it possible to isolate the people who make up their minds early and those who decide late. These groups can be reinterviewed and examined for other distinguishing characteristics. More important, perhaps, those voters who change their minds during the campaign can be identified and studied. If a panel of respondents can be reinterviewed over a number of years and a series of elections, it may become possible to discover directly why some people change their voting habits from election to election.

NOTES

1. See Seymour M. Lipset, Paul F. Lazarsfeld, Allen H. Barton, and Juan Linz, "The Psychology of Voting: An Analysis of Political Behavior," in *Handbook of Social Psychology*, ed. Gardner Lindzey (Cambridge, Mass., 1954), pp. 1124–1175; Paul F. Lazarsfeld, Bernard Berelson, and Hazel Gaudet, *The People's Choice*, 2nd ed.

(New York, 1948), pp. 87–93; and Bernard Berelson, Paul F. Lazarsfeld, and William N. McPhee, *Voting* (Chicago, 1954), pp. 16–17.

2. See Warren E. Miller, "The Political Behavior of the Electorate," *American Government Annual: 1960–61*, ed. E. Latham (New York, 1960), pp. 40–61, and Fred I. Greenstein, *The American Party System and the American People* (Englewood Cliffs, 1963), Chapter 3, both of which give findings of surveys conducted primarily under academic auspices. Gallup data also bear out the same general conclusion: "If every potential voter in the country had to register with either party, the figures projected by survey findings would be Democrats: 56,800,000; Republicans: 40,020,000; Undecided: 6,-200,000." (American Institute of Public Opinion News Release, "Republicans Outnumbered by 16 Million, Poll Finds," October 16, 1960.) The number of "undecideds" may have been reduced by assigning a party affiliation to people who expressed a faint preference for one or the other party.

3. There is another possibility: That voters who turn out only by being dinned at by the media are likely to be less stable in their political orientations and will therefore vote less for the party and more for the candidate whose name or personality seems more familiar to them. This, in a year when an Eisenhower is on the ticket, might well mean Republican votes.

4. See Angus Campbell, Philip E. Converse, Warren E. Miller, and Donald E. Stokes, *The American Voter* (New York, 1960), pp. 124, 552–553. Table 6-1 on p. 124 summarizes the highly consistent results of seven separate national sample surveys taken by the Survey Research Center from October, 1952 to October, 1958. In October, 1958, the S. R. C. figures were:

Strong Republicans	13%
Weak Republicans	16%
Independent Republicans	4%
Independents	8%
Independent Democrats	7%
Weak Democrats	24%
Strong Democrats	23%
Apolitical, don't know	5%

5. See Philip E. Converse, Angus Campbell, Warren E. Miller, and Donald E. Stokes, "Stability and Change in 1960: A Reinstating Election," *American Political Science Review* 55 (June 1961), 269–280, esp. p. 274.

6. See Campbell *et al.*, *The American Voter*, pp. 537–538 and Herbert H. Hyman and Paul B. Sheatsley, "The Political Appeal of President Eisenhower," *Public Opinion Quarterly* 19 (Winter 1955–56), 26–39.

7. For indications that this strategy is feasible despite the existence of general stereotypes, see Campbell *et al.*, *The American Voter*, pp. 44–59, 179–187. See also American Institute of Public Opinion News Releases, February 6, 1963, October 9, 1964, and October 25, 1964.

8. For a striking demonstration of this, see Ithiel de Sola Pool, Robert P. Abelson, and Samuel Popkin, *Candidates, Issues and Strategies* (Cambridge, Mass., 1964), pp. 117–118.

9. Recall Senator Dirksen's famous castigation of Thomas E. Dewey at the Republican Convention of 1952: "We followed you before, and you took us down the path to defeat."

10. For indications that this is so, see in particular Herbert Mc-Closky, Paul J. Hoffman, and Rosemary O'Hara, "Issue Conflicts and Consensus Among Party Leaders and Followers," *American Political Science Review* 54 (June 1960), 406–427.

11. Good accounts of debates over strategy among Republicans can be found in such sources as Charles O. Jones, *The Republican Party in American Politics* (New York, 1965); Robert Donovan, *The Future of the Republican Party* (New York, 1964); Malcolm C. Moos, *The Republicans: A History of Their Party* (New York, 1956); Robert Novak, *The Agony of the G.O.P. 1964* (New York, 1965); and Conrad Joyner, *The Republican Dilemma* (Tucson, 1964).

12. Another example is the common practice of declaring special dividends on G.I. insurance to put more money in circulation in order to increase income and decrease unemployment.

13. Campbell *et al.*, *The American Voter*, pp. 525–527.

14. A useful source on the Nixon campaign is *The Speeches of Vice-President Richard M. Nixon, Presidential Campaign of 1960*, Report 994, Part II, 87th Congress, 1st Session, U.S. Senate (Washington, 1961).

Party Best Suited to Keep the United States Out of War

SOURCE: Adapted from the *Gallup Political Index,*

15. The report of the speech in the New York *Times,* October 6, 1956, gives no indication of how it was received. The authors heard it delivered.

16. Thomas Flinn, "How Nixon Took Ohio," *Western Political Quarterly* 15 (June 1962), 276–279.

17. See footnote 2 and, for examples of this Democratic strategy in operation in 1960, see *The Speeches of Senator John F. Kennedy, Presidential Campaign of 1960,* Report 994, Part I, 87th Congress, 1st Session, U.S. Senate (Washington, 1961).

18. See Nixon's speeches in Report 994, Part II. For example, on p. 266, in a speech at Lafayette, La., Sept. 24, 1960, Mr. Nixon said:

ELECTION
YEAR

ELECTION
YEAR

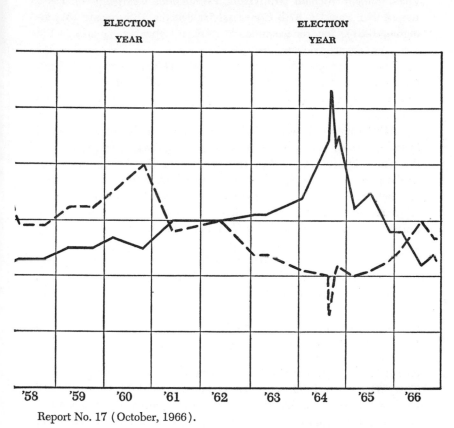

'58   '59   '60   '61   '62   '63   '64   '65   '66

Report No. 17 (October, 1966).

"I say further that what we adopted in our platform in Chicago is closer to the views of Democrats in not only the South, but in California, where there are many more Democrats than Republicans, incidentally . . . on oil depletion, . . . Mr. Kennedy's position was not in agreement with the Democratic platform."

19. See, for example, the American Institute of Public Opinion News Release of September 3, 1964 in which 53% of a national sample said that the Democrats were the party best able to keep the country prosperous. Only 21% picked the Republicans. See also, Campbell *et al., The American Voter,* pp. 44–59.

20. *The Joint Appearances of Senator John F. Kennedy and*

Vice-President Richard M. Nixon, Presidential Campaign of 1960, Report 994, Part III, 87th Congress, 1st Session, U.S. Senate (Washington, 1961). See, for example, Mr. Nixon's opening remarks in the first joint television debate, pp. 75–78.

21. See, for example, Campbell *et al., The American Voter,* pp. 44–59 and Angus Campbell, Gerald Gurin, and Warren E. Miller, *The Voter Decides* (Evanston, 1954), pp. 44–45, especially Table 4-3, p. 45.

AIPO surveys show the fifteen-year trend on this issue indicated in the graph on pages 164–165. This graph indicates, first, that over the whole fifteen-year period, the position of the Republican party as the party of peace has steadily been eroded. It also indicates that just before elections, voters' expressions of their accustomed stereotypes are at their strongest, which we would expect owing to the polarization in voters' attitudes that takes place during the heat of battle. A dramatic reversal took place at the time of the 1964 election, no doubt owing to Senator Goldwater's extreme foreign policy positions and to President Johnson's relative moderation. However, the progressive escalation, under President Johnson, of the Vietnam war since 1964 seems to have had an impact on public opinion, and the Republican party once more seems to have regained its status, by a small margin, as the party of peace.

22. The most well-publicized clashes over foreign policy occurred in the second and third television debates; see the New York *Times,* October 8, 1960, pp. 1, 12; October 9, 1960, Pt. IV, p. 10; and October 14, 1960, p. 22. The impression of journalists and political observers that Nixon gained in these confrontations (see, for example, the New York *Times* for October 17, 1960) was corroborated by surveys of the viewers (see the references in footnote 24, following) and by Pool, Abelson, and Popkin, *Candidates, Issues, and Strategies,* p. 118.

23. Converse *et al.,* "Stability and Change in 1960: A Reinstating Election," 269–280.

24. Elihu Katz and Jacob J. Feldman, "The Debates in the Light of Research: A Survey of Surveys," in *The Great Debates,* ed. Sidney Kraus (Bloomington, 1962), pp. 201–202. Bear in mind, however, that *issues* as such do not strongly influence voting behavior. Katz and Feldman conclude: "First of all, it seems safe to say that the debates

—especially the first one—resulted primarily in a strengthening of commitment to one's own party and candidate. This was much more the case for Democrats than Republicans, but the former had much greater room for improvement" (p. 208).

25. See Theodore H. White, *The Making of the President, 1960* (New York, 1961), pp. 269–275 and his, *The Making of the President, 1964* (New York, 1965), *passim*.

26. Department of Marketing, Miami University, Oxford Research Associates, *The Influence of Television on the Election of 1952* (Oxford, 1954), pp. 151–160.

27. See White, *The Making of the President, 1960*, pp. 282–283, and Herbert A. Seltz and Richard D. Yoakum, "Production Diary of the Debates," in *The Great Debates*, ed., Sidney Kraus, pp. 73–126.

28. *Ibid.*; see also Richard Nixon, *Six Crises* (New York, 1962).

29. Earl Mazo, *Richard Nixon* (New York, 1959), pp. 21–22.

30. See Katz and Feldman, "The Debates in the Light of Research: A Survey of Surveys," pp. 173–223.

31. See William L. Rivers, "The Correspondents After 25 Years," *Columbia Journalism Review* 1 (Spring 1962); Nixon, *Six Crises*; and especially White, *The Making of the President, 1960*, for a discussion of two candidates' contrasting attitudes toward their "camp" of reporters. For the 1964 election, see White, *The Making of the President, 1964*.

32. For further examples see Hugh A. Bone, *American Politics and the Party System*, pp. 457–469. Readers may not be aware that Al Smith had thought of moving the Vatican to Washington or that Herbert Hoover had a Negro concubine, yet these ridiculous allegations were made (p. 458).

33. Robert E. Sherwood, *Roosevelt and Hopkins* (New York, 1948), p. 821.

34. See Flinn, "How Nixon Took Ohio."

35. New York *Times*, August 1, 1948, p. 49.

36. See Jules Abels, *Out of the Jaws of Victory* (New York, 1959).

37. Robert Alford, "The Role of Social Class in American Voting Behavior," *Western Political Quarterly* 16 (March 1963), 180–194; Campbell *et al.*, *The American Voter*, Chapter 13.

38. White, *The Making of the President, 1960*, pp. 203–204.

39. *Ibid.*, p. 315.

40. Nixon, *Six Crises.*

41. See, for example, Samuel Lubell, *The Future of American Politics* (Garden City, 1956), and his, "Personalities and Issues," in *The Great Debates,* ed. Sidney Kraus, pp. 151–162, and Joseph Alsop, "The Negro Vote and New York," New York *Herald-Tribune* (and elsewhere) August 8, 1960.

42. Louis H. Bean, *Ballot Behavior* (Washington, 1940).

43. IBM published a pamphlet, *The Fastest Reported Election,* in 1961 describing their operations.

44. These suggestions are drawn in part from a reading of the Report of a Committee of the Social Science Research Council, Frederick Mosteller *et al., The Pre-Election Polls of 1948,* Social Science Research Council Bulletin 60 (New York, 1949).

45. Joseph Alsop, "The Wayward Press: Dissection of a Poll," *The New Yorker* (September 24, 1960), pp. 170–184.

46. There are several sources about the technology and tactics of polling. George Gallup has published *A Guide to Public Opinion Polls* (Princeton, 1948). More recently, see *Opinion Polls, Interviews by Donald McDonald with Elmo Roper and George Gallup* (Santa Barbara, 1962).

47. Sherwood, *Roosevelt and Hopkins,* p. 86.

48. As a matter of fact, this method produced a correct prediction in 1932, when the *Literary Digest* said that Roosevelt would win. Sampling error is tricky; an atypical sample may still give the correct prediction—by luck, but sooner or later, the law of averages is bound to catch up with it.

49. Mosteller *et al., The Pre-Election Polls of 1948.*

50. See Paul F. Lazarsfeld, "The Use of Panels in Social Research," *Proceedings of the American Philosophical Society* 92 (November 1948), pp. 405–410.

Chapter 4

The 1964 Election

THUS FAR we have talked about the strategies of candidates and election outcomes as though they were related in a particular way, and, in a sense, they are. Experience and accumulated knowledge suggest that there are strategies that are best for Democrats and for Republicans, for incumbents and for challengers, for front-runners and for dark horses, and so on. An underlying assumption we have been using—for the sake of simplicity—is that, when a player knows the payoffs attached to various available alternatives, he will, on the whole, choose the alternatives that are likely to bring him the maximum payoffs. This is more or less what all "rational man" theories predict, in economics, game theory, or politics.

But in 1964, the Republican party chose a number of alternatives manifestly disadvantageous to its chances of winning the election. It nominated a relatively unpopular candidate who alienated not only independents and borderline Democrats, but even many traditional Republicans by the kind of campaign he conducted. The results of the 1964 election suggest that our understanding of the merits of various strategies available to Republicans is not faulty: Goldwater did lose badly, as the prevailing theory would predict; but it is still necessary for us to try to understand why the Republicans chose as they did;

why they, in effect, rejected alternatives promising greater pay-offs in favor of less promising alternatives.

Two explanations are possible. On one hand, it may be that Republicans misperceived the payoffs, that they believed they *were* pursuing a winning strategy. On the other hand, perhaps Republicans were not trying to win the election but had other payoffs in mind, which dictated a choice of alternatives quite different from a strategy in which winning public office is the paramount goal.

If some Republicans did not care about winning, or thought that Goldwater might win, other Republicans did care about winning and knew that Goldwater would lose. Why, then, did the Republican party nominate Barry Goldwater?

It is clear that our explanation of the Goldwater phenomenon must come in two parts. We must first understand the nature of Goldwater's supporters. Why did they care so little about win-ning or so badly misperceive their candidate's electoral chances? Second, even if we can understand why some Republicans pre-ferred to back Goldwater, we still need to know why these Republicans triumphed within the party as a whole.

We shall deal with these two points in turn. Then we shall see how Goldwater's nomination decisively affected the campaign. Finally, we shall assess the impact of 1964 upon the future of the competitive, two-party system in the United States.

MISPERCEIVING THE OUTCOME:
THE HIDDEN VOTE HYPOTHESIS

Did Republicans believe that Barry Goldwater could actually win the election? An argument was made by Goldwater support-ers that he could win, based upon the possibility that he could put together a coalition in the Electoral College of Southern and Western states, and, in particular, upon the notion of a hidden vote.

The classic Republican criticism of "me-too" strategies argues that such strategies merely alienate potential Republican voters while failing to attract sufficient Democrats. Alienated Republicans, so goes this argument, seeing no difference between the policies espoused by the major parties, withdraw from politics into apathy. This is the hidden vote that a thoroughgoing conservative Republican campaign is supposed to attract. But did this hidden vote exist—or was this argument an instance of misperception on the part of those who believed it and supported Goldwater thinking he could win?

The resulting disastrous consequences for the Republican party at the congressional and state levels[1] invites the exercise of hindsight on the question of the hidden Republican vote. But, for once, hindsight merely confirms foresight. It was apparent before the election as well as afterward that there are only very weak factual grounds supporting the notion that there is a hidden Republican vote, waiting to be tapped by an unequivocally conservative candidate.

Let us examine the evidence. First, we must ask where the Republican vote could be hidden that this strategy seeks to tap. Presumably not among Democrats, at least outside the South, since this approach relies so heavily upon sharpening the cleavage between the two parties. Nor can there be much of a hidden vote among disaffected conservative Republicans who fail to turn out, since the best knowledge we have of Republicans is that they do turn out and vote Republican.[2]

The only other possible location for the hidden vote is among those who profess to no regular party affiliation—roughly 25% of the potential electorate. What do we know about these people that might lead us to conclude that they can be moved to vote Republican by a highly ideological appeal based on conservative and right-wing doctrines?

There is, in fact, no reason at all to suspect that these people can be reached in this way. All the information we have on party neutrals indicates that they are much less interested, less informed, less likely to seek information about politics, and much less likely to vote than are regular partisans. Non-affiliates are relatively unconcerned about issues and are only dimly aware of political events.[3] Efforts to reach this population, to attract their attention, are likely to fail. Attempts to outline issue positions to them, to engage their support in behalf of any self-consistent philosophical and political position, seem on a par with the famous campaign to sell refrigerators to Eskimos.

There is a well-known suspicion, voiced from time to time by imaginative writers, that conservative elements of the population are in fact alienated from politics and sit in the wings, frustrated, immobilized and without party loyalties, until someone pursuing a Goldwater-like strategy gives them the "choice" they are looking for. This is probably a canard. What fragments of evidence we have point to the probability that the dedicated conservatives and right-wing ideologues who are sufficiently interested in politics to hold strong opinions about public policy do in fact belong to political parties and participate actively in them. Outside the South, it seems certain, these people are almost all Republicans. Thus, the hidden vote that Goldwater hoped to attract was probably hidden inside the vote Richard Nixon received in 1960.[4]

Another assumption underlying the hidden vote theory is that in 1964 it would have been possible to attract this mythical vote in substantial numbers without losing the allegiance of large numbers of more moderate people who supported the almost-successful candidacy of Richard Nixon in 1960.

In fact, this proved impossible to accomplish. An enormous number—probably around 20%—of Nixon's 1960 supporters voted for Lyndon Johnson in 1964.[5] But this outcome might have been extrapolated from poll and primary election data in the pre-convention period which showed that, even among Republican voters, Goldwater enjoyed far from overwhelming support.[6]

In addition, Goldwater aroused great antipathy among the general population. According to the Gallup poll in mid-September, 38.3% of respondents expressed definite hostility to Goldwater (including 14.7% expressing the most extreme hostility on an 11-point scale) while only 8.1% expressed any antipathy at all toward President Johnson.[7] Likewise, on a number of issues, Louis Harris surveys found that sizable majorities in the general population defined themselves as opposed to positions that they believed Senator Goldwater held.[8]

ALTERNATIVE PAYOFFS:
PURISTS vs. PROFESSIONALS

Yet even if Goldwater's supporters could convince themselves that his cause was not utterly hopeless, the fact that they chose him in the face of reasonably strong evidence of his slight chance of victory suggests that winning the election was not uppermost in their minds. Politicians have been accused of many things; until now it has not been usual to accuse them of wishing to lose elections. But perhaps in specifying only the paramount goal of winning, we have been taking a narrow view of the matter. Interviews held with Goldwater delegates to the Republican Convention may help to clarify this problem.[9]

One Goldwater delegate said: "The delegates are for Goldwater because they agree with his philosophy of government. That's what you people will never understand—we're committed to his whole approach." He was undoubtedly correct. There was a remarkable fit between Goldwater and a substantial majority of his followers. What they liked about Goldwater, however, was not merely or even primarily his policy positions but rather his "approach," his style of operation. When we asked Goldwater delegates to tell us what they most liked about their candidate only a few mentioned his position on the issues, and those who did were content with brief references to constitutional principles like states' rights.

By far the most frequent delegate characterizations of Goldwater referred to his consistency, honesty, integrity, and willingness to stick by principles.[10] It was not so much his principles (though these were undoubtedly important) but the belief that he would stick to them that counted most with his supporters. "He can be trusted." "He is straightforward." "He does not compromise." "He doesn't pander to the public; he's against expediency." "He is frank." "He has courage." "He stands up for what he believes." "He won't play footsie with the people." "He votes his convictions when he knows he's right." "He doesn't go along with the crowd." "He meets issues head-on." "Goldwater speaks about things others avoid. Most politicians like to avoid issues." "He keeps promises." "He doesn't change his mind." "He is not confused." As one of Goldwater's supporters perceptively observed, "He's different from most politicians." And so were most of Goldwater's followers different from most politicians.

Many Goldwater delegates held attitudes quite different from those characteristic of American politicians. We can refer to these delegates as "purists"—political activists whose attitudes about politics have strongly moralistic overtones. Here is an example. This Goldwater purist was a delegate from a rural area in Pennsylvania attending his first convention.

> Interviewer: What qualities should a Presidential candidate have?
>
> Delegate: Moral integrity.
>
> I.: Should he be able to win the election?
>
> D.: No; principles are more important. I would rather be one against 20,000 and believe I was right. That's what I admire about Goldwater. He's like that.
>
> I.: Are most politicians like that?
>
> D.: No, unfortunately.
>
> I.: What do you like about Goldwater?
>
> D.: I am in sympathy with many of his philosophies of government, but I like him personally for his moral integrity. I always believed that a candidate should carry out his promises. Scranton didn't do that. But now, for the first time in my life, we have a candidate who acts as he believes. He doesn't change his position when it is expedient.

I.: Do you think that if the party loses badly in November it ought to change its principles?

D.: No. I'm willing to fight for these principles for ten years if we don't win.

I.: For fifty years?

D.: Even fifty years.

I.: Do you think it's better to compromise a little to win than to lose and not compromise?

D.: I had this problem in my district. After we fighters had won [the nomination for] the Congressional seat the local [Republican] machine offered to make a deal: They wouldn't oppose our candidate if we didn't oppose theirs. I refused, because I didn't see how I could make a deal with the men I'd been opposing two years ago for the things they did. So I lost, and I could have won easily. I've thought about it many times, because if I had agreed I could have done some good at least. But I don't believe that I should compromise one inch from what I believe deep down inside.

Here we begin to see the distinguishing characteristics of the purists: their emphasis on internal criteria for decision, on what they believe "deep down inside"; their rejection of compromise; their lack of orientation toward winning; their stress on the style and purity of decision—integrity, consistency, adherence to internal norms.

The professionals looked at politics quite differently. Here is a California delegate strongly for Goldwater, with more than fifteen years in party work, attending his third Republican Convention.

Interviewer: You seem different from many of the Goldwater supporters. How would you characterize your position in comparison with them?

Delegate: Yes, I'm more practical. I realize you have to live together. For example, I'm going up now to a meeting of the California Republican committee and we've got to handle a liberal candidate and an ultra-conservative. I'm going to urge them to accept the liberal because we've got to work together. We [the Republicans] are a minority party in California and we can't afford to squabble amongst ourselves. The art of politics is the art of compromise. If I can get a whole loaf, I'll take it. If not, I'll take half rather than lose it all.

> I.: What would Goldwater do about the Cuban situation?
> D.: Well, it's there now, and we'll just have to live with it.
> I.: The Berlin Wall?
> D.: He won't tear it down; I know him very well.
> I.: Social Security?
> D.: We've had it for a long time. It's part of our system. That's something some of these Goldwater people don't realize. They're a new breed and sort of naive on things like this. They think you can suddenly shift the whole range of government to the right. What they don't realize is that you can only bend a little back away from the left.
> I.: What if Goldwater loses by a landslide?
> D.: Well, I don't think that will happen.
> I.: Suppose it does?
> D.: Well, then, maybe the people aren't ready for a change. . . . Yes, we'll have to try to change, maybe a little more toward the liberal side.

The belief in compromise and bargaining; the sense that public policy is made in small steps rather than big leaps; the concern with conciliating the opposition and broadening public appeal; and the willingness to bend a little to capture public support are all characteristic of the traditional American politician.

Having sketched some of the essential attributes of purists and professionals, we can proceed to a closer examination of these two types, with special emphasis on the purists.

Winning Elections

"I've talked to some of the California delegates," a citizen who observed the convention informed us, "and I don't understand them at all; they talk like they don't care if we win." In a sense he was wrong, because the delegates desperately wanted Goldwater to win. But our informant was essentially correct in the sense that these delegates cared more about maintaining their purity—"I would rather lose and be right"—than about winning. The essential element of this style is a devotion to principles, especially the principle that men in politics should have, maintain, and cherish their principles.

When asked why they entered politics, Goldwater delegates often answered, "For the same reason as any man—principles." When asked if the party should change some of its policies if Goldwater lost badly, the delegates responded by reiterating their devotion to principles. "God, no. These are American principles; these are what we stand for." "No, we want a clear party which will represent principles to the people." "I'd rather stick by the real principles this country was built on than win. Popularity isn't important; prestige isn't important; it's the principles that matter."

Although the professionals, on the other hand, put a high premium on popularity with the electorate, there were things that even they would not do and ways they would not prefer to win. A Scranton delegate, in politics for many years in Philadelphia, pointed out that in his white, upper-class ward he and his party had benefited from a white backlash issue in a local election. "But we don't want that; that divides the country. We don't want whites and blacks to fight; it's not good for the country." A New Jersey delegate with many years of political experience did not really like any of the candidates for the nomination and feared that the party would fare badly at the polls if Goldwater were nominated. Yet he felt that things could happen: "a white backlash building up if the Negroes have a lot of big demonstrations in the cities; or if Vietnam blew up in our faces. But I'd rather lose than have those things happen. I'd rather lose than have race fights or war."

One great difference between the purists and the professionals lay in what they considered valid grounds for preferring not to

win. The professionals emphasized specific unfortunate consequences, such as race riots and war. The purists emphasized
departures from internal principles—such as consistency, integrity, and standing firm—held by their party leaders. The professionals were oriented toward what might happen to other people,
the purists toward their own consciences.

Emphasizing Differences

An important component of the Goldwater style was the
guiding principle that the parties ought to be different. The
maintenance of wide and sharp differences between the parties
was seen as a fundamental purpose of engaging in politics. As
an enthusiastic woman from New Jersey put it, "I think everything should be an issue, civil rights should be an issue, Cuba
should be an issue. This is the first time a campaign will be on
issues; I think it's wonderful. It's just terrible the way personality
has been in politics, like Kennedy winning on his hair and teeth
and Nixon losing because there was a shadow on his chin. . . .
It's ridiculous."

Hence when Goldwater supporters were asked whether they
should balance the ticket with a liberal as Vice-President, they
replied: "We don't want a blurred image, we've been a 'me-too'
party for too long. We want to take a clear position." If, in order
to provide clear differences between the parties, the Republicans
lost, that was all right. For "even if the party loses at least we
have presented a clear alternative to the people. At least we'll
have a strong party." What is meant by "strong"? "Cohesive,
united on principles." The chorus of Goldwater purists rose to a
crescendo when they insisted, in almost identical words, "We
don't want to become a 'me-too' party; we don't want to be the
same as the Democrats." There is a definite possibility, therefore,
that, if they had been offered accommodations or compromises
on issues, they would have rejected them because they wanted
to be different.

The ideal party of the purists is not merely a conservative

party; it is also a distinct and separate community of co-believers who differ with the opposition party all down the line. To this extent their style merges with that of the liberal Democratic reformers in some big cities who wish to see the parties represent clear and opposing alternatives and to gain votes only through appeals based on policy differences rather than on such "irrational" criteria as personality, party identification, or ethnic status.[11] But the Goldwater purists went even further in their willingness to cast aside whole groups of voters who did not agree with them. "We won't get Negro votes anyway, so there's no point in trying." "They can vote for the other party for all I care." "We won't change our principles just to get a few votes from Negroes." In the same spirit, Barry Goldwater suggested that people who favored the kind of government the United States has had since 1932 should not vote for him.

For the professionals, the desire to win is intimately connected with the belief that a political party should try to get as much support from as many diverse groups as possible. In describing the qualities a Presidential candidate should have, a professional would say, "He should be diplomatic. He should be able to gather support from a lot of groups underneath him. That's what Eisenhower had, that's what Kennedy had, and that's what Johnson has. You know there's one thing about politics, there's no such thing as second place, you don't get anything for coming in second."

Hence the professionals were concerned with the possible loss of a substantial part of the small Negro vote they had received in the past. "You just can't go around throwing away votes. The object of a party is to draw voters together to the party, not to push them away." A delegate from Philadelphia was more specific. He had "nothing personal against Goldwater" but feared that if Goldwater were to run "we'll get the hell kicked out of us. We've been out of [state] power for ten or twelve years. Now we're getting some of the Polish vote and the Italians don't treat us too bad. The Jews and the Negroes go about 75%

against us, but at least we get part of the Negro vote and that helps us hold the line in the state generally."

To their dichotomous view of political parties and their belief that issue preferences are the only moral way to choose between the parties, the purists added a strong desire to simplify political choice: a party for the growth of government and a party against; a party which believes in standing up to the enemy and one which believes in appeasement; a party which believes in private initiative and one which wishes to stifle it; a party of free enterprise and a party of socialism.

The desire to dichotomize and simplify found expression in ways of locating political supporters and opponents. Perhaps the most charming example came from a California delegate who expressed the wish to see all liberals in the East and all conservatives in the West. Presumably then, if one knew where a man came from, one could immediately discern his political tendency. Many delegates voiced the desire to divide friend from foe by simple criteria and then do joyous battle.

THE PRIVATIZATION OF POLITICS

We may sum up the purist style by saying that it represents a virtually complete privatization of politics. The private conscience of the leader—rather than his public responsibilities—becomes the focal point of politics. Internal criteria—possession of, devotion to, and standing up for private principles—become the standards of political judgment. Constituents disappear, and we are left with a political leader determining policy on the basis of compatibility with his private principles.

From this perspective we can better understand why Goldwater voted against the Civil Rights Act of 1964 despite his agreement with the view that the race issue should not become a matter of political partisanship. Goldwater's conscience dictated that he vote against an Act which contained two sections that he believed violated the Constitution. Although he knew that the

Act would pass anyway, he was simply unwilling to sacrifice his private conscience in order to achieve what he agreed was the public good. Nor would he or his supporters agree to make rather innocuous concessions in the civil rights plank of the Republican platform in order to placate Negroes because that would have suggested compromise; and compromise suggests that one has not stuck to one's principles.

Once the platform became identified as a Goldwater platform, presumably derived from careful scrutiny of conscience, it became a matter of principle not to permit any alteration whatsoever, even if this refusal to compromise meant rejecting important segments of the party. The very idea that the Republican party should try to balance its ticket with a less conservative Vice-Presidential candidate was uniformly regarded as immoral and despicable. Such thoughts reeked of inconsistency, "metooism," expediency, and other political vices stemming from the lack of conscience in politics.

Conspicuously missing from purist thought is any consideration of the voters. The political party is defined entirely without reference to the people who would have to vote for it. To be sure, the purists believed that there was a hidden Republican vote, and they fully expected a huge upsurge of support as these Americans discovered that a party embracing their most cherished principles had at last appeared on the scene. But the "real Republican party," as they were fond of calling it, was far removed from vulgar pandering for votes. It stood on its principles. It did not change to attract votes. Voters would be attracted to it when people changed.

One can see the privatization of politics at work when Goldwater delegates expressed their feelings about President Johnson and former President Eisenhower. Extremely hostile feelings were voiced about both men because they were seen as traditional politicians, given to compromise. Goldwater's castigation of Johnson as a "faker," for example, was regarded by the delegates interviewed as accurate and appropriate. "Originally and historically," a delegate told us, "Johnson was a conservative, but he's willing to do things, to change to stay in power. This shows weakness of character."

The purists did not think it appropriate for a man to act differently as President than as Senator: If a public official need consult only his private conscience, of course, there should be little change in his actions in different offices. If Johnson acted differently in the two offices this could only be because "he has no principles. L.B.J. is a consummate politician. He is inconsistent and immoral." Goldwater was different: "He doesn't talk from both sides of his mouth."

If the essence of politics is to be found in the relationship between leaders and their principles rather than between leaders and constituents, one would ask quite different questions and give much different answers to queries about the positions taken by candidates. When we asked delegates about Goldwater's position on racial matters, the purists would always respond by saying that Goldwater himself was not bigoted. They knew the exact percentage of employees in the Goldwater department store in Phoenix who were non-Caucasians and pointed with pride to this statistic as evidence of their candidate's favorable disposition toward Negroes. There was no mention of what Goldwater might do as President; there was no understanding that the public role of a Presidential aspirant might be of interest. The Negro delegates we interviewed, to be sure, could not have cared less about Goldwater's personal predilections. They wanted to know what he would do for Negroes in his capacity as President of the United States. That Goldwater shared his supporters' perspective became evident during the campaign when he asked if Negroes would not rather have a President who dealt with race relations as a matter of conscience than as a political football. Since these days political action is a major method of redressing Negro grievances, it is not surprising that Goldwater failed to get his conscience accepted as a substitute for favorable Presidential action.

The privatization of politics leads to a fundamentalist approach to politics. Problems are dealt with by stating one's first principles and assuming that they must be relevant to whatever issue is at hand. One gets no sense whatsoever that Goldwater purists approached problems and inquired how special circumstances might be taken into account in order to achieve desirable results. The pragmatic spirit is completely lacking. Indeed, the purists manifested amazingly little interest in specific issues. In our interviews at the convention, we simply could not get them to talk about anything concrete, unless references to welfare-statism and too-much-government are considered specific replies. The purists did express strong belief in the importance of being interested in issues, but this was not reflected in their own interests in specific issues.

WHY THE REPUBLICAN PARTY
NOMINATED BARRY GOLDWATER

Republicans in 1964 did not first settle upon a grand strategy and then look around for a candidate to carry it out. The strategy was adopted from the beginning by those within the party who first decided to advance the Goldwater candidacy. By choosing Goldwater at the national convention, the Republican party thereby chose Goldwater's strategy of sharp and general opposition to the incumbent Democratic administration on such matters as government intervention in the economy, the extension of government-sponsored welfare and medical benefits, and the use of the powers of the Federal government to further the cause of civil rights. Goldwater expressed it in Phoenix in January, 1964,

> After asserting that a majority of Republicans believe "in the essential emphasis on individual liberty," he continued:
> "I have been spelling out my position now for ten years in the Senate, for years before that here in my own state. I will spell it out even further in the months to come. I was once asked what kind of Republican I was. I replied that I was

not a 'me-too' Republican. That still holds, I will not change my beliefs to win votes. I will offer a choice, not an echo." [12]

If this strategy for victory was transparently untenable, and Senator Goldwater's showing in the public opinion polls and in Presidential preference primaries indifferent, how did the Republican party come to nominate him?

There are five principal reasons for Goldwater's success in his campaign for the nomination: the weakness of his opposition within the Republican party; the lack of hierarchical control within state Republican organizations; President Johnson's immense popularity and seeming invincibility; Goldwater's own strength among Republican party professionals; and the unusual influx of political amateurs—almost all favoring Goldwater—into Republican politics.

First, there was the weakness of Goldwater's opposition within the Republican party. For the first time in thirty years there was no moderate Republican candidate who was both popular with the voters and willing to contest the nomination actively. There was a fatal flaw, for example, in the candidacy of Nelson A. Rockefeller. As each new incident unfolded in Governor Rockefeller's private life—his divorce, his remarriage, and the birth of Nelson A. Rockefeller, Jr. just days before the California primary—his Presidential candidacy became less and less promising. [13]

Henry Cabot Lodge, who won the early-bird New Hampshire primary as a write-in candidate with 35% of the vote and who showed write-in strength in the Massachusetts, Texas, Illinois, and Nebraska primaries, refused to resign his ambassadorship to Vietnam in order to come home to campaign. This may have cost him the Oregon primary, which he lost narrowly to Rockefeller. Lodge's strategy could be defended on the grounds that he is an indifferent campaigner and hence was less likely to damage his candidacy by his absence. On the other hand, it cast grave doubts upon the seriousness of his interest in the nomination. To party professionals, these doubts seemed to have reinforced preexisting antipathies toward certain of Lodge's personal manner-isms, and, in addition, many professionals still nursed resentments over Lodge's active role in securing Eisenhower's nomination in 1952.

The attractive, though inexperienced, William Scranton adopted a Stevensonian posture of reluctance. But unlike Steven-son in 1952, who was the designated successor of President Truman, Scranton could never manage to win more than qualified encouragement from General Eisenhower. No doubt the Scranton campaign was delayed not only by the hesitancy of the candidate, but also by the hope that Rockefeller and Goldwater would effectively cancel one another out in the primaries. This hope was dashed by the unexpected Rockefeller defeat in California. By the time the Scranton campaign got started, too many people had been otherwise committed. Only a *force majeure,* such as the Eisenhower blessing, could have shaken the situation loose, but instead, Eisenhower's main impact was to delay Scranton's entry into the race until after the crucial Governor's Conference in early June, giving him less than a month to campaign before the convention began.

Finally, Richard Nixon's candidacy seems to have been hampered to a remarkable degree by his own activities since his narrow loss of the Presidency in 1960. In 1962, he ran for Governor of California and lost. This by itself was bound to create some skepticism in the minds of party leaders about Nixon's continued popularity with the voters. He then com-pounded his problem by his immediate reaction to this defeat. His bitter, recriminatory remarks about press coverage of the gubernatorial race were given wide publicity. On-the-spot radio and television records of this unfortunate event put a potent weapon into the hands of his future political opponents. Shortly after this debacle, he gave up his titular leadership of the California Republican party and moved his residence to New York City, where he entered private law practice. But unlike Thomas E. Dewey, in whose steps he seemed to be following,

Nixon retained a sufficient interest in public officeholding to embark upon a low-key campaign for the Presidency which consisted—in the absence of any more tangible resources—of statements reminding Republicans of his ideological acceptability to all wings of the party and of his general abilities as an experienced campaigner and public servant. These statements were understandably received with something less than enthusiasm by party leaders who had made commitments to other candidates, but even when this was not the case, as, for example, at the Cleveland Governor's Conference, Nixon seemed to have created a predominantly negative impression by efforts in his own behalf that could not be energetically seconded by some identifiable bloc of troops at the national convention.[14]

Participation in Presidential primaries is usually the preferred strategy of aspirants who cannot be chosen by compromise at the national conventions. Men like Kennedy and Humphrey in 1960 or Goldwater and Rockefeller in 1964 actively contest many primaries because they have to establish overwhelming support before the conventions meet in order to have a chance. Candidates like Nixon, Lodge, and Scranton, however, may reasonably hope to be the choice of the convention after the front-runners have demonstrated that they cannot win. So they stay out of the primaries and wait to pick up the pieces. This waiting strategy proved disastrous in 1964, because Nelson Rockefeller was unexpectedly unable to play the role allotted to him; he failed to defeat Goldwater in the California primary, and the contest was over before it was supposed to have started.

In addition to the various flaws in the candidacies of Goldwater's potential opponents, the Republican party in 1964, on a state-by-state basis, was somewhat more loosely organized than usual. Normally, state party organizations are unified by incumbent Governors. Without the centralizing forces of state patronage and coherent party leadership embodied by a man in the Governor's chair, state parties tend to fragment into local satrapies or territorial jurisdictions which can be played off one against another by astute aspirants for the Presidential nomination. The lack of strong leadership at the state level also means that a set of Presidential preferences and strategies for pursuing them is less likely to be worked out in advance and agreed upon by all elements of the state party. Decentralized state parties thus become happy hunting grounds for early starters in the Presidential sweepstakes. They can move into a vacuum, make alliances and receive commitments, and build delegate strength from the ground up.

There were Republican state leaders in 1964 who winced at the thought of a disastrous defeat in November, but there were fewer such leaders than there might have been precisely because the Republicans are a minority party. There were only sixteen Republican Governors at the Republican Convention. (See the table on p. 188.) The advantages to Goldwater's early candidacy under these circumstances are obvious. Governors might have had sufficiently hierarchical control over their delegations to keep them from precipitously joining the Goldwater bandwagon. The absence of central leadership on a state-by-state basis meant that delegates were freer to follow their personal preferences and also free to weigh ideological considerations more heavily than they could have if they had been responsible to a leader who would suffer badly if Republicans were defeated for state offices.

This factor may continue to weigh heavily in the future. There has been a little noticed but important secular decline in the number of Governorships that are up for election in years during which Presidents are also running for office, as the table on page 188 indicates. From a starting point of thirty-three governorships that were open to election in 1944, the number will decline to twenty-five in 1968. Many states are changing the two-year gubernatorial term to a four-year term and are providing for the gubernatorial election in the middle of the President's term of office. This is intended to isolate gubernatorial elections from national electoral currents. But it may also mean that the number of state delegations to national party conventions controlled by Governors will decrease as the motivation of Governors to protect their own fortunes by finding popular Presidential candidates also decreases. This trend thus far has had its most pronounced effect upon the Republican party, where the number of Republican Governors up for election in Presidential years has declined from twenty in 1944 to seven in 1964. (See the table on p. 189.)

Decline in the Number of Republican Governors in Office During Presidential Election Years (Excluding Hawaii and Alaska)

Year	Number of Republican Governors
1944	26
1948	24
1952	25
1956	21
1960	14
1964	16

Decline in the Number of Gubernatorial Elections in Presidential Election Years (Excluding Hawaii and Alaska)

Year	Number of Elections
1944	33
1948	31
1952	31
1956	31
1960	27
1964	26
1968	25

Decline in the Number of Republican Governors Up for Election in Presidential Election Years (Excluding Alaska and Hawaii)

Year	Number of Republican Governors Up for Election
1944	20
1948	19
1952	15
1956	16
1960	11
1964	7

SOURCE: *World Almanac*, 1944, 1948, 1952, 1956, 1960, 1964.

Another factor, which helps to explain the nomination of Senator Goldwater, was the strength of the Democratic party. In 1964, reasonable Republicans might well have asked themselves whether the nomination of their party was worth fighting for, or whether it was, in the words of one Eastern liberal delegate, "a ticket on the Titanic." Less than a year before, a Democratic President had been martyred. John F. Kennedy's hairline margin of victory in 1960 suddenly had been replaced as a point of reference by a massive bipartisan wave of sympathy, remorse, and retrospective popularity following his assassination.[15] Kennedy's chosen successor, Lyndon Johnson, had had only eight months on the job, and by astute management, he had prolonged his honeymoon with Congress, the press, and the people.[16] These factors had to be added to the normal advantages which accrue to Democrats by virtue of their majority of supporters and to incumbent Presidents because of their access to publicity, their command of the resources of the entire government for political purposes, and the various emotional linkages of the populace with them—feelings of dependency, demands for "security," and so on—all of which were no doubt magnified by the Kennedy assassination. The universal expectation that no Republican candidate had much of a chance of beating Lyndon Johnson also reduced the persuasiveness of the usual argument that the Republican party should put up a popular candidate who might win. Goldwater's opponents had to content themselves with the weaker argument that another candidate might lose by less.

The belief that the Republican party was bound to lose the election opened up the possibility of using the conflict over the nomination as a means of gaining control of the various state parties. Party leaders still cared about winning, but their notion of the relevant contest changed. Wherever Goldwater had strong support among Republican activists, opposing party factions could be beaten down in the name of support for him. Had there been a popular candidate to oppose Goldwater, the opposition might have decided to fight the battle around this champion. In the circumstances, however, they were faced in many states with the choice of Goldwater or nothing. Some Republican leaders, as was apparently the case with Charles Percy in Illinois, decided to try to maintain their influence within the party by rolling with the Goldwater tide and thus living to fight another day. This is precisely what Governor DiSalle of Ohio did in 1960 when a hostile faction of the Democratic party threatened to use John F. Kennedy's popularity as a club with which to beat him. By supporting Kennedy, he was able to hold at bay his opponents within the party.

In addition, Goldwater's own strength among Republican party professionals should be recalled. Goldwater had been building a base of support at the Republican grass roots for some time. He was chairman of the Republican Senatorial Campaign Committee for the elections of 1956, 1960, and 1962. After the 1960 election, while Richard Nixon was pinned down in California, and Governor Rockefeller was engrossed in domestic problems, he became the most active party leader on the national banquet circuit, helping to raise money for local candidates and parties and not incidentally widening still further his acquaintance with state and local party leaders. Furthermore, there is no doubt that he struck a responsive chord with many of these leaders not only because he is personally charming and likeable, but also because he expressed many of their own views on public policy.

Finally, there is the factor of increased amateur participation in politics. By slow increments, the image of politicians in this country as cynical manipulators devoid of interest in public policy is giving way to a more complicated description in which practicality and patronage are mixed with idealism and issue orientation.[17] In an era of economic prosperity and great opportunities in the private sector, recruitment into political involvement and leadership is bound to contain a more important component of issue orientation than would be true when the government is a major source of direct income through the distribution of jobs and favors.[18] In fact, a high degree of interest in party politics usually is associated with a high level of political information and strong policy preferences. Among Republican political activists, even allowing for diversity of opinion, these preferences can in general be characterized as definitely conservative, and apparently, on a very large number of issues, as more conservative than the views not only of Democratic activists, but also of ordinary citizens who classify themselves as habitual Republican voters.[19]

Our explanation of Goldwater's nomination does not fully account for what others saw at the Republican National Convention: a kind of amateur take-over of the Republican party. The journalist Murray Kempton commented at the time: "The Goldwater forces seem in fact to have captured a number of state conventions with the device of mass amateur influx which Dewey and Henry Cabot Lodge used to seize so many Southern states from Taft in 1952. A mountain state Republican Senator, who had assumed that he would be his delegation's favorite son, was shocked to find that his state convention had elected a Goldwater delegate slate. 'There were people at the convention,' he said, 'that I've never seen before.' " [20]

One assumption underlying this idea of amateur take-over seems to be that professional politicians would never, if left to their own devices, have supported a candidate who promised to be as weak as Goldwater. Even if they entertained small hope of winning the Presidency, these politicians had a stake in the preservation of party competition further down on the ballot, where the right candidate for the Presidency could at least attenuate the effects of the Johnson coattail. Such considerations, it is suggested, are bound to be less salient to amateurs, who are more likely to value ideological purity above all other considerations.

But the 1964 Republican Convention is not good evidence for this notion. Regular Republican activists may well have preferred Goldwater anyway, on ideological grounds. In addition, there was no doubt an influx of amateurs into the state conventions which helped turn the tide in his favor. County Chairmen certainly represent an important part of the activists of the Republican party. An Associated Press poll of Republican County Chairmen, taken in April, 1964, showed that 722 chose Goldwater as their personal preference compared to 301 for Nixon.[21] But the nature of the activists at the conventions may have changed somewhat. In the state of Washington, for example, Goldwater forces won control by the simple expedient of showing up and being elected precinct delegates when nobody else wanted the jobs.[22] F. Clifton White headed a secret committee which undoubtedly tried similar maneuvers in other states, but we do not know to what extent they were successful.[23] One clue may be found by determining the proportion of delegates who were at the Goldwater convention but not at previous conventions.

We are accustomed to reading about new faces at national conventions. Each election year, so it seems, some leading politician well known to members of the press is irked to discover that his delegation has been taken over by strangers. Indeed, at the Republican conventions of 1952 and 1956—one a hard-fought contest among factions of the out-party, the other a love-feast dedicated to the renomination of an incumbent—a majority of the regular delegates had not served at the previous convention.[24] Nevertheless, the Republican Convention of 1964 was extraordinary: 74.3% of the delegates had not been at *either* of the two preceding conventions. Thus the proportion of new faces was high, and so also, we may surmise, was the number of amateur persons moved by passionate conviction and relatively insensitive to demands for compromise or the necessities of team play with copartisans whose general orientation to politics, or whose policy preferences, differed from their own.

The question arises as to whether the Goldwater delegates were a special breed of activist who came out in 1964 to support their hero or whether, as we believe, they are representative of a large proportion of Republican activists. It is clear that Republican activists have been more conservative than Republican voters at least since 1952. In that year the Gallup organization polled both County Chairmen and ordinary Republican voters. While the activist Chairmen preferred Taft over Eisenhower by 61% to 31%, the voters preferred Eisenhower by 46% to 31% for Taft.[25] That nothing has changed since then is made clear by a comparison of the preferences of County Chairmen in 1964 with the voters in the New Hampshire Republican primary. In this case Goldwater received 48% of the preferences of the party professionals; he received only 22% of the Republican votes.[26] When the 1960 Republican delegates were queried about their preference in 1964, Goldwater was far and away the strongest candidate.[27] A comparison of the Goldwater and Rockefeller slates of delegates in California[28] gives us no reason to believe that the Goldwater people were novices to the Republican party. On the contrary, 41% of the Goldwater slate had attended previous national conventions compared with 21% of the Rockefeller people. The Goldwater men averaged slightly greater years of active service to the Republican party (16 to 15), and far more of them held an official party position in the state (61% to 39%) than did the supporters of Nelson Rockefeller. Taken together with Mc-Closky's poll of 1956 Republican delegates and voters, these data suggest that Goldwater's nomination was but another manifestation of a historical trend in which Republican voters have become much more moderate in their preferences than Republican activists.

Let us summarize our analysis of why Goldwater won the Republican nomination by taking a close look at the state delegations that supported and opposed him. A major part of the explanation, we believe, lies in the underlying commitment of a substantial proportion of Republican activists to strong conservative views. On top of this, we have argued, there was some infusion of new conservative activists into the party in several states. Finally, there were splits within the ranks of the moderate and liberal Republicans, and they relied on a weak reed in Nelson Rockefeller to defeat Goldwater in the primaries. The table that follows tells most of the story.[29] The existence of

Percent of Vote for Conservatives	Taft States[1]	Swing States[2]	Progressive States[3]
1952	83.6%	18.6%	13.0%
1964	95.1%	92.8%	16.0%

[1] 23 states for Taft and Goldwater.
[2] 12 states against Taft but for Goldwater.
[3] 13 states against Taft and Goldwater.

persistent conservative tendencies is dramatically demonstrated by the fact that Goldwater carried all but one of the twenty-three states that Taft had won in 1952. In addition, Goldwater won back the three states (Texas, Louisiana, and Georgia) that Taft had lost to Eisenhower in their famous credentials fight. What this shows is that when Republican conservatives have a candidate, he can count on a good deal of support. In order to win, however, Goldwater had to turn Eisenhower majorities into Goldwater majorities in nine swing states: California, Colorado, Delaware, Iowa, Kansas, Missouri, Oklahoma, Washington, and Wyoming. The poll data make it clear that Goldwater would not have won the primary in California had he run against Lodge instead of Rockefeller.[30] Goldwater's capture of the border states of Missouri, Oklahoma, and (to some extent) Delaware may represent two phenomena: the impact of the race issue and the influx of conservatives into weak Republican party organizations. We know that Goldwater backers organized to prevail in Washington, and they may have done the same in Colorado, Iowa, Wyoming, and Kansas. While it is difficult to give a precise estimate of the exact importance of each of the various factors we have mentioned, it does appear that the conservatism of Republican activists provided a strong base from which to consolidate gains in the South and make incremental advances in the Mid and Far West. When joined to Rockefeller's weakness in California, the combination was irresistible.

CAMPAIGN STRATEGIES

Fought between a political purist and a traditional politician, the 1964 election campaign was most peculiar by recent American standards. Questions of personality and morality—did Goldwater lack responsibility and Johnson, integrity?—seemed to dominate the campaign. For the first time in many years, the Republicans made more appeals based on party identification than did the Democrats. The change in direction that this represented for professional Republicans was not accomplished without cost. Many Negro delegates to the Republican National Convention expressed dismay at the turn of events, so did party leaders and candidates from the urban Northeast, who were beaten back in attempts to strengthen the civil rights plank of the platform and to insert a plank criticizing "extremism."

The Goldwater Strategy

Senator Goldwater, throughout the platform battle and thereafter, adhered to an uncompromising line with impressive fidelity. He and his allies withstood all attempts to amend the platform from the floor. As his running mate, Goldwater "balanced" his ticket by choosing a man almost as conservative as he is, Representative William E. Miller of New York. And when the time came to bind up his party's wounds and unite it for action against the Democrats—which is one traditional function of the acceptance speech—Senator Goldwater spoke these words (seemingly to his fellow Republicans):

> Anyone who joins us in all sincerity we welcome. Those, those who do not care for our cause, we don't expect to join our ranks in any case. And let our Republicanism so focused and so dedicated not be made fuzzy. . . .

Immediately thereafter came his famous allusion to the platform battle:

> I would remind you that extremism in the defense of liberty is no vice.

> And let me remind you also that moderation in the defense of justice is no virtue.[31]

Throughout the campaign, the Goldwater-Miller ticket continued to differentiate itself sharply even from those Democratic policies likely to be favored by audiences the candidates were addressing. On Labor Day, Representative Miller criticized liberalized immigration policies in South Bend, Indiana, an industrial community heavily populated with immigrants and their children. Before the American Political Science Association on September 11, Senator Goldwater criticized the Supreme Court of the United States as, among the three branches of the government, "least faithful to the constitutional tradition of limited government, and to the principle of legitimacy in the exercise of power." On September 16, in Knoxville, Tennessee, Senator Goldwater said,

"I know that you know, and most of you share my faith in private initiative and private enterprise. . . . Now what I said with respect to TVA is within the general framework of that philosophy and I stand by it." Two days later, in the economically-depressed Appalachian region, he attacked the Administration poverty program as "phony," "cynical," and "irresponsible," and called for free enterprise to combat poverty. At the National Plowing Contest in North Dakota, Goldwater said that "a gradual decline would be good for you" in farm price supports. Contrast this last statement with a more conventional Republican campaign: General Eisenhower's pledge at this same gathering during the 1952 campaign to work for farm price supports at 100% of parity.[32]

Another atypical feature of the Goldwater campaign was his unequivocal bid for support from the South and his forthright sacrifice of Negro votes. Whereas Vice-President Nixon did his best in 1960 to appeal to *both* Southerners and Negroes,[33] Goldwater's campaign was marked by attacks on the Supreme Court, reminders that he had voted against the Civil Rights Act of 1964 because he believed sections of the bill were unconstitutional, and promises that a Goldwater Presidency would restore "law and order" in the streets and would not tolerate civil disobedience and demonstrations of a kind associated by many of his listeners with the civil rights movement.[34] In all of these particulars, Senator Goldwater's campaign represented a sharp departure from Republican tactics of the recent past.

There can be little doubt that in addition to his unimpeachably conservative voting record in Congress, Goldwater made a general appeal based on ideological considerations, laying emphasis upon issues of morality and rightness "in your heart" and on complaints about an unidentifiable malaise in American society. These sorts of appeals can be contrasted with the identification of specific issues, the making of promises about the content of policies, and the suggestion of concrete steps to be taken. This latter approach can be used when there is a specific coalition of interest groups to be put together. But Senator Goldwater took a novel public posture with respect to interest groups: "If I had to cater to every special interest in the country to get elected, I wouldn't want the job." [35]

The campaign speeches of Barry Goldwater are a testimonial to the extraordinary importance he assigned to political style. One would have to go far to find another candidate so insistent that people not vote for him if they did not share his views. Rarely has so much attention been given to these sorts of reasons for supporting a candidate. Let us take one major speech (which epitomizes this approach) delivered at a rally at Madison Square Garden, and observe the overwhelming emphasis on matters of individual style.

Goldwater began by saying that although he knew what statements would get him the most votes, he was not going to make them.

> I can't help wondering if you've asked why my campaign is what it is.
>
> I wonder, my fellow Americans, if you think I don't know what views would be most popular. Do you think I don't know what labor wants to hear, what management . . . what housewives and diplomats and white-collar workers want to hear?
>
> Do you honestly think, after all these years in politics, that I don't know the easy ways to get votes? The promises to make? The subjects to talk about—and the ones to avoid? Well, I do!

He then proceeded to tell his audience why he didn't "take the easy way."

> First of all, if I just went around telling people what they wanted to hear, I'd sound like Lyndon Baines Johnson. And I still think the American people are entitled to a choice.
>
> But more important, if I had to cater to every special interest in the country to get elected, I wouldn't want the job.

Like many of his followers, Goldwater was a political purist who objected to telling people what they wanted to hear, catering to "special interests," or being like the other party in order to gain popularity.

As a political purist, Goldwater was careful about the kind of people who should and should not support him. The Nazi and Fascist types, the Communists and left-wing radicals, are clearly beyond the pale. Goldwater also excluded "the lazy, dole-happy people who want to feed on the fruits of somebody else's labor" and people who believe in promises and those "who are willing to believe that Communism can be 'accommodated.' " Most revealing, for our purposes, was his characterization of the people he believed would vote for him.

> People who take the trouble to reread, thoughtfully, the Declaration of Independence and the Constitution of the United States will vote for me. . . .
>
> People who have learned to be suspicious of neverending promises of "something for nothing"—they will vote for me.
>
> People who have the courage and the intelligence to listen to the truth, and think about it. People whose votes can't be bought. They'll vote for me.
>
> People who are sick to death of politicians coming out in favor of happiness and declaring war on misery. People who are fed up with so-called leaders of government promising to legislate worry out of existence. People who will listen for a little while to such transparent, vote-grabbing demagoguery and say "Baloney." They'll vote for me.
>
> But most of all, it will be the people who know that something must be done.[36]

Goldwater thought that the people who would vote for him were not merely those who agreed with him on specific issues. Rather, they would be the people who hark back to fundamental principles, such as may be found in the nation's venerable documents, people who are suspicious of promises, who have courage, who are "sick to death of politicians," and who know that something must be done.

The Democratic Strategy

If Senator Goldwater's nomination was unexpected and his campaign strategy unorthodox, the Democratic strategy was a model of orthodoxy, and scarcely needs either description or explanation.

Most of the resources available to President Johnson have already been mentioned: incumbency, the halo effect that resulted from the trauma of his predecessor's assassination and that undoubtedly prolonged his honeymoon with the press and with Congress, and his leadership of what, after all, is the majority party.

Johnson's main problem, standing in his way when he sought the nomination in 1960, was the fact that he is from the South. Indeed, labor and civil rights groups had opposed even his nomination as Vice-President in that year.[37] But the passage of the Civil Rights Act of 1964 with his vigorous support served as no honeyed words alone could possibly have served to underscore to liberal Democrats that Johnson understood the necessities of the times as they understood them and demonstrated that he was ready, like President Truman and Adlai Stevenson before him, to sacrifice the demands of the South where they conflicted with the demands of the rest of the Democratic coalition.

The Democratic Convention of 1964 seated representatives of the predominantly Negro Freedom Democratic party of Mississippi in a White House-approved compromise. Television viewers whose memories ran back to the 1960 convention remembered Joseph Rauh, a prominent leader of the liberal Americans for Democratic Action and delegate from the District of Columbia. When the word went out that Senator John Kennedy wanted Lyndon Johnson for his running mate, Rauh seized the nearest microphone and pleaded over nationwide TV, "Don't do it, Jack." In 1964, appearing as counsel for the Freedom Democrats, Rauh flayed the regular Mississippi delegation for repudiating the leadership of "our great President Johnson." Thus far had Johnson come in allaying the fears and winning the support of his party's liberal activists. The choice of Senator Hubert Humphrey as his Vice-Presidential candidate sealed the bargain. In this way President Johnson solved his major problem—how to unite the Democratic party behind him—before the campaign began. Once the campaign was under way, it rapidly became apparent that Johnson had no further problems. He needed only to refrain from rocking the boat to win.

On the Democratic side, the campaign was unexciting. A comprehensive statement of the President's views in a book published for the campaign was justly hailed by critics as comparable only to the prose of Warren G. Harding in unexceptionable blandness.[38] The President prudently refused to debate with his challenger on nationwide television. He shook thousands of hands and exuded hospitality and sympathy for disaffected Republicans—some of whom turned out to be prominent businessmen and former members of the Eisenhower Administration who endorsed him publicly. For once, the Democratic party had less difficulty than their opponents in financing the campaign.

All the Democratic nominee had to do was pounce on the weaknesses of his Republican opponent. The fact that Senator Goldwater was so far to the right of most Republican voters gave President Johnson the opportunity to detach a significant portion of that party's traditional supporters. In search of this Republican vote, Johnson eschewed the usual partisan appeals. Instead, he went out of his way to praise the good old Republican party of yesteryear and to ask the electorate to reject the extremists who had temporarily taken control of it. While maintaining his party's historic position on welfare issues, Johnson carefully toned down his comments so as not to give moderate Republicans an excuse for voting against him. If he could not positively attract Republicans, he would do nothing to repel them. So the President adopted the stance of national unity, calling insistently on Americans to get together against certain demagogues and hotheads who might get the United States into a nuclear war or foment racial strife.

Goldwater's conservatism and his unwillingness to change course to get votes made it difficult for him to make any appeal on welfare matters. As a result, Lyndon Johnson was placed in the unique position of being able to make gains on two issues—prosperity and poverty—even while playing down an aggressive pro-welfare stand in order not to alienate Republicans.

In the realm of foreign policy, the Democrats are subject to attack as "the party of war" because they were in office during the three major wars of this century. Given Goldwater's proclivity for an adventurous foreign policy, however (in part a product of the style of "stand up and be counted"), he was not in a position to gain votes on the war issue. Rather, he seemed to advocate extension of military conflict in South Vietnam, Berlin, Cuba, and other places. In 1952, General Eisenhower made political capital out of promising "to bring the boys back from Korea," not by promising to send more of them over there. Goldwater, on the other hand, had the extraordinary task of having to assure voters that he would not launch a nuclear war immediately upon assuming office.

Thus, Goldwater could not pick up votes on either foreign policy or on the broad spectrum of domestic welfare policy. At the same time, he could not count on full support from normal Republican identifiers. What kind of appeal, then, could he make and to whom?

He could appeal to ordinarily Democratic working- and lower-middle class voters on the racial issue, references to which were put in terms of safety on the streets and in the scarcely veiled suggestions that women would know what he was talking about. Yet this approach also created problems for Goldwater. As a self-professed constitutional conservative eager to retain a consistent position, he could hardly call for a Federal police force or for national action in an area explicitly reserved to state and local government except, perhaps, to advocate the appointment of tougher judges. His running mate, William Miller, could suggest that the jobs of workers would be taken by hordes of immigrants who would be let in by new immigration procedures proposed by the Johnson Administration. But many of the workers who might have been influenced by this type of appeal came from ethnic groups sensitive to selective limitation of immigration.

A surface reading of the election returns suggests that outside the South the so-called "white backlash" could not have been very large. The workers whose "authoritarian tendencies" presumably left them responsive to a racial appeal were among the most fervent supporters of the Democratic party on "pocketbook" issues.[39] Racial feelings would have had to be highly salient and intense for them to vote against their traditional party and the social welfare legislation which is so important to them. If a group had felt its jobs threatened by Negroes, or if it was desperately trying to ward off Negro encroachment on its residential areas, it might have been sufficiently moved to change the direction of its vote. But there simply were not enough people in this position. Apparently more Republicans were frightened by Goldwater than whites were frightened by Negroes.

MORALITY

The focus of the campaign upon problems of personal competence was directly connected with the existence of profound differences on public policy. Candidates find it hard to differ more and more over issues while saying nicer and nicer things about each other. Once Goldwater had moved rather far away from positions traditionally taken by Republican Presidential candidates, Johnson seized the opportunity to gain Republican votes by denouncing Goldwater as an "extremist." A candidate is likely to be called an extremist when he leads his party far from positions it has previously espoused, especially if the new position is far from where the voters are. Goldwater raised the morality issue and, by using the Bobby Baker episode, tried to undermine Johnson. If one believes that politics should be concerned with the private conscience of the political leader and his stock of basic principles, as the Goldwater people did, then the morality of the candidates necessarily assumes prime importance. The politician is immediately condemned as immoral by virtue of his usual practices. He is immoral because he alters his policies to suit different constituencies. Even when the politician hangs onto his fundamental position but gives a little to assure a wider consensus he is immoral because of his inconsistency and vacillation. Because Lyndon Johnson epitomized the practicing politician, famed for his love of bargaining, maneuver, conciliation, and consensus, his morality was questionable for the political purists.

There is still another way in which concentration on political style made morality a central focus of the campaign. Goldwater purists believed that difficulties facing America, particularly in foreign affairs, were due to forces largely within the control of leaders. They thought that if the leaders of the United States had the right approach, if they stood up for what they believed and enunciated their principles with sufficient force, most of the nation's problems would be solved. This was presumably what Goldwater meant when he said that he had a "rational solution" to the Cold War, without specifying what it was, or when he insisted that our foreign policy difficulties are not complex but simple; if the world situation was not exactly rosy, therefore, the blame lay with immoral leaders who behaved as politicians instead of as purists. They sold out their country because they either did not have the right American principles or did not stand up for them or both. From the Goldwater point of view, one needed only to look at the state of the world to see that American political leaders were immoral. Reasoning from effect to cause, the purists would be bound to place the simple moral test—

does the candidate have the right political style?—at the heart of a campaign taking place when decay had set in from the remotest Asian principality to the nearest city street.

DISCUSSION OF ISSUES

Although the candidates in 1964 were not subjected to the kind of abuse that was typical of the early days of the American republic, one has the impression that there was more personal vilification than in the past decade or two. Of greater importance for our purposes, however, is the undoubted fact that in a campaign in which the parties were further apart on issues than they have been in our time, at least since 1936 and possibly in this century, there was relatively little discussion of issues. Certainly, the existence of wide and deep policy differences did not, as has sometimes been thought, lead directly to a campaign focusing on specific issues. Why not?

Perhaps when candidates are virtually identical in their views, there is little else for them to talk about except differences in their respective personalities. When they are too far apart, discussion also turns on personalities, because issue differences are generalized to differences in basic values. When they are moderately far apart, separated by marginal but real differences on the issues, the possibility for discussion may be at its highest point. For the parties are then far enough apart to make debates meaningful and yet close enough together so that a real dialogue is possible. Both the candidates and attentive publics can understand what a marginal change from one proposal to another might mean.

The experience of the 1964 Presidential campaign suggests that the old proposition—the greater the differences on issue positions, the greater the discussion of specific issues—might be replaced with a new hypothesis: Discussion of issues varies directly with moderate, marginal disagreements on issues and inversely with the extremes of total agreement or total disagreement. Such has been the situation in France where election campaigns typically involve disagreements among the parties closest to each other and little or no direct confrontations among the parties furthest apart in ideology.[40]

THE FUTURE

The existence of a political elite, in a position to control a major national party, which holds views widely at variance both with the general voting population and its own followers, presents a major political problem in the United States. Goldwater's nomination and defeat was merely a sign of an old problem, but one which has been hidden by the normal operation of the party system. What are some of the consequences for American political parties?

One possibility is that the Republican party will return to its previous course and seek out popular candidates whose moderate views will give it a chance to win Presidential elections. If, on the other hand, the Goldwater movement is not a temporary aberration, but represents a profound current within the Republican party, we cannot expect that the moderates and liberals in the party will automatically gain control simply because Goldwater lost badly. Nearly a majority of party activists may now support the political tendency that Goldwater represents.[41] While it is always possible that they will alter their behavior, if the chances of defeating these conservatives are to be consistently high, they will have to be challenged by a rival, moderate elite, willing to engage in the daily tasks of political organization. The vast majority of Republican votes in 1964, of course, were traditional Republicans who would undoubtedly support almost any candidate of their party.

Goldwater supporters were saying after it was all over that the twenty-six million people who voted for their man constituted an endorsement of right-wing Republicanism. But Goldwater's total represented a decline of over seven million in the vote for the Republican candidate since 1960, and was a stunning sixteen million fewer than voted for the winner. (By way of contrast, Lyndon Johnson received the largest percentage of the major party vote in any twentieth-century Presidential election.) Students of messianic movements and of other organizations heavily dependent upon faith rather than rational calculation as a method of achieving internal cohesion would not be surprised at the reaction shown by the Goldwaterites.[42]

But political parties in the United States cannot long survive solely as vehicles for drastically unpopular doctrines, no matter how passionately these doctrines are upheld by the minority of activists who believe in them. Indeed, after the election, a clamor among Republicans for a new image was not long in coming. A month after the election, the Republican Governors met for two days in Denver and issued a statement endorsing civil rights and condemning radicalism "whether of the right or left." Writing in the January, 1965 issue of Fortune, Republican Representative Gerald R. Ford of Michigan suggested that, in the House, his party abandon its attempts to coordinate plans with leaders of the Southern Democrats.[43] In spite of the misgivings of some of his colleagues about the import of this article, Ford, running on a new image platform, successfully displaced Charles Halleck of Indiana as Republican leader of the House at the start of the 89th Congress. And Barry Goldwater's hand-picked chairman of the Republican National Committee, Dean Burch, was at the same time forced out of office. His successor, Ray Bliss of Ohio, is preeminently a rational, calculating, organization politician, who is used to testing his personal preferences against political realities.

To an outside observer, the lesson of this election for Republicans seems to be remarkably clear; a question remained as to who within the Republican party would be charged with interpreting that lesson. Normally, this task falls to officeholders of the defeated party. No one could believe, on the record of their past performance and preferences, that the elevation to leadership of Mr. Ford and Mr. Bliss heralded a drastic leftward turn in the policies espoused by the leaders of the Republican party. However, both men recognized the need to strike a bargain with reality. Whether merely giving ground before popular sentiment will be enough to transform the Republican party from a minority to a majority party may be doubted, but such a leadership is capable of attracting a larger share of the voting population than candidates and leaders who are unwilling even to accommodate that much.

It may be that some pro-Goldwater Republicans recognized that their chances of winning the election were slim but believed that even a debacle in 1964 would enhance their long-run chances of controlling the Republican party and in possibly pushing political dialogue in this country to the right. Judging from the activity of the 89th Congress and from the tendency of political parties to cohere around elected officeholders rather than defeated candidates, this seems to have been a gross miscalculation.

The possibility cannot be ruled out that the Republican party will continue to nominate conservatives like Goldwater and will continue to lose badly. A noted study of state party systems has shown that when one party dominates the political scene and nomination becomes tantamount to election, there is a strong tendency for voters to move into the primaries of this party in order to gain some influence over its decisions.[44] The minority party loses its moderates and becomes the preserve of the diehards. Hence it becomes increasingly difficult for a candidate who might appeal to the whole electorate to win nomination in the minority party. As the majority party grows in relative size and importance, it becomes more diverse; at the same time the weakness of the opposition removes a powerful incentive to majority party cohesion.

Should this vision of the future materialize, we can expect an end to a competitive, two-party system. In its place we will have a modified one-party system with a dominant Democratic party. As its leaders find that their potential for controlling policy decisions has enormously increased, they may also discover that their capacity for united action has precipitously decreased due to vastly intensified internal factionalism. The Republican party, much diminished in size, will find that its greater potential for unity is accompanied by a drastically reduced capacity to get its preferences translated into government policy. It will have gained cohesion in exchange for impotence. The 1964 election may yet turn out to be a disaster for conservative Republicans and a Pyrrhic victory for liberal Democrats.

At the same time it must be remembered that the Republican party scored an impressive victory in the 1966 elections. In part, this victory appears magnified by the extent of their defeat in 1964. But in any event, the Republicans did snap back in 1966, winning several key governorships and regaining much of the strength they had lost in the House of Representatives.

The results have important consequences for the 1968 Presidential election. The larger the number of Republican governors, the greater the chance that a moderate candidate will be nominated. This follows not only because of the moderation of most of the governors, but because governors in general have a stake in protecting the electoral chances of their party. They also have the resources to control delegates who might otherwise vote their own ideological preferences. But whether or not 1966 will be looked upon as a significant break in the trend toward continual diminution of Republican strength, or merely a minor deviation, will depend on whether Republicans are able to find attractive candidates in 1968 and future years.

Despite the results of the 1966 elections and various measures within the Republican party to mend the damage caused by Senator Goldwater's candidacy, the events and efforts may be insufficient to prevent an effective shift in this country to a one-and-one-half party system, a shift that has been in the making for some time.[45] While this may be a deplorable development to defenders of a vigorous two-party system, the health of the system depends ultimately upon the capacity of the two parties to agree on most issues and at the margins to offer alternatives attractive to slightly different components of the population. This makes for disagreement on live issues, not on issues already settled and part of an overriding national consensus. There seems to be little incentive for voters to reward with public office an out-party that fails to seek new opportunities to appeal to the preferences of voters.

In any event, a serious problem for Republicans is whether the opportunity will soon arise for them to capture the loyalties of enough voters to return them to power for any lengthy period of time. We are speaking now not of a momentary aberration but of the creation of long-term party loyalties. The great historic opportunities for the creation of party loyalty seem to have been associated to a certain extent with domestic disasters, but even more important, with the entry into suffrage of great numbers of similarly situated people. The prospects for civil war seem dim; we are now growing accustomed to the role of the government in putting a floor on many aspects of the economy which heretofore were capable of combining and producing drastic depressions. And so the Republican chances to create lasting adherents among those who now vote Democratic, on account of domestic crisis, must be rated as slim. What is worse from a Republican standpoint, the Goldwater candidacy seems to have solidified a trend, visible since the New Deal, away from the Republican party of the last great bloc of voters to enter American political life: the Negro voters. Once Negroes everywhere vote, the long march toward universal suffrage in America will have ended. Even allowing for the past instability of the Negro vote, the future loyalties of the Negro seem likely to be predominantly Democratic. Seen in this light, and projected into the medium-range future, the Goldwater candidacy was a disastrous bargain for the Republican party. It is much easier for a political party to win new friends than to convert old antagonists. The decision of

Senator Goldwater and his advisors to lock the Negro out of his historic home may have had a greater impact on the Republican party's future fortunes than any other strategic choice of 1964.

NOTES

1. *Congressional Quarterly*, November 20, 1964, p. 2709, estimated that Republicans lost more than 500 seats in state legislatures in the 1964 election. Republicans gained one Governor (for a total of 17), lost two United States Senators (reducing their senatorial representation to 32), and sustained a net loss in the House of Representatives of 38 seats (reducing their strength to 140 members, the lowest since the Roosevelt landslide of 1936).

2. See, for example, Charles O. Jones, *The Republican Party in American Politics* (New York, 1965), pp. 66–71. The Michigan Survey Research Center estimates that an overwhelming 96% to 98% of such Republicans typically vote. Philip E. Converse, Aage R. Clausen, and Warren E. Miller, "Electoral Myth and Reality: The 1964 Election," *American Political Science Review* 59 (June 1965), 322–323.

3. This point has been confirmed as often as any in the entire literature of voting behavior. See Bernard Berelson, Paul F. Lazarsfeld, and William McPhee, *Voting* (Chicago, 1954), pp. 333–347, e.g., propositions 39, 50, 51, 66, 68, 69, 70, 71, 78, 79; Angus Campbell, Philip E. Converse, Warren E. Miller, and Donald E. Stokes, *The American Voter* (New York, 1960), pp. 142–145.

4. The study of right-wing ideologues and their supporters is more speculative than empirical. Nevertheless, there are a few straws in the wind, and all blow in the same direction. In 1962, Raymond E. Wolfinger and his associates administered a questionnaire to 308 "students" at an anti-Communism school conducted by Dr. Fred Schwarz's Christian Anti-Communism Crusade in Oakland, California. Among the findings of this study were that 278 of the 302 persons in this sample who voted in 1960 (or 92% of those who voted) had voted for Nixon, and that 58% of those who answered the question chose Goldwater over Nixon for 1964. At about the same time, a nationwide Gallup poll showed Goldwater the choice of only 13% of

Republicans. Raymond E. Wolfinger, Barbara Kaye Wolfinger, Kenneth Prewitt, and Sheilah Rosenhack, "America's Radical Right: Politics and Ideology" in *Ideology and Discontent,* ed. David Apter (New York, 1964), pp. 267–269. Analysis of various election returns and of a 1954 Gallup poll suggest that support for the late Senator Joseph McCarthy was importantly determined by party affiliation, with Republicans far exceeding Democrats or independents in the ranks of his supporters. See Nelson W. Polsby, "Towards an Explanation of McCarthyism," *Political Studies* 8 (October 1960), 250–271.

5. AIPO News Releases of September 6, 1964 and October 16, 1964 suggested that Republican defections would run as high as 30%, but the Release of December 11 indicated that a 20% defection figure was more accurate. This compares with defections by Republican voters of 5%, 4%, and 8% in the three previous elections. Democratic defections in this election were also high—13% of those calling themselves Democrats voted for Goldwater—but these were confined mostly to the Southern states.

6. In early July, the Gallup poll (AIPO News Release, November 11, 1964) showed the following figures among Republican voters:

Preferring:

Goldwater 22%	Scranton 20%
Lodge 21%	Rockefeller 6%

Just before the Republican Convention, the figures among Republicans were:

Scranton 60%	Undecided 6%
Goldwater 34%	

Goldwater received 23% of the vote in the New Hampshire primary; 18% in Oregon; 8% in Pennsylvania (fourth in a field of five write-ins); 10.5% in Massachusetts; 71% in Indiana, where Harold Stassen received the remainder; only 49% in Nebraska, where Goldwater's name alone was on the ballot; 51.4% in California; 76% in Texas, running in a trial heat with only Rockefeller; 31.9% in South Dakota; and a bit better than 60% in Illinois, where he was opposed on the ballot by only Margaret Chase Smith and where there is no law requiring election officials to tabulate write-in votes.

Gallup trial heats (AIPO News Release, July 1, 1964) before the

Republican Convention showed Goldwater running a poorer race against President Johnson than either Scranton or Nixon, e.g.:

Goldwater 18%	Scranton 26%	Nixon 27%
Johnson 77%	Johnson 69%	Johnson 70%
Undecided 5%	Undecided 5%	Undecided 3%

7. AIPO News Release, September 13, 1964.

8. Louis Harris Survey News Releases, July 13, 1964 and September 14, 1964. Some of the Harris survey findings on foreign affairs were:

Issue		Voters Describe Goldwater Position		Describe Own Position	
		July	Sept.	July	Sept.
Go to war over	For	78%	71%	29%	29%
Cuba	Against	22%	29%	71%	71%
Use atomic bombs	For	72%	58%	18%	18%
in Asia	Against	28%	42%	82%	82%
United Nations	For	42%	50%	82%	83%
	Against	58%	50%	18%	17%

9. The interviews were conducted in the lobby of the Fairmont Hotel in San Francisco—where the California, Illinois, and New Jersey delegations were housed—by Aaron Wildavsky, Judy Gordon, Maralyn Millman, James Payne, and Joseph Paff. While these unstructured interviews in no way represent a systematic sample of the delegates, they were undertaken because they have one great advantage over the usual mail questionnaire: They can elicit spontaneous information about respondents' attitudes that a more structured method might well miss.

10. This is borne out by findings of the Michigan Survey Research Center. Integrity was the personal quality most admired in him by his supporters. See Angus Campbell, "Interpreting the Presidential Victory," in *The National Election of 1964*, ed. Milton C. Cummings, Jr. (Washington, 1966), p. 261.

11. See James Q. Wilson, *The Amateur Democrat* (Chicago, 1962).

12. Robert D. Novak, *The Agony of the G.O.P. 1964* (New York, 1965), pp. 268–269.

13. Here, and in the following paragraphs, we rely on contemporary newspaper coverage in the New York *Times, Wall Street Journal,* Washington *Post* and *Star,* on accounts in *Congressional Quarterly Weekly Reports,* on Robert Novak's excellent *The Agony of the G.O.P. 1964,* and also upon a manuscript account being prepared for publication by Professor John Kessel of Allegheny College, tentatively titled *The Goldwater Coalition.*

14. See Rowland Evans and Robert Novak, "The Unmaking of a President," *Esquire* (November 1964), 91 and J. F. Ter Horst, "Nixon Hopes as GOP Unifier Clouded by June Maneuvers," Washington *Star,* December 2, 1964.

15. See Bradley S. Greenberg and Edwin B. Parker, eds., *The Kennedy Assassination and the American Public: Social Communication in Crisis* (Stanford, 1965).

16. Before the nominating conventions, pro-Johnson sentiment in national sample surveys was expressed by well over 70% of the voting public. See a summary in the Washington *Post,* November 2, 1964.

17. For a good example of this sort of description at the state level, see James D. Barber, *The Lawmakers* (New Haven, 1965).

18. See Wilson, *The Amateur Democrat* and Fred I. Greenstein, "The Changing Pattern of Urban Party Politics," *Annals* 353 (May 1964), 1–13.

19. See Herbert McClosky, Paul J. Hoffman, and Rosemary O'Hara, "Issue Conflict and Consensus Among Party Leaders and Followers," *American Political Science Review* 54 (June 1960), 406–427. This article compares the responses on a long self-administered mail questionnaire of three populations: 1,788 delegates to the Democratic Convention of 1956, 1,232 delegates to the 1956 Republican Convention, and 1,484 persons in two successive waves of American Institute of Public Opinion national cross-section surveys in January, 1958.

20. *The New Republic* (July 11, 1964), 6.

21. New York *Times,* April 26, 1964, 18.

22. Theodore H. White, *The Making of the President, 1964* (New York, 1965), p. 134.

23. *Ibid.* p. 92ff. and pp. 132–138.

24. Paul T. David, Ralph M. Goldman, and Richard C. Bain, *The Politics of National Party Conventions* (Washington, 1960), pp. 349, 350.

These turnover figures raise an interesting question as to the proper inferences one can make from the McClosky data discussed previously on party leaders who attended the 1956 convention. A substantial number of delegates to the 1964 convention did not attend the convention of 1956. In fact, 153 of 1,308 delegates to the 1964 convention were delegates or alternates at the 1956 convention according to a comparison of the two convention rosters. Therefore, we would have to take the McClosky findings as indicative rather than demonstrative of attitudes of a much larger—and somewhat different —group of party activists. Because the 1956 Republican nominations were a foregone conclusion, enlivened in the event only by the brief candidacy of one "Joe Smith" for Vice-President, the number of party insurgents at this convention must have been unusually low. This gives a greater plausibility to the use of responses from the delegates to this convention as in some sense accurately representative of regular Republican activist sentiment.

25. AIPO News Release, June 20, 1952 (poll of County Chairmen) and July 2, 1952 (poll of Republican voters). Out of 2,774 County Chairmen polled by mail, 1,480 responded.

26. *Ibid.*, March 29, 1964. Out of some 3,000 County Chairmen polled, 1,840 responded.

27. Novak, *The Agony of the G.O.P. 1964* (New York, 1965), p. 174.

28. Edmond Costantini (University of California, Davis) and Kenneth Craik (University of California, Berkeley), preliminary breakdowns of questionnaires received from Goldwater and Rockefeller delegates.

29. Frank Munger and James Blackhurst, "Factionalism in the National Conventions, 1940–1964: An Analysis of Ideological Consistency in State Delegation Voting," *The Journal of Politics* 27 (May 1965), 379n. For purposes of analysis, the Taft vote was combined with a handful of votes for Douglas MacArthur.

30. Converse, Clausen, and Miller, "Electoral Myth and Reality: The 1964 Election," 324–325.

31. Shortly after the convention, in a meeting at Hershey, Pennsylvania, Goldwater made a half-hearted attempt (and his only attempt) to unify the party behind him.

32. New York *Times,* September 7, 1952.

33. See the discussion of this in Theodore H. White, *The Making of the President, 1960* (New York, 1961), pp. 203–204, 315. See also pp. 128–129.

34. See Goldwater statements on September 3, 10, and 15, summarized in *Congressional Quarterly Weekly Report,* October 2, 1964, 2323–2324.

35. Speech at Madison Square Garden, New York City, October 26, 1964. Contrast this with General Eisenhower's final TV appearance in 1952, November 4, 1952.

36. New York *Times,* October 27, 1964, 30.

37. See Philip Potter, "How LBJ Got the Nomination," *The Reporter* (June 18, 1964).

38. Lyndon B. Johnson, *My Hope for America* (New York, 1964). See, for example, the review by Murray Kempton, "The People's Choice," *New York Review of Books* (November 5, 1964), 3–4.

39. Seymour Martin Lipset, "Democracy and Working-Class Authoritarianism," *American Sociological Review* 24 (August 1959), 482–501.

40. See Philip M. Williams, *Crisis and Compromise: Politics in the Fourth Republic* (Hamden, Conn., 1964) and Maurice Duverger, *Political Parties, Their Organization and Activity in the Modern State,* trans. Barbara and Robert North (New York, 1959).

41. It might be well to recall the Associated Press poll of Republican County Chairmen, taken in April, 1964, which showed that 722 chose Goldwater as their personal preference compared to 301 for Nixon. See also McClosky, Hoffman, and O'Hara, "Issue Conflict and Consensus Among Party Leaders and Followers."

42. See Leon Festinger, Henry Riecken, and Stanley Schachter, *When Prophecy Fails* (Minneapolis, 1956).

43. Gerald R. Ford, "What Can Save the G.O.P.?" *Fortune* (January 1965), 140.

44. V. O. Key, Jr., *American State Politics: An Introduction* (New York, 1956), pp. 169–196.

45. There is some indication, for example, that the number of noncompetitive Democratic Congressional seats has increased over the years. See Charles O. Jones, "Inter-Party Competition for Congressional Seats," *Western Political Quarterly* 17 (September 1964), 461–476.

Chapter 5

Reform?

THE POLITICAL PROCESSES we have been describing have, from time to time, come under severe criticism from people who believe that our political system can be made more responsive to popular demands, more equitable and more effective. One clarion call asserts: "The American government today suffers from three weaknesses:

1) its difficulty in generating sustained political power;
2) its difficulty in developing a flow of imaginative, informed, consistent and power-related responses to pressing national and world issues;
3) its difficulty in making policy truly accountable to a national popular majority." [1]

If these implied goals were enunciated in the abstract, few people would disagree with them, assuming that they could be achieved at all, or at a less than exorbitant cost. It is to the credit of critics of the party system that they have made suggestions recommending specific changes in specific institutions. A recent commentator has a list which includes recommendations 1) to centralize electoral campaign finance in the hands of national party leaders, 2) to expand two-party competition in Congressional elections by strengthening the role of the national (i.e., Presidential) party in campaign finance and other campaign

218

services, 3) to enlarge the staffs of the party national committees and to create permanent advisory councils to the national committees, 4) to build offices for the two major political parties on Federal land, situated in Washington between the White House and Capitol Hill, 5) to repeal the 22nd amendment to the Constitution, which limits the President to two terms, 6) to amend the Constitution so that Congressmen and Senators are always elected at the same time as Presidents, 7) to centralize the Congressional parties by means of frequent party caucuses and effective policy committees, and 8) to "find a mathematical formula for computing Congressional seniority which will give added weight to those legislators who come from competitive two-party districts and states." [2]

There is a kind of fascination to a list such as this one. Sweeping constitutional amendments and trivial building programs are suggested with equal seriousness. Machinery, such as Congressional party caucuses, is proposed which already exists but does not do the job contemplated by reformers. Other machinery, such as the "mathematical formula," would undoubtedly do the job assigned to it, but how would such machinery be put into effect? On this question, reformers customarily are silent, relying only on the extremity of the national "need," as they interpret it, to evaporate any possible opposition to their schemes.

Taken all together, the position of party reformers constitutes a coherent picture or view of the functions of a party system. The concreteness of their proposals makes it possible for others to examine them and to ask such questions as whether or not they will in fact accomplish the ends in view, whether they can be achieved under the political conditions which prevail, or whether changing these conditions would not lead to consequences more costly than the alleged mischiefs of the status quo. This general view can also be compared and contrasted with an alternative view, whose implications for party reform would diverge from the party reformers' ideal model.

THE POLITICAL THEORY OF PARTY REFORM

There is a general political theory which is implied in the proposals of party reformers, a theory that contains a conception of the proper function of the political party, which evaluates the legitimacy and the roles of the Congress and the President, and which embodies a particular definition of the public interest. This theory is stated with greater or lesser elaboration by different advocates of reform; some reformers leave out certain features of it, and some are disinclined to face squarely the implications of the measures they espouse. We shall try here to reproduce correctly a style of argument which, though it ignores the slight differences separating party reformers one from another, gives a coherent statement of the party reform theory and juxtaposes and contrasts it with the political theory which critics of the party reform position appear to advance.[3]

Party reformers suggest that democratic government requires political parties which 1) make policy commitments to the electorate, 2) are willing and able to carry them out when in office, 3) develop alternatives to government policies when out of office, and 4) differ sufficiently between themselves to "provide the electorate with a proper range of choice between alternatives of action." [4] Party reformers thus come to define a political party as "an association of broadly like-minded voters seeking to carry out common objectives through their elected representatives." [5] In a word, party is based on policy.

Virtually all significant party relationships are, for reformers, mediated by policy considerations. The electorate is assumed to be policy motivated and mandate conscious. Policy discussion among party members is expected to create widespread agreement upon which party discipline will then be based. Pressure groups are to be resisted and accommodated only as the overall policy commitments of the party permit. The weaknesses of parties and the disabilities of governments are seen as stemming from failure to develop and support satisfactory policy programs.

Hence it seems sensible to refer to the theory of party reform which predominates in this country as a theory of "policy government." This theory suggests "that the choices provided by the two-party system are valuable to the American people in proportion to their definition in terms of public policy." [6]

Opponents of party reform believe that democratic government in the United States requires the minimization of conflict between contending interests and social forces.[7] Their ideal political party is one which serves as a mechanism for accomplishing and reinforcing adjustment and compromise among the various interests in society to prevent severe social conflict. Where reformers desire parties which operate "not as mere brokers between different groups and interests but as agencies of the electorate," their critics see the party as an "agency for compromise." Opponents of party reform and policy government hold that "the general welfare is achieved by harmonizing and adjusting group interests." [8] In fact, they sometimes go so far as to suggest that "the contribution that parties make to policy is inconsequential so long as they maintain conditions for adjustment." [9] Thus, the theory of the political party upheld by critics of the party reform position is rooted in a notion of "consensus government."

A basic cleavage between advocates of policy government and consensus government may be observed in their radically opposed conceptions of the public interest. For advocates of consensus government, the public interest is defined as whatever emerges from the negotiations, adjustments, and compromises made among conflicting interest groups. They suggest no external criteria by which policies can be measured in order to determine whether or not they are in the public interest. So long as the process by which decisions are made consists of intergroup bargaining, within certain specified democratic "rules of the game," they regard the outcomes as being in the public interest.

For advocates of policy government, the public interest is held to be a discoverable set of policies which represents "something more than the mathematical result of the claims of all the pressure groups." [10] While they suggest that there are, in principle, ways of judging whether a policy is in the public interest, apart from the procedural test applied by supporters of consensus government, these methods are never identified. This lack of concrete criteria spelling out the public interest would not present great difficulties if it were not for the fact that policy government advocates demand that an authoritative determination of party policy be made and that party members be held to it. Information about the policy preferences of members is supposed to flow upward and orders establishing and enforcing final policy decisions are supposed to flow downward in a greatly strengthened pyramid of party authority. Without criteria of public interest clearly in mind, however, the party leaders are in a position to define the public interest in any terms they find convenient.

It would be wrong to suppose that policy government advocates do not believe in the advisability of some compromise, or that consensus government supporters do not recognize the necessity that the parties sponsor some policies and programs. Nonetheless, each gives heavy stress to its own particular concern and admits qualifications only with reluctance. The respective positions are clearly a response to their adherents' deeply held views on the most basic needs of our times.

"In an era beset with problems of unprecedented magnitude at home and abroad," party reformers declare, "it is dangerous to drift without a party system that helps the nation to set a general course of policy for the government as a whole." [11] The failure to establish policy government may well "lead to grave consequences in an explosive era." [12] Reformers seek to awaken the people to untold dangers that lie ahead, to "growing public cynicism" that may lead to the "disintegration of the two major parties," and to the eventual destruction of constitutional government.[13] It is no wonder that with the apparent need so great, the supporters of policy government feel that a way must be found to institute their essential life-or-death reforms of our present system.

The advocates of consensus government do not evidence so great a sense of urgency, because our present party system comes much closer to meeting their requirements. This is to a certain extent an artifact of their whole mode of argument, which tends to define that which is as inevitable and that which is inevitable as good. "It is the party system, more than any other American institution," they assert, "that consciously, actively and directly nurtures consensus." [14]

While advocates of policy government fear the continuation of the present party system, their opponents fear that the introduction of policy government would destroy the underlying social consensus and perhaps even lead to civil war. They hold that while our nation possesses "a degree of consensus that is more than adequate for maintaining the present political system . . . [it] might be quite inadequate for maintaining a different system . . ." such as reformers suggest.[15] Americans are agreed, in general, upon the rules governing the exercise and transfer of political power, the main outlines of our economy, and the desirability of maintaining the conditions under which they can continue to enjoy their material prosperity. But civil war is still possible because this consensus could be threatened by sharp disagreement over economic issues ("The domestic battles of American practical politics are not sham battles");[16] by the diversity of our economic, racial, religious, ethnic, and sectional groupings; by our "restless and immoderate people"; and by the tendency of a nontraditional society to "push political conflict to its most unfortunate logical conclusion." [17]

The civil war is a living nightmare to those who insist that we maintain consensus government. But as in the case of party reformers, there is less proof of the factual assumptions lying behind their arguments than one might like. "Greater differences in party platform than those . . . [in 1948]," one writer assured his readers, "would impose a burden which politicians in a republican system could not be expected to bear." [18] In the same vein, other advocates of consensus parties have argued, "the day that some major elements completely desert one party in favor of the other, the stage will have been set for the kind of conflict that leads to civil war." [19] But we are never told in detail why policy government would lead to severe social conflict under other than the most extreme conditions.

THE BIAS BEHIND PARTY REFORM

It should be obvious that party reforms are generally not politically neutral. They are designed almost entirely to strengthen the President and to weaken Congress, especially as Congress is presently constituted. More specifically, reforms of the party system are generally designed to help Democrats and weaken Republicans. The reasoning is this: Republican Presidents represent a party generally unsympathetic to innovation and increased activity by the Federal government. Hence, they will be inclined to ask less of Congress, and thus they run less risk of being stymied by a recalcitrant Congress. Democratic Presidents, on the other hand, in behalf of the more liberal, more activist, and more innovative party, ask much more of Congress and customarily have to settle for much less of what they ask.

It seems to us quite understandable that agitation for party reform, which during the late 1940's so excited the liberal academicians who are its chief proponents, died away to a whisper during the Eisenhower decade. Now, once again, frustrated liberals are taking up their cudgels in the cause of righteousness, "responsibility," and Presidential prerogative. The underlying aim, it seems to us, is to speed up social changes that they desire by trying to rig the rules of the game more in favor of that political institution, the Presidency, which shares their policy preferences.

At the moment, of course, many rules of the game favor policies defending the political, economic, and social status quo;

however, we suggest that it is not some abstract (and unexplicated) conception of equity which prompts this renewed plea for reform, but rather the policy preferences of reformers. We are ourselves sympathetic to many—indeed, perhaps, most—of the social measures covertly advocated by party reformers. Rent supplements and the negative income tax are two examples. But as political scientists, rather than political advocates, we think it proper to spell out the political implications of proposals such as those put forward by party reformers, and not pretend, as party reformers sometimes do, that their suggestions are designed to make everyone happy.

IS BROAD-GAUGED PARTY REFORM POSSIBLE?

If we were to have parties that resembled the ideal of the party reformers, what would they be like? They would be coherent in their policies, reliable in carrying them out, and accountable to the people, sharply differentiated, and in conflict with each other, disciplined and hierarchical internally. Let us see, then, what it would take to create a party system of this kind.

For the parties to carry out the promises they make, the people responsible for making promises would have to be the same as (or in control of) the people responsible for carrying them out. This means, logically, one of two alternatives: 1) either the people who controlled party performance all year round would have to write the party platforms at the national conventions; or 2) the people who wrote the platforms would have to be put in charge of party performance. In the first case, the party platforms would have to be written by leaders such as the Congressmen who presently refrain from enacting laws favored by both national conventions. State and local political leaders would write their respective platforms. Thus, very little formal, overall coordination or policy coherence seems likely to emerge. Logically coherent, unified policy is the main point of policy government because this is regarded by party reformers as the main method of mobilizing public support for government, and so we must reject the first alternative as a possible way to fulfill the demands of party reformers.

In fact, it is the second alternative which is most often recommended by advocates of policy government. National conventions must be newly arranged to make policy that will be enforced on national, state, and local levels by means of party discipline, and the people who write the convention platforms must be put in charge. This arrangement also has a fatal defect: It ignores the power of the people who do not write the platforms. How are independently elected Congressmen to be bypassed? Will present-day sectional and state party leaders acquiesce in this rearrangement of power and subject themselves to discipline from a newly constituted outside source? Generally, we assume they will not. Getting politicians to exchange some political power for none is a task the magnitude of which has surely been underestimated. When reforms have to be carried out by those who would stand to lose the most from them, their practicality is dubious. A Democratic Congressman has written of the institutional factors which, in the House of Representatives, make his party leaders shy of party cohesiveness: "The Democrats don't meet to talk things over, to be persuaded, to be sold. We don't meet in caucus because the Leadership fears that it would irreparably breach the tenuous links with the South. . . . [House leaders] lead, but they lead only because they win. If they cannot be certain of winning, they don't want to go. Latent power, negative power, is so much better than power committed that lacks victory as a capstone. Hence the legislative timidity of the Congress. . . . Hence the great time lags for consideration of legislation . . . while the Leadership waits for the pressures to build. . . . Hence the distaste for short cuts . . . distaste for battle just for the sake of battle, distaste for The Discharge Petition, and for Calendar Wednesday, and for the Democratic Caucus." [20]

One reformer says: "As for the clash of personal political ambitions in the United States, they are being completely submerged by the international and domestic concerns of the American public. War and peace, inflation and depression are both personal and universal issues; tariffs, taxes, foreign aid, military spending, federal reserve policies, and hosts of other national policies affect local economic activities across the land. Politicians who wish to become statesmen must be able to talk intelligently about issues that concern people in *all* constituencies. . . ." [21]

But is it necessarily the case, as party reformers suggest, that the increasing importance of national issues will inevitably lead to placing greater power in the hands of party leaders with national (that is to say, Presidential) constituencies? There is no necessary connection between political power in the national arena and the national scope of issues. National political power may rest upon local control of nomination, alliances with locally based interest groups, and many other bases. Even if national issues become more important, this may only enhance the powers of the local interests best able to influence national policy.

The people who have the most to lose from party reforms are, of course, the leaders of Congress. As of now, the major electoral risks facing national legislators are local. This does not mean that they will necessarily be parochial in their attitudes and policy commitments. But it does mean that they are not necessarily bound to support the President or national party leadership on issues of high local saliency. In order to successfully impose discipline, the national party must be able either to control sanctions presently important to legislators, such as nomination to office, or to impose still more severe ones upon him. At the moment, our system provides for control of Congressional, state, and local nominations and elections by geographically localized electorates and party leaders. Presidents are not totally helpless in affecting the outcomes of these local decisions, but their influence is in most cases quite marginal.

In the light of this, one obvious electoral prerequisite of disciplined parties is that the local voters must be so strongly tied to national party issues that they will reward rather than penalize their local representatives for supporting national policy pronouncements, even at the expense of local advantage. The issues on which the national party makes its appeal must either unify a large number of constituencies in favor of the party or appeal at the least to some substantial segment of opinion everywhere. But even if this could be accomplished, it would be strategically unwise for parties to attempt to discipline their members who lived in areas which were strongly against national party policy. This would mean reading the area out of the party. Thus, reformers must show how they intend to contribute to the national character of political parties by enforcing national policies upon members of Congress whose local constituencies are drastically opposed to national party policy, or whose constituents do not pay attention to issues but care more for the personality or the services of the Congressman.[22] Insofar as leeway exists, let us say, for Republicans in the Northwest to support public power and for Southern Democrats to oppose civil rights, the parties shall, in fact, have retained their old, "undisciplined," "irresponsible" shape. Insofar as this leeway does not exist, splinter groups of various kinds are encouraged to split off from the established parties, surely a consequence regarded as undesirable by most party reformers.

IS BROAD-GAUGED PARTY REFORM DESIRABLE?

An Appraisal of the Nomination Process

Although reform of the party system may be impractical, this does not necessarily mean that it is undesirable. If we believed that such reform were a vital necessity, we might still advocate it and hope that the unfolding of events would lead others to share our viewpoint. But we suspect that achievement of many of the specific objectives of party reformers would be detrimental to their aims and to those of most thoughtful citizens. Let us consider, for example, two specific reforms of governmental machinery, commonly advocated in order to make the parties more responsive to popular will and more democratic, but which might well have the exactly opposite effects. Party reformers often advocate a variety of changes in the nomination process and modification or abolition of the Electoral College.

In order to evaluate the nominating process, it would be helpful to suggest a set of goals which most Americans would accept as desirable and important.[23] The following six standards appear to meet this test: Any method for nominating Presidents should 1) aid in preserving the two-party system, 2) help secure vigorous competition between the parties, 3) maintain some degree of cohesion and agreement within the parties, 4) produce candidates who have a likelihood of winning voter support, 5) lead to the choice of good men, 6) result in the acceptance of candidates as legitimate.

We may first look at some suggested alternatives to the system that presently relies so heavily upon decision-making by party leaders at national conventions.

A national direct primary has often been suggested. This, however, would have serious disadvantages. It is quite probable that as many as ten candidates might obtain enough signatures on nominating petitions to get on the ballot. Nor would it be surprising if they divided the vote equally. The victor would then have to be chosen in a special run-off primary. By following this procedure, the United States might have to restrict its Presidential candidates to wealthy athletes. No man without enormous financial resources could ever raise the millions required for the nominating petition, the first primary, the run-off primary, and the national election; and no one who was not superbly conditioned could survive the pace of all these campaigns.

National primaries might also lead to the weakening of the party system. It is not unusual for a party to remain in office for a long period of time. If state experience with primaries is any guide, a prolonged period of victory for one party would result in a movement of interested voters into the primary of the winning party where their votes would count more.[24] As voters deserted the losing party, it would be largely the die-hards who were left. They would nominate candidates who pleased them but who could not win the election because they were unappealing to a majority in the nation. Eventually, the losing party would atrophy, thus seriously weakening the two-party system and the prospects of competition among the parties. The winning party would soon show signs of internal weakness as a consequence of the lack of opposition necessary to keep it unified.

A national primary might lead to the appearance of extremist candidates and demagogues who, unrestrained by allegiance to any permanent party organization, would have little to lose by stirring up mass hatreds or making absurd promises. A George Wallace might well find a fertile field in a national primary, an opportunity sufficient to raise the temperature of American politics to explosive levels even if he did not win. On the whole, the convention system rules out these extremists by placing responsibility in the hands of party leaders who have a permanent stake in maintaining the good name and integrity of their organization. Some insight into this problem may be had by looking at the situation in several Southern states where most voters vote only in the Democratic primary and where victory in that primary is tantamount to election. The result is a chaotic factional politics in which there are few or no permanent party leaders; the distinctions between the "ins" and "outs" become blurred; it is difficult to hold anyone responsible; and demagogues sometimes arise who make use of this situation by strident appeals.[25] The fact that under some primary systems an extreme personality can take the place of party in giving a kind of minimal structure to state politics should give pause to the advocates of a national primary.

We believe, in short, that widespread use of direct primaries would weaken the party system because only the wealthiest candidates could possibly enter a large number of them; they would encourage prospective candidates to bypass regular party organizations in favor of campaigns stressing personal publicity; and they would throw nominations entirely into the hands of persons whose stake in the workings of the political process is not great enough to ensure that the eventual nominee would be qualified for the Presidency by experience, qualities of mind, or by virtue of political alliances with others professionally engaged in political activity. The use of primaries at the state level has produced a variety of anomalous experiences; totally unqualified candidates whose names have resembled famous politicians have been nominated by innocent voters in primaries; ethnic minorities concentrated in one party have defeated attempts by party leaders to offer "balanced tickets," thus dooming to defeat their entire ticket in the general election; and palpable demagogues have defeated responsible candidates for public office. All of these consequences may not persuade reformers that an increase in the use of direct primaries is not a good idea, but they must be faced. If we value political parties, as reformers often profess, then we must hesitate to cut them off from the process of selecting candidates for public office, to deprive them of incentives to organize, and to set them prematurely at the mercy of masses of people whose information at the primary stage is especially poor.

This is not, we suggest, an elitist doctrine. Responsible political analysts and advocates must face the fact that party identification for most people provides the safe cognitive anchorage around which political preferences are organized. Set adrift from this anchorage, as they are when faced with an intra-party primary election, most voters have little or nothing to guide their choices. Chance familiarity with a famous name or stray feelings of ethnic kinship under these circumstances seem to provide many voters with the only clues to choice.[26] Given the conditions of popular interest and participation which prevail, we would question throwing the future of the party system entirely and precipitously into the hands of primary electorates.

Another alternative is nomination by one of the branches of Congress. This, though, would be out of the question. The caucus system of nomination has been rejected since Andrew Jackson's time, because it did not give sufficient representation to the large population groups whose votes were decisive in the election.[27] Furthermore, the large fluctuations of party membership in Congress lead to serious difficulties. If a party happened to do very poorly for a few years in several sections of the country, the representation in Congress from those areas would be small and they would, in effect, be deprived of a voice in nominating a President. Thus, if Northern Democrats suffered a serious reversal one year, the Southern members of that party would be in complete control. This nominating procedure would advertise itself as being national in scope, but it would be far more likely than the present system to produce candidates with a limited sectional appeal. The attempts of leaders in areas where the party is weak to strengthen themselves by nominating a candidate who might help increase their vote would be stymied.

Perhaps, it may be argued, what is required is not some radically new method of nominating candidates, but reform of some of the more obnoxious practices of the present system. High on the list of objectionable practices would be the secret gathering of party leaders in the smoke-filled room. Some liken this to a political opium den where a few irresponsible men, hidden from public view, stealthily determine the destiny of the nation.[28] Yet it is difficult to see who, other than the party's leaders, should be entrusted with the delicate task of finding a candidate to meet the majority preference. Since head-on clashes of strength on the convention floor usually do not resolve the question, the only alternative would be continued deadlock, anarchy among scores of leaderless delegates splitting the party into rival factions, or some process of accommodation.

Let us suppose that the smoke-filled room were abolished and with it all behind-the-scenes negotiations. All parleys would then be held in public, before the delegates and millions of television viewers. As a result, the participants would spend their time scoring points against each other in order to impress the folks back home. Bargaining would not be taking place since the participants would not really be communicating with one another. No compromises would be possible; leaders would be accused by their followers of selling out to the other side. Once a stalemate existed, it would be practically impossible to break, and the party would probably disintegrate into warring factions.

An extensive system of state primaries in which delegates were legally compelled to vote for the candidate who won in the state would lead to the disappearance of the smoke-filled room without any formal action. Since delegates could not change their positions there would be little point in bringing their leaders together for private conferences. Sharply increasing the number of pledged delegates would introduce great rigidity into the convention because of the increased likelihood of stalemates which could not be overcome because no one would be in a position to switch his support.

Much criticism has been leveled at the raucousness of demonstrations that take place on the convention floor while candidates are being nominated.[29] Criticism of demonstrations on the grounds that they are unseemly and vulgar seem to us to be trivial. There is no evidence which would substantiate a claim that the final decision is in some way worse than if demonstrations were banned.

In still another way the demonstrations help meet the need of many delegates for an active function which they can perform.[30] As in almost any large political gathering (the number of delegates and alternates were approximately 2,600 for the Republicans and 5,260 for the Democrats in the 1964 conventions), only a small number actively participate in planning strategy or in trying to influence other people. The rest often find that they have no well-defined political role other than casting one vote out of many and they may feel at a loss to explain their lack of activity to themselves as well as to the people back home. The demonstrations provide an opportunity for the delegate to enhance his feelings of importance by active participation in a colorful event which he can recount when he returns. Since one of the advantages of the convention is to gather the party faithful and imbue them with a sense of belonging to a national party, a mechanism which increases the delegate's sense of satisfaction is by no means unimportant.

Undoubtedly, the demonstrations have been overdone and might be cut short. This task can safely be left to the requirements of television. As the conventions of the last few years have shown, television dictates briefer demonstrations to retain the attention of the vast audience which the party would like very much to influence in its favor.

The convention, as we have said, aids party unity in a variety of ways. It provides a forum in which initially disunited fragments of the national party can come together and find common ground as well as a common nominee. The platform aids greatly in performing this function. In order to gain a majority of electoral votes, a party must appeal to most major population groups. Since these interests do not want the same thing in all cases, it is necessary to compromise and, sometimes, to evade issues which would lead to drastic losses of support. And since the parties must contain somewhat conflicting interests, internal accommodation is essential to avoid splits. A perfectly clear, unequivocal, consistent platform on all major issues presupposes an electorate and a party system which divides neatly and more or less evenly along ideological lines, and that is not the case in this country.

The concern of reformers with party platforms stems primarily from two assumptions: first, that there is a significant demand in the electorate for more clear-cut differences on policy; second, that elections are likely to be a significant source of guidance on individual issues to policy-makers. Yet both these assumptions are either false or highly dubious. On a wide range of issues, leaders in both parties are much further apart than are ordinary members who, in fact, are separated by rather small differences.[31] To the degree that party platforms do spell out clear and important differences on policy, and these were considerable in 1960 and extraordinarily large in 1964, this probably results far more from a desire of party leaders to please themselves or from misinformation about what the voters desire than from any supposed demand from the electorate. In any event, it is exceedingly difficult (if not impossible) to discover just what an election means in terms of the policy preferences of a majority. About all that one can expect from a platform is an indication of the general direction in which a candidate and the dominant factions in his party intend to go, and the present party platforms do reasonably well in this respect.

Some critics object to the normal convention's stress on picking a winner rather than the "best man" regardless of his popularity. This doctrine is not compatible with the democratic notion that voters should decide who is best for them and communicate this decision in an election. Only in dictatorial countries do a set of leaders arrogate unto themselves the right to determine who is best regardless of popular preferences. An unpopular man can hardly win a free election. An unpopular President can hardly secure the support he needs to accomplish his goals. Thus, popularity can be regarded as a necessary element for obtaining consent in democratic politics. Only if one assumes that it is the characteristic behavior of parties in a two-party system to disregard their chances of winning, does it make sense to speak of popularity in a derogatory way.

Although popularity is normally a necessary condition for nomination, it should not be the only condition. The guideline for purposes of nomination should be to nominate the best of the popular candidates. But "best" is a slippery word. A great deal of what we mean by "best" in politics is "best for us" or "best represents our policy preferences" and this can hardly be held up as an objective criterion. What is meant by "best" in this context are certain personal qualities such as experience, intelligence, and decisiveness. Nevertheless, it is not at all clear that an extreme conservative would prefer a highly intelligent liberal to a moderately intelligent candidate who shared his conservative policy preferences. Personal qualities are clearly subject to discount based on the compatibility of interests between the voter and the candidate.

Insofar as the "best man" criterion has a residue of meaning, we believe that it is possible to argue that the criterion has largely been followed in recent times. Looking at the candidates of both parties since 1940—Roosevelt, Truman, Stevenson, Kennedy, Johnson for the Democrats, and Willkie, Dewey, Eisenhower, Nixon for the Republicans—there is not one man among them who could not be said to have had some outstanding qualities or experience for the White House. Without bothering to make a formal declaration of the fact, American political leaders and their followers have apparently agreed on at least one hidden requirement of availability. They have restricted their choice to those popular candidates who give promise of measuring up to the formidable task of the President as preserver of the nation and guardian of prosperity. The nominee whose sole virtue is his innocuousness or pleasant smile seems to have disappeared.

As usual, Goldwater presents a special problem because in many important ways he is a man of extreme views, something, we have argued, the present nominating process normally discourages. It is unlikely that any system of nomination—total primary, total convention, mixed, or even action by Republicans in Congress—would have resulted in a different choice. For the nomination of Goldwater is, in part, the result of an underlying trend, working since the New Deal period, through which Republican activists have become separated in their preferences from Republican voters and from the electorate as a whole. It required only the temporary disarray of the moderate opposition for this trend to manifest itself in the visible presence on the ticket of Senator Goldwater. No system of nomination, indeed no political system, can be expected to forever run counter to the desires of the activists who have the most say about running it. It is not the convention system but the desires of the activist core of the Republican party that produced an exception to the rule in 1964.

It might be argued, however, that the criterion of ability has been violated because nominations have come to be determined by popularity, that is, by expressions of mass preferences as reported in polls and state primaries.[32] Merely defining the candidate who won the nomination as most popular is not sufficient to prove the thesis; it must be shown that the voters agreed who was the most popular candidate, that this was communicated to the delegates, and that they nominated him. It would be hard to say that William Howard Taft, Warren Harding, Alfred Landon, Wendell Willkie, and Thomas Dewey, to name a few, were indisputably the most popular Republican candidates. (Goldwater was clearly an unpopular candidate.) Dwight Eisenhower might fit in this category (though he had to fight for the nomination), but he represents just one case and is counterbalanced by the very popular Theodore Roosevelt's failure to obtain the nomination in 1912. There is no evidence to suggest that, among Democratic candidates, Woodrow Wilson was more popular than Champ Clark in 1912, that James M. Cox and John Davis fitted the most popular criterion, or that Franklin Roosevelt could have been placed in that category with certainty before his first nomination. If any Democrat was most popular in 1952 it was Estes Kefauver and not Adlai Stevenson.

A surface view of the 1960 Democratic Convention might suggest that John F. Kennedy's nomination was due to an irresistible current of public opinion. When other factors are taken into account, however, this "mass popularity" thesis loses much of its force. To begin with, Kennedy's excellent organization was not matched by any other candidate. We must also take into account the difficulty which Democratic leaders would have faced in refusing the nomination to a Catholic who had won important primaries, and whose defeat in the convention might easily have been viewed as a sign of religious prejudice which would damage the party's chances for years to come. Still a third factor operative in securing Kennedy's nomination is suggested indirectly by the 1960 Republican race for the Presidential nomination. We have never discovered whether or not Nelson Rockefeller was more popular with the voting public than Richard Nixon, because the latter had such strong support among party professionals that the former decided it was not worth running. A crucial difference between the two conventions was that there was no Democrat to oppose Kennedy who could claim a widespread preference among party leaders as was the case with Nixon in the Republican party.

Presidential primaries have also been subjected to much criticism. What, we may ask, is the overall effect of the primary in Presidential nominating politics? In theory, the primary election is supposed to have the effect of bringing the nominating process to the people, but in practice it does not work quite that way at all. What really happens in primary elections is governed by a number of contingencies not at all anticipated by those who advocate primaries as the solution to a variety of political problems.

First, not all serious candidates run in primary elections. They may not want to run the risk, although they are avowed candidates. They may not wish to tip their hand, if they are not. They may not have the time to make what they regard as an adequate campaign, or they may not be able to raise the money to do so.

Second, many people do not vote in primary elections. These stay-at-home voters tend to be less well-educated, less informed and less interested, and less closely tied to regular party organizations. The voting in primary elections is, in other words, a rather imperfect representation of public sentiment.

President Truman, after hearing the results of the 1952 New Hampshire primary, which Estes Kefauver had just won without serious opposition, referred to primaries (with unexpected mildness) as "eyewash." In this sense he was correct: Primaries are far from what their proponents would like them to be. But they do serve the useful purpose of providing politicians at national conventions with some information about the relative popularity of candidates in a series of admittedly artificial "trial heat" settings. Most often, so it seems, primaries kill off promising contenders before the convention. This, at any rate, seems to have been the fate of Hubert Humphrey, who was a casualty in West Virginia in 1960, Harold Stassen, who lost in Oregon in 1948, Wendell Willkie in Wisconsin in 1944, and Nelson Rockefeller in California in 1964. Kennedy's long-shot parlay paid off in 1960, it is true, but the rather discouraging example of Kefauver was the best recent historical evidence he had on the fate of primary winners.

The primaries, though held in different sections of the country and in different kinds of states, are by no means a perfect representation of the electorate. Another criticism of primaries is that they are held at widely separated intervals so that some candidates do not declare themselves in time to enter and others are exhausted by a grueling series of campaigns. But if primaries were all held at the same time they would take on the aspect of a national primary with all its disadvantages and without the one great advantage of being open to all interested voters in the nation. Candidates like Hubert Humphrey and Estes Kefauver could not have afforded the enormous expenditures required to put their views before the public in so many places at once.

The conclusion we would draw is that the primaries, together with other methods of delegate selection which give predominance to party activists, provide one reasonably viable balance between popularity and other considerations which party leaders deem important. Without denying an element of popular participation, the decision is ultimately thrown into the hands of the men who ought to make it if we want a strong party system—the party leaders.

For some critics the defects of conventions lie not only in their poor performance in nominating candidates but also in their failure to become a sort of "superlegislature" enforcing the policy views in the platform upon party members in the executive branch and Congress. We have previously indicated that such enforcement is most unlikely to be achieved.

Let us suppose, nevertheless, for the purposes of argument, that the conventions could somehow become much more influential on matters of national policy. How could either party retain a semblance of unity if the stakes of convention deliberations were vastly increased by converting the platform into an unbreakable promise of national policy? If one believes that an increase in heated discussion necessarily increases agreement, then the problem solves itself. Experience warns us, however, that the airing of sharp differences, particularly when the stakes are high, is likely to decrease agreement. For example, at the 1964 Republican Convention, Negro delegates, bitter about the defeat of Governor Scranton's proposed amendment on civil rights to the GOP education plank, held a protest march around the Cow Palace and, when Goldwater was nominated, announced that they would sit out the campaign.[33] Today, the choice of nominees at the convention is accepted as legitimate by all but a few delegates. The fact that platforms are *not* binding permits the degree of unity necessary for the delegates to stay long enough to agree on a nominee. By vastly increasing the number of delegates who would bitterly oppose platform decisions, and who would probably leave the convention, the proposed change would jeopardize the legitimacy of its nominating function. Paradoxically, in such circumstances, the temptation to make the platform utterly innocuous so as to give offense to no one would be difficult to resist.

There are also good reasons for opposing the desires of those who love the conventions so well that they would like to see them convene once every year or two years. For without a Presidential candidate to nominate, they would have little to do. If the purpose of these meetings is to give free advice, there would seem to be little point to them. Congressmen are likely to pay as little attention to convention talk as they would to the pronouncements of any advisory committee that does not appreciate the context within which they operate. After all, Congressmen are subject to different risks and sanctions than are most delegates, get little help from the national party in securing nomination and election, and have no reason to be beholden to it for suggesting policies which may get them into trouble. As they have uniformly decided in the past, Congressional leaders will probably refuse to participate in organizations whose policies they cannot control but whose proposals they are committed to support. The notion of getting delegates together under circumstances where their disagreements are certain to come out into the open, merely for the purpose of making recommendations, does not seem promising. It is doubtful whether most delegates, who could not be expected to take an active part in formulating proposals, would feel it worthwhile to participate in a convention which lacked its major rationale and interest—the choice of a Presidential candidate.

Although we hope to have avoided the error of assuming that whatever is is right, the superiority of national conventions to the available alternatives is clearly demonstrable. Only the convention permits us to realize in large measure all the six goals— the two-party system, party competition, some degree of internal cohesion, candidates attractive to voters, good men, and acceptance of nominees as legitimate—which we postulated earlier would commonly be accepted as desirable. It is a rare occasion indeed that we fail to get good candidates rather than extremists who would threaten our liberties or convert our parties into exclusive clubs for party ideologists. Leaders are usually motivated to choose popular candidates who will help maintain vigorous competition between the parties but who are unlikely to split them into warring factions. As a matter of fact, the two major party splits in this century occurred while an incumbent was securing his own renomination. The Progressive split in the Republican party which Theodore Roosevelt led against President Taft in 1912 and the revolt Dixiecrats led against President Truman in 1948 indicate that incumbent Presidents, as hierarchical leaders, are perhaps more prone to underestimate the costs of their actions to party unity than are the party leaders who are forced to bargain with one another in the smoke-filled rooms.[34]

The element of popular participation in the present nomination process is strong enough to impress itself upon party leaders but not sufficiently powerful to take the choice out of their hands. The convention is sufficiently open to excite great national interest, but it is not led into perpetual stalemate by pseudo-bargaining in public. Voters have a choice between conservative and liberal tendencies—a choice which is not absolute because a two-party system can be maintained only if both parties moderate their views in order to appeal to large population groups in the country. In our view, the very unusual experience of 1964 only serves to reinforce strongly this conclusion.

An Appraisal of the Electoral College

In the case of the Electoral College, two proposals are offered. One would abolish the Electoral College outright, and weigh votes everywhere equally. The net effect of such a proposal would be to undermine slightly the current strategic advantage enjoyed by populous, two-party, urbanized states. The second proposal would retain the apportionment of the Electoral College (which gives numerical advantage to the small, rural states) but abolish the unit rule electoral vote (which operates strongly in favor of populous states). This proposal is most extreme in its import, which would be to confer an additional political bonus upon states already overrepresented in positions of Congressional power.[35]

The Constitution provides that each state, regardless of its population, shall be represented by an equal number of Senators. This means that the eight largest states, with 54 per cent of the voters, have just sixteen Senators. In the course of legislative proceedings, these Senators can be canceled out by the sixteen votes of the Senators from the eight least populous states, with less than 3 per cent of the voters. In the House of Representatives, Nevada has nearly fifteen times as much representation as it would have if representation were apportioned strictly according to the number of voters, and New York has only one-sixth as much representation as it would have if voters were equally represented. Thus, in elections for the House, an average vote in Nevada has eighty-five times as much weight as an average vote cast in New York, other things being equal.[36]

We recognize the merit in allowing a rural minority to have at least *some* protection from their more numerous city brethren. But the fact that most of our people live in or near cities provides a sufficient reason to resist changes in the "balance of power" which would give greater weight to the needs and preferences of a dwindling rural population.

Any proposal to equalize the weight of voters would have to attack both the Presidential and Congressional problems simultaneously. To do otherwise would be to reduce the Presidential advantages of urban voters while maintaining the Congressional advantages of rural voters. If one problem is tackled before the other, an imbalance might well be created that would be most difficult to correct. But that difficulty may shortly be dissolved. In a series of decisions beginning with *Baker* vs. *Carr,* and extending through *Wesberry* vs. *Sanders* and *Reynolds* vs. *Sims,*[37] the Supreme Court has set in motion a train of events that eventually should lead to gradual rearrangement of districts represented by members of the House of Representatives. These new districts are designed to come into closer accord with the principle of "one man, one vote" and thus give greater weight in the House to presently underrepresented metropolitan areas, especially the rapidly growing suburbs. Hence the major contemporary rationale for the retention of the Electoral College is slowly being removed. If rural, sparsely populated areas are no longer so grievously overrepresented in the House, there is much less need to give metropolitan areas special advantages in the election of Presidents.

Allowing a majority (or plurality) of voters to choose a President has a great deal to commend it. This is the simplest method of all; it would be most easily understood by the greatest number of people; and it comes closest to reflecting intuitive notions of direct popular sovereignty through majority rule. But to end the matter there would be too simple-minded. There is more than one political lesson to be learned by a closer examination of the Electoral College and available alternatives to it.

Some plans to change the Electoral College would have greater effect than others on the rural-urban balance in national politics. The outright abolition of the Electoral College, and the substitution of the direct election of the President, would certainly reduce the importance of the larger states. It would not, however, completely obliterate urban influence. A vote is a vote wherever it is found, and more votes will continue to be found in the cities. But the one-party states would take on a new importance. In some states where one party's organization is nonexistent, large majorities for the other party are easier to turn out at election time, and special rewards would be forthcoming for party leaders who could provide a large margin of victory for their candidate. The emphasis would not be on which candidate is going to win, already a foregone conclusion, but by how many votes he is going to win.

In two-party states, however, voters are cross-pressured in many ways and a candidate can seldom count on defeating his opponent by a very large margin. The emphasis, again, is on the *difference* in popular vote between the two candidates, and states which are able to provide large differences are more likely to be rewarded. For example, in 1960 Senator Kennedy won in Illinois by 6,000 votes, but in Louisiana his margin was 170,000 votes. If Kennedy had distributed his gratitude in proportion to his popular margin, the "Solid South" would have risen once again to play an extremely significant role in Democratic Presidential politics. Let us examine 1960 as the latest example of the usual operation of Presidential elections and 1964 as an unusual instance of how this *difference* effect works.

The table on p. 245 shows the extent in 1960 to which

Southern States Yield a Greater Difference in Popular Votes for the Winner Than Do Larger States

(Large states and Southern states ranked together in order of the margin of votes given to the winner of each state, 1960)

State	Two-Party Voting Population	Margin for Winner
Massachusetts	2,462,680	511,680
New York	7,258,901	404,535
Ohio	4,151,051	269,445
Louisiana	610,740	170,414
Georgia	647,853	155,615
Pennsylvania	4,907,002	130,158
Alabama	523,829	73,699
Tennessee	1,025,051	73,073
North Carolina	1,352,914	66,092
Michigan	3,299,448	65,134
Texas	2,157,086	45,264
Virginia	759,757	40,503
Mississippi	173,531 (votes for unpledged Electors excluded)	33,269
Arkansas	367,413	31,881
Florida	1,494,073	28,321
New Jersey	2,747,614	22,454
California	6,425,262	13,160
South Carolina	383,835	8,139
Illinois	4,744,093	6,397

Southern states, despite their smaller size, yielded a harvest of popular votes for the winner comparable to that of the large states. Only New York, Ohio, and Massachusetts led all the Southern states in popular vote margins delivered to the winner of the state, while at the other extreme, ten of the eleven Southern states exceeded the large states of Illinois, California, and New Jersey in popular vote margins. This table confirms our expectation that the large, two-party states would not be wholly eclipsed by doing away with the Electoral College, but it is also apparent that the one-party states such as those of the South could expect to become a great deal more important in the calculations of party leaders and Presidential candidates, especially Democrats.

However, in 1964, an election which overturned numerous political axioms, the margin for Johnson was greatest in the larger urbanized states and least in the small Southern states. The reason for this exception is obvious: The Southern states were the only ones with a sizable minority to whom Goldwater's stand on civil rights appealed; Johnson won dramatically in all other areas. In effect, the South became an area of two-party states and the North of one-party states for the duration of that single election. If a man is going to win as easily as Johnson did, he is going to bury normal divisions in the popular vote as handily as he buries his opponent.

But 1964 was unusual; in normal elections in the past, the South has delivered lop-sided Democratic majorities. Yet, curiously, the rise of the South is precisely what many Electoral College reformers want to prevent. They are horrified at the spectre of unpledged Southern Electors throwing a Presidential contest into the House of Representatives. They apparently take no comfort from the inability of the South to make good its threat both in 1948 and again in 1960. And they are particularly slow to recognize that these repeated Southern failures occur primarily because of the unit rule of the Electoral College, not in spite of it. Reformers are attempting to do away with the very system which helps to prevent the election of the President by one-party states. To change the present manner of electing the President would play directly into the hands of the Southern states and other one-party states as well.

Another proposal, once embodied in the unsuccessful Lodge-Gosset Resolution, is seen by some reformers as an acceptable "compromise" between outright abolition of the Electoral College and its retention.[38] In this scheme, the electoral vote in each state

Southern States Yield a Smaller Difference in Popular Votes for the Winner Than Do Larger States

(Large states and Southern states ranked together in order of the margin of votes given to the winner of each state, 1964)

State	Two-Party Voting Population	Margin for Winner
New York	7,166,015	2,669,597
Pennsylvania	4,818,668	1,457,336
California	7,050,985	1,292,769
Massachusetts	2,344,798	1,236,695
Michigan	3,203,102	1,076,463
Ohio	3,969,196	1,027,466
New Jersey	2,846,770	903,828
Illinois	4,702,000	890,887
Texas	2,626,811	704,619
Mississippi	409,038	303,856
Alabama[1]	689,817	268,353
North Carolina	1,424,983	175,292
Tennessee	1,144,046	126,082
Louisiana	896,293	122,157
Georgia	1,139,157	94,043
South Carolina	524,748	93,348
Arkansas	560,426	70,933
Virginia	1,042,267	70,704
Florida	1,854,481	42,599

[1] Unpledged Democratic Electors.

is split between the candidates according to their proportion of the popular vote. This is not a compromise, but the most extreme "reform" of all. Under this system, large, urban, two-party states would no longer be able to deliver large blocs of electoral votes to the winning candidate in the state. In fact, the electoral vote in two-party states would be quite evenly divided between the two candidates, neither one receiving more than a margin of two or three electoral votes. Hence, the bargaining position of these states at national conventions would be drastically reduced and Presidential nominees would begin to follow a different strategy in their campaigns, giving special attention to those states in which they felt a large difference in electoral votes could be obtained.

Once again, the proposed reform throws the emphasis on the amount of difference within the state between the winner and the loser. In this case, however, it is the electoral votes of the states which are divided rather than the popular votes. This effectively cancels out the advantage of the large states. The fact that the Electoral College underrepresents the large states in the first place even further reduces their influence. The following table shows how, under normal political conditions, the large states are in effect neutralized by proposals to divide the electoral vote proportionally between the candidates. There is no point in dealing with the special case represented by 1964, because the Democratic victory was so overwhelming that it is difficult to imagine a remotely democratic method of recording votes that would have altered the outcome.

**Larger States Lose Influence
When Their Electoral Vote Is Split**

Electoral vote advantage given to the winning candidate:

State	Under present system	If electoral votes were split proportionately in 1960
New York	45	2.475
California	32	.064
Pennsylvania	32	.864
Illinois	27	.027
Ohio	25	1.6
Texas	24	.48
Michigan	20	.4
Massachusetts	16	3.2
New Jersey	16	.128

The reduction in influence suffered by the large states under this proposal might mean, in effect, that the overrepresentation of sparsely populated and one-party states in the Congress would entirely dominate the national lawmaking process, unchecked by a President obliged to cultivate urban and two-party constituencies.

Most of the current criticisms of the Electoral College come about because it is claimed that majority rule is endangered. People ask: "Isn't there something inherently wrong with a system which makes it possible for a President to be elected by something less than a majority of the American electorate?" Twelve times in our history a President of the United States has been elected by a majority of the Electoral College but by less than a majority of the popular vote. Three times the winner received fewer popular votes than the loser. Those who believe in majority rule deplore these facts and want to change our Constitution accordingly. On the whole, we favor the rule of the majority. We believe, however, that most people tend to forget the extent to which our Constitution is in fact designed to thwart majority rule.

In our form of government, majority rule does not operate in a vacuum but within a system of "checks and balances." The President, for example, holds a veto power over Congress, which, if exercised, requires a two-thirds vote of each House to override. Treaties must be ratified by two-thirds of the Senate, and amendments to the Constitution must be proposed by two-thirds of Congress or of the state legislatures and ratified by three-fourths of the states. Presidential appointments, in most cases, must receive Senatorial approval. The Supreme Court passes upon the constitutionality of legislative and executive actions. Involved in these political arrangements is the hope that the power of one branch of government will be counter-balanced by certain "checks" from another, the result being an approximate "balance" of forces. In the past the Electoral College had its place within this system. Originally designed to check popular majorities from choosing Presidents unwisely, the Electoral College provided a "check" on the overrepresentation of rural states in the legislative branch by giving extra weight to the urban constituencies of the President.

Majority rule should be placed in proper perspective by considering other aspects of democratic government, such as the principle of political equality. We want majority rule, but we also want all sectors of the population to have an equal voice in government. Overrepresentation of rural interests in Congress inhibited political equality. To check this inequality we had to either alter the circumstances which promoted such inequality or provide some other means of preventing rural interests from dominating the political system. Now that the method of determining the composition of Congress is undergoing change, we can consider abolishing the Electoral College and turn to majority (or plurality) voting in electing Presidents. Other things being equal, a simpler and more direct method is preferable to a device that has outlived its usefulness.

Party Differences and Political Stability

The case for the desirability of party reform often rests on the assumption that American political parties are identical, that this is confusing and frustrating to American voters, and that it is undesirable to have a political system where parties do not disagree sharply.

We would suggest, rather, that there are enough differences between the political parties to give voters a choice, but that many wide policy differences between the parties would be undesirable from the standpoint of the stability of the political system. The parties could well be somewhat further apart on a few issues, however, without necessarily decreasing the stability of the system. Our conceptual tools are too rough to say much about small departures from the existing situation; let us consider only extreme changes of the kind advocated by the proponents of policy government.

Imagine for a moment that the two parties were in total and extreme disagreement on every major point of public policy. One group would appease the U.S.S.R.; the other would court nuclear war. One group would stop Social Security; the other would expand it drastically. One group would raise tariffs; the other would abolish them entirely. Obviously, one consequence of having clear-cut parties with strong policy positions would be that the costs of losing an election would skyrocket. If parties were forced to formulate coherent, full-dress programs and were forced to carry them out "responsibly," then people who did not favor these programs would have no recourse. Clearly, their confidence in a government whose policies were not to their liking would suffer, and, indeed, they might feel strongly enough about preventing these policies from being enacted to do something drastic, like leaving the country, or not complying with governmental regulations, or, in an extreme case, seeking to change the political system by force. This, bear in mind, assumes a more or less even distribution of extreme opinions in the population, which is unrealistic; what really happens is that nobody votes for the unpopular side.

In fact, we have a political system that is kind to losers. Why? Because both Presidential parties usually agree on a wide variety of issues; because people other than the President have to pass on policies before they are enacted by law, and these people are not bound by the Presidential platform.

This is, we suggest, not necessarily a bad thing. Suppose that each major political party were composed solely of people who supported it because, and only because, it represented their views on a wide range of policies. The surface attractiveness of this idea diminishes rapidly once we consider the consequences. The most immediate results would be extraordinary instability in the party system. For as soon as people changed their minds or the party changed its position, vast numbers of its adherents would leave. Great swings in party strength might take place, leaving the minority party on occasion virtually without representation. Who, then, would take on the burdens of party opposition? Who would take the lead in introducing rival policies to compete for public favor?

The existence of a one-party system would be the least of our troubles. What would be the point in building up a party organization if it were doomed to come tumbling down with every significant change of opinion? None at all. So the function of nominating and electing candidates would become a matter for shifting groups of individuals varying from issue to issue and place to place. Naturally, those groups with the best organizations, the most money, and the greatest interest in the policies of the day would predominate. No longer would it be possible to use party identification as a shortcut, as a means of reducing information costs about candidates. Unless voters spent most of their time finding out precisely what officeholders were doing, they would have little idea how to vote. Nevertheless, their votes might be more important to them because the dizzying alternation of policy would have created such political chaos as to disrupt normal patterns of life. We need go no further to make the point that the existence of a hard core of party adherents who do not easily switch party allegiance from year to year provides an element of stability for the party system and thus for the whole political system as well. Paradoxically, the attempt to make issues all-important as a means of increasing the rationality of public decisions greatly decreases the chances for making any sort of meaningful decisions at all.

Party platforms written by the Presidential parties should be understood not as ends in themselves but as means to obtaining and holding public office. It would be strange indeed if one party found policies like Social Security and unemployment compensation to be enormously popular and yet refused to incorporate them into its platform.[39] This would have to be a party of ideologues who cared everything about their pet ideas and nothing about winning elections. Nor would it profit them much since they would never get elected and never be in a position to do something about their ideas. Eventually, ideologues have to make the choice between pleasing themselves and pleasing others.

Actually, party platforms do change over a period of time in a cyclical movement. The differences between the parties may be great for one or two elections until innovations made by one party are picked up by the other. The net change from one decade to the next, however, is substantial. Let us begin when platforms are more or less alike. Their similarity begins to give way as it appears that certain demands in society are not being met. The minority party of the period senses an opportunity to gain votes by articulating and promising to meet those demands. The majority party, reluctant to let go of a winning combination, resists. In one or two elections the minority party makes its bid and makes the appropriate changes in its platforms. Then, in the ensuing elections, if the party which has changed its platform loses, it drops the innovation. If it wins, however, and wins big, the other party then seeks to take over what seem to be its most popular planks, and the platforms become more and more alike again.

We can see this cycle clearly in the New Deal period. The 1932 Democratic platform, though hinting at change, was much like the Republican, especially in its emphasis on balancing the budget. A great difference in platforms could be noted in 1936 as the Democrats made a bid to consolidate the New Deal, and the Republicans stood pat. The spectacular Democratic triumph signaled the end of widely divergent platforms. By 1940 the Republicans had concluded that they could not continue to oppose the welfare state wholesale if they ever wished to win again. By 1952 the parties had come much closer to one another, as the Republicans adopted most of the New Deal. Though the platforms of the major parties were similar to each other in both 1932 and 1952, the differences between 1932 and 1952 for either party were enormous.[40]

Sometimes, reformers deplore what they regard as an excessive amount of mud-slinging in campaigns, but also ask that differences among the major parties be sharply increased in order to give the voters a clear choice. The two ideas are incompatible to some extent. It would be surprising indeed if the parties disagreed more sharply about more and more subjects in an increasingly gentlemanly way. A far more likely outcome would be an increase in vituperation as the stakes of campaigns increased, passions rose, tempers flared, and the consequences of victory for the other side appeared much more threatening than had heretofore been the case. The 1964 campaign is a good case in point.

Those who claim American elections are a fraud and wish to see great things decided in these contests all the time often point to Great Britain as a shining example of the right way to do things. There, in that wiser country, where the fires of class warfare are held (fortunately) to burn more fiercely, the voters have real choices. They vote a government in or out, and the victorious party goes about making great changes in order to carry out its mandate.

This tale may be a pretty one, according to one's taste for conflict, but it is quite exaggerated. The truth in it occurs every once in a great while, much as American party platforms present sharp and profound differences about that often. Such was the case in 1945 when the Labour Party staged its great bid to bring the full welfare state to Britain and to nationalize what it could. The overwhelming Labour victory did its work. The Conservatives soon decided to adopt all the most popular parts of the Labour Party program—medicare, increased pensions—and left Labour holding the unpopular bag of nationalization. By 1955 the two major parties in Britain were presenting much the same program. By 1958 the only difference we could find was that Labour offered sixpence more on the pension. Most of the time, in fact, in Britain as in the United States, the great parties lean toward the undivided middle.[41]

The Labour Party's reaction to the problem of nationalization is instructive. The party was reluctant to leave behind its heritage in this respect; nor was it certain that this issue alone caused its electoral defeats after 1950. Nevertheless, it moved, however painfully, away from a strident position on the subject. There were pleas from those who put ideological consistency first and felt that the lesson to be learned from each defeat was to propose more of the same. Parties do not usually choose to die in this way, however, and Labour politicians who hoped one day to gain office won out over their more ideologically inclined colleagues. Indeed, since regaining office in 1964, the Labour Party leadership has carefully avoided a showdown in Parliament over nationalization of industry.

IS PARTY REFORM RELEVANT?

Even if reform were successful and the political system did not suffer detrimental effects such as we have outlined, many of the problems at which reform is aimed still would not be closer to solution. Thus, it can be argued that the achievement of party government is beside the point.

Can we say, for example, that the present system shows marked or widespread party incoherence in Congress? This is perhaps an overstated problem for, in fact, on roll call voting, party allegiance is the strongest cohesive force in Congress. It has been demonstrated that party is stronger than other bases of allegiance, stronger than sectionalism, rural versus urban, native versus foreign born.[42] Party cohesion depends, to be sure, on the nature of the issue. On the organization of Congress itself and on patronage matters, each party is aligned 100 per cent against the other. Defense policies and appropriations usually show widespread agreement among members of both parties, a situation which is widely regarded as desirable. Some issues like race relations may split each of the parties down the middle. On the economic and welfare issues, where the general label of liberal is commonly attributed to Democrats and conservative to Republicans, cohesion, while not perfect, is high; the labels make sense. If we look at votes on public housing, medical care for the aged, private versus public power, and so on, we can discover that a preponderant majority of both parties takes opposing views. Cohesion does exist and it is important. Since it is not perfect, however, and one party rarely has an overwhelming advantage, it is often necessary to gain some votes from the opposing party in order to make up a majority. Party, therefore, cannot properly be viewed as a drag on unified policy-making. It is most often a force making for greater cohesion than would be the case without it. By itself, it does not supply all the agreement necessary for the making of policy. In the American context of separated and fragmented powers, based on a population divided along many lines, this is no small accomplishment.

Consider now the realm of foreign policy, where decisions made at any moment literally involve our survival and possibly that of the human race. How would policy government help us? The answer, presumably, is that the United States government would be able to follow more consistent, less internally contradictory, policies and that these would lead to happier results. This assumes first that inconsistent policies are, in themselves, undesirable, a proposition which has never been convincingly demonstrated. In fact, inconsistency, "imbalance," and incoherence may in many instances be beneficial because of the necessity for satisfying a variety of diverse interests both at home and abroad through various policies of the government. Inconsistency in its policies is often a way in which the government gains the legitimacy and support which are necessary to govern at all. A second assumption of the reformers is that the lack of party cohesion has been a major problem in foreign affairs. But this is simply not the case. In fact, it appears that virtually every single major policy initiative of a President in the last twenty years—the blockade of Cuba, the Marshall Plan, NATO, the Eisenhower Doctrine, intervention in Korea and Vietnam, nonintervention in

Indochina in 1954—has been supported by Congress, in most cases promptly and enthusiastically. Slight rumblings of dissent no doubt exist, but they do not appear in any major instance to be a consequence of the party system.

The difficulties facing the United States may be traced to causes for which the party system cannot be blamed. The rise of the Soviet Union and Communist China as great powers generally hostile to America, nationalist revolutions all over the world, the break-up of colonialism, the creation of weapons of unparalleled destructiveness—all these developments have neither been hastened nor delayed by the character of our party system. American makers of foreign policy have found that they could not solve these problems primarily because of the enormous difficulties involved, not because Congress refused to accept the correct policies. Presidents and Secretaries of State today find that the world is intractable; there are so many things they can do little or nothing about. They have to deal with a worldwide range of problems, make decisions of enormous technical complexity, gain consent of allies with differing interests, take account of huge forces arrayed against them, obtain popular support at home to a degree, all largely independent of the party system. If only they can decide what to do, if only their policies prove viable, they can expect to be strongly supported. It would be pure fantasy to claim that our Presidents and their advisors have had wonderful ideas for making the world a better place only to have them frustrated by lack of ability to command support in Congress.

The Chief Executive has unique opportunities for leadership in foreign affairs if only he can decide in what direction the nation ought to move. His is the single most commanding voice in the nation. He is visible and trusted above all others. He has the information, the opportunity to deal with foreign governments, the formal powers, and the acknowledged right to lead. Others may clamor but in the post-World War II environment at least, he is the one who will be heard. All of us are dependent upon the President for guidance in a fantastically complicated world where our personal experience rarely proves a reliable guide. Perhaps this is why the President's popularity rises sharply whenever he acts in an international crisis, even in cases like the invasion of Cuba and the Suez crisis, which were, from our point of view, disasters.[43] Rather than seeing danger in our President's being thwarted by hostile Congresses, the more likely danger is that few, except the President, will have much to say about the most vital foreign policy decisions which may have to be made in a terribly short time.

Perhaps the most significant area with impact on foreign policy in which some contradiction among party policies appears is in the area of tariffs.[44] The United States seeks the stability of nations like Japan, on the one hand, and sets up tariff barriers which may help undermine this stability on the other. Interests which find themselves disadvantaged seek a sympathetic hearing in Congress, where members are less attuned to foreign policy considerations than is the President.

It would not, in any event, be surprising if governments were concerned about protecting the interests of domestic industries to some extent. Looking at nations like Britain, France, and Germany, whose governments can command automatic support in parliament, we find that they are also interested in protecting their domestic industries and the workers who depend on them. The negotiations on the Common Market made this abundantly clear. If party government, let us say, on the British model were suddenly to appear in the United States, there would still be the necessity of bargaining with interests within the majority party, and no one doubts that the impact of tariff levels on industry would have to be considered. The United States has, for the most part, been moving toward a tariff position more consonant with its foreign policy objectives. At least we have done no worse than other democratic nations with different party systems.

There is an unfortunate tendency to blame the American decentralized party system for all sorts of things which cannot properly be laid at its door. In 1960, after the U-2 incident blew up the summit meeting in Paris, many recriminations were voiced about the lack of coordination in Washington. Wasn't it terrible, these critics cried, that in this crisis we were let down by our fragmented political system which permitted so many spokesmen to go off in different directions? A careful review of these events reveals, however, that the charges were wholly erroneous. The problem was not at all one of lack of coordination. Just the opposite. All the responsible officials were following whatever instructions they had; the trouble was that these instructions turned out to be poor ones. The apparent inconsistencies, the clumsy efforts to cover up, resulted from the defective instructions. "Lack of coordination" presumably means that the officials involved all went their separate ways without regard to what the President wanted; it cannot properly be taken to mean that they did badly, because the central directions they followed turned out not to be appropriate.

When we turn to Great Britain, where policy government has long been established, we do not find that ability to command a certain majority in the House of Commons helps Prime Ministers solve foreign policy problems better than Presidents. Her Majesty's Government is in at least as much turmoil as ours because its problems are as difficult. The Prime Minister may be better able to disregard criticism but this is not necessarily an advantage.

The most notorious example of failure of democratic leadership in recent times comes not from the United States but from Great Britain. There, in the 1930's, Stanley Baldwin and Neville Chamberlain led their country to the brink of ruin when they failed to inform the people of the growing danger of Nazi Germany, partly because they thought their people were profoundly pacifist and would defeat them at the polls. These men were patriots who wished their country well; they had devoted their lifetimes to its service. Had they realized the full implications of their actions (or failures to act), they undoubtedly would have done otherwise. Uncertain as to the course of events, prone to underestimate the fury of their foes abroad, they allowed themselves to be swayed by the notion that the people would not stand for the truth, no matter how essential that truth was. Surely the existence of a cohesive party system, with sharp policy differences between the parties, did nothing to avoid this disaster. If anything, party cohesion permitted Baldwin and Chamberlain to proceed with impunity against the attacks leveled by Churchill and others who vainly sought to alert the nation. So strong was party unity that it took the calamitous events of 1940, threatening the very existence of the nation, to bring about a change in government.

Policy government is not, however, irrelevant for purposes of domestic politics, and we will want to define more precisely its likely impact. But before we proceed in this direction, it is necessary to modify the policy government proposals so that they are more defensible. For so long as its proponents insist that the parties be both popular and extremely far apart on many policies, the contradictions in this approach do grave damage to the consistency and validity of their proposals. Let us agree to modify the reformers' proposals by stating that the major Presidential parties should be able to propose coherent policies to the electorate and to carry them out after they assume office, regardless of whether their policies are or are not similar.

Now we are in a position to write a sort of profit and loss statement on what would be involved in the realm of domestic politics if policy government were instituted. The benefits would accrue almost entirely to liberals (and the interests they represent) with superior access to the President who would have a better chance of securing the enactment of the welfare and civil rights measures they prefer. Conservatives would stand to lose their power and their policy preferences as their Congressional bastion was weakened if not rendered wholly useless. Liberals in Congress would gain more of their preferred policies at the cost of losing Congressional power. Where the present system enables them to maintain their power as Congressmen while achieving some of their policies, they would have to choose between power and their other preferences under policy government. People who prefer more welfare policies and a traditionally powerful Congress would have to weigh their competing preferences carefully. Beyond this point we see dimly at best. In order to achieve somewhat greater party cohesion on domestic affairs we would risk an unspecified increase in social conflict and a somewhat greater likelihood of producing splinter parties. And if these consequences materialized, they might act to reduce the considerable area of agreement which has been achieved in foreign affairs. What the citizen has to decide is whether the benefits are worth the costs.

We think that the supporters of policy government over estimate by far the magnitude of the problem from their own viewpoint. It is not true that the parties are basically lacking in cohesion and certainly not true that no welfare legislation is passed by Congress. What is true is that medical care for the aged, aid to education, and greater attention to problems besetting urban areas have had a rough road in Congress. The recent passage of much forward-looking legislation dealing with these problems weakens the argument that there was a serious need for basic reform of the party system. It seems excessive to us to contemplate far-reaching changes in the party system which are exceedingly difficult to achieve and whose desirability is at least questionable, when there are much less drastic and much more desirable means available for securing the kinds of legislation which the proponents of policy government want so badly.

A basic difficulty is that the policy government people are so enchanted with the mystique of the Presidency, and so annoyed with Congress, that they do not perceive the excellent opportunities available to them for altering the pattern of legislation. Let us consider some of the activities which give promise of bearing results: (1) continued attack on the problem of apportionment toward the end that metropolitan areas receive greater representation in Congress; (2) efforts to secure from liberal strongholds in the cities candidates who will make a career out of service in Congress, rather than regarding their service as a stepping-stone toward a judgeship or some other such position. There is no need for conservatives to enjoy their present superiority of seniority, skill, and dedication; (3) greater attention by national party leaders to the distribution of Congressional committee positions so that liberal majorities on crucial committees may be more readily achieved. The recent success at the start of the 88th Congress in permanently expanding the House Rules Committee and putting men favorable to welfare legislation on House Ways and Means and Appropriations Committees are good examples of what might be done; (4) development of strategies which show the mass of people, especially urban people, the stake they have in welfare legislation and which bring home to them the importance of presenting their views to their Congressmen. No doubt it seems easier to talk blithely about a revolution in the party system than to actually do something to increase the support which the mass of people give to legislation which is presumed to benefit them. Action in any one or all of these directions would, in our opinion, do more to secure welfare legislation than talk about policy government or taking actions which are bound to be futile. Knowing what we know now, in 1967, we can well understand why the clamor for Congressional party reform has died down after the 89th Congress passed an enormous amount of the legislation that liberals had tried so hard to get in the 1940's and 1950's. The major reason these bills passed was that the Democrats were able to elect an extraordinary majority (particularly in the House) in 1964. Indirectly, of course, Barry Goldwater's candidacy was responsible for putting enough liberal Democrats in Congress to virtually complete the New Deal. It should also be said, however, that years of effort, begun half a decade before, that altered the composition of crucial Congressional committees, was also important in securing this result.

To summarize: Most of the reforms suggested by students

of the party system are, we believe, designed to give greater power to liberal Presidents to enact their domestic programs and to diminish, correspondingly, the power of Congress. For the conduct of foreign affairs these changes would, we believe, be largely irrelevant. With respect to the stability and inclusiveness of the two major parties themselves, the reforms might well be detrimental, owing to the encouragement they might well give to splinter parties. And finally, we observe that the case for party reform has certainly not been made. The enunciation of large national problems does not in and of itself demonstrate the linkage of these problems to the party system. The prescription of reforms does not in and of itself provide the strategy or the power or the inducements to carry them out. Until these key links in the argument are forged, the advocacy of party reform will continue to be an academic exercise, appealing to the frustrations of unsophisticated audiences but without practical effect.

NOTES

1. Stephen K. Bailey, *The Condition of Our National Political Parties* (New York, 1959), p. 3.

2. *Ibid.*, pp. 12–16.

3. There are many examples of the party reform school of thought. See for example, Woodrow Wilson, *Congressional Government* (Boston, 1889); Henry Jones Ford, *The Rise and Growth of American Politics* (New York, 1898); A. Lawrence Lowell, *Public Opinion and Popular Government* (New York, 1913); William MacDonald, *A New Constitution for a New America* (New York, 1921); William Y. Elliott, *The Need for Constitutional Reform* (New York, 1935); E. E. Schattschneider, *Party Government* (New York, 1942); Henry Hazlitt, *A New Constitution Now* (New York, 1942); Thomas K. Finletter, *Can Representative Government Do the Job?* (New York, 1945); James M. Burns, *Congress on Trial* (New York, 1949); Committee on Political Parties, American Political Science Association, *Toward a More Responsible Two-Party System* (New York, 1950); Bailey, *The Condition of Our National Political Parties;* and James M.

Burns, *The Deadlock of Democracy* (Englewood Cliffs, 1963). The work of the Committee on Political Parties, representing the collective judgment of a panel of distinguished political scientists in 1950, is the statement we shall refer to most often.

4. Committee on Political Parties, *Toward a More Responsible Two-Party System*, p. 1.

5. *Ibid.*, p. 66.

6. *Ibid.*, p. 15.

7. A sample of this literature might include Pendleton Herring, *The Politics of Democracy* (New York, 1940); Herbert Agar, *The Price of Union* (Boston, 1950); Malcolm C. Moos, *Politics, Presidents and Coattails* (Baltimore, 1952); Austin Ranney and Willmoore Kendall, *Democracy and the American Party System* (New York, 1956); David B. Truman, *The Governmental Process* (New York, 1953); John Fischer, "Unwritten Rules of American Politics," *Harper's Magazine* (November 1948), 27–36; Peter Drucker, "A Key to American Politics: Calhoun's Pluralism," *Review of Politics* 10 (October 1948), 412–426; Ernest F. Griffith, *Congress: Its Contemporary Role* (New York, 1951); Murray Stedman and Herbert Sonthoff, "Party Responsibility: A Critical Inquiry," *Western Political Quarterly* 4 (September 1951), 454–486; Julius Turner, "Responsible Parties: A Dissent from the Floor," *American Political Science Review* 45 (March 1951), 143–152; William Goodman, "How Much Political Party Centralization Do We Want?" *The Journal of Politics* 13 (November 1961), 536–561; and Austin Ranney, *The Doctrine of Responsible Party Government* (Urbana, 1954).

8. Herring, *The Politics of Democracy*, p. 327.

9. *Ibid.*, p. 420.

10. Committee on Political Parties, *Toward a More Responsible Two-Party System*, p. 19.

11. *Ibid.*, p. 17.

12. *Ibid.*, p. 92.

13. See *ibid.*, and especially Burns, *The Deadlock of Democracy, passim.*

14. Ranney and Kendall, *Democracy and the American Party System*, p. 508.

15. *Ibid.*, p. 476.

16. Herring, *The Politics of Democracy*, p. 345.

17. Robert A. Dahl, *A Preface to Democratic Theory* (Chicago, 1956), p. 151; Don K. Price, "The Presidency: Its Burdens and Its Promises," *Strengthening America's Institutions* (Ithaca, 1949), p. 110.

18. Turner, "Responsible Parties: A Dissent from the Floor," p. 144.

19. Ranney and Kendall, *Democracy and the American Party System*, p. 509.

20. Clem Miller, *Member of the House*, ed. John W. Baker (New York, 1962), pp. 53, 91–92.

21. Bailey, *The Condition of Our National Political Parties*, p. 20.

22. This is, of course, not at all uncommon. See, for instance, examples in Raymond Bauer, Ithiel Pool, and Lewis A. Dexter, *American Business and Public Policy* (New York, 1963), Chapters 16, 18, and 19; Donald E. Stokes and Warren E. Miller, "Party Government and the Saliency of Congress," *Public Opinion Quarterly* 26 (Winter 1962),531–546; Jacob K. Javits, "How I Used a Poll in Campaigning for Congress," *Public Opinion Quarterly* 11 (Summer 1947), 222–226.

23. This section is adapted from Aaron B. Wildavsky, "On the Superiority of National Conventions," *Review of Politics* 24 (July 1962), 307–319.

24. See V. O. Key, Jr., *American State Politics* (New York, 1956), Chapter 6.

25. V. O. Key, Jr., *Southern Politics* (New York, 1949), e.g., Chapter 3 (Alabama) and Chapter 9 (Arkansas).

26. Key, *American State Politics*, p. 216.

27. See Edward Stanwood, *A History of the Presidency from 1788 to 1897* (Boston, 1898), pp. 125–141.

28. A classic statement is M. Ostrogorski, *Democracy and the Party System* (New York, 1910), pp. 158–160. See also, Elmo Roper, "What Price Conventions?" *Saturday Review* (September 3, 1960), 26.

29. Ostrogorski, *Democracy and the Party System*, pp. 141–142.

30. See Aaron Wildavsky, "What Can I Do? Ohio Delegates View the Democratic Convention," in *Inside Politics: The National*

Conventions, 1960, ed. Paul Tillett (Dobbs Ferry, N.Y., 1962), pp. 112–130.

31. Herbert McClosky, Paul J. Hoffman, and Rosemary O'Hara, "Issue Conflict and Consensus Among Party Leaders and Followers," *American Political Science Review* 54 (June 1960), 406–427.

32. See, for example, William Carleton's argument, "The Revolution in the Presidential Nominating Convention," *Political Science Quarterly* 72 (June 1957), 224–240.

33. New York *Times,* July 16, 1964, 1.

34. This is often a cost characteristic of hierarchy. See Nelson W. Polsby, "Decision-Making at the National Conventions," *Western Political Quarterly* 13 (September 1960), 609–619, and Robert A. Dahl and Charles E. Lindblom, *Politics, Economics and Welfare* (New York, 1953), pp. 247–261, especially pp. 254–255.

35. Numerous proposals for Electoral College reform have been made, and most of them have been more complicated and ingenious than those reported here, although most are designed to produce effects roughly similar to those we discuss. See Hearings before the Subcommittee on Constitutional Amendments on the *Nomination and Election of President and Vice-President,* Four Parts (Washington, 1961).

36. Dahl, *A Preface to Democratic Theory,* pp. 112–118. This does not take account of the selective effects of turnover, or of the seniority system in Congress, which also tend to give advantage to one-party states.

37. *Baker* vs. *Carr,* 369 U.S. 186 (1962); *Wesberry* vs. *Sanders,* 376 U.S. 1 (1964), and *Reynolds* vs. *Sims,* 377 U.S. 533 (1964).

38. Roscoe Drummond, "Perils of the Electoral System," Washington *Post,* November 14, 1960. An argument in some ways parallel to our own is contained in Anthony Lewis, "The Case Against Electoral Reform," *The Reporter* (December 8, 1960). See also Allan P. Sindler, "Presidential Election Methods and Urban-Ethnic Interests," *Law and Contemporary Problems* 27 (Spring 1962), 213–233.

39. Despite popular misconceptions, even the 1964 Republican platform, written by supporters of Barry Goldwater, contained explicit promises to preserve these programs.

40. See Kirk H. Porter and Donald Bruce Johnson, *National*

Party Platforms 1840–1956 (Urbana, 1956). There are immense differences between both party platforms of 1932 and 1952. Note, for example, the subheadings under domestic policy in the 1952 platforms dealing with a range of topics entirely missing in 1932. The Democratic 1952 platform includes subheadings on full employment, price supports, farm credit, crop insurance, rural electrification, the physically handicapped, migratory workers, river basin development, arid areas, wildlife, recreation, Social Security, unemployment insurance, public assistance, needs of our aging citizens, health, medical education, hospitals and health centers, costs of medical care, public housing, slum clearance, urban redevelopment, aid to education, school lunches, day care facilities, specific steps under civil rights, and many other subjects completely absent in 1932. Most of these worthy causes were also supported in the 1952 Republican platform and were missing from the 1932 Republican platform. Nevertheless, there are differences *between* the parties in 1952 in regard to use of the public lands, public housing, labor legislation, farm legislation, public power, aid to education, and much more. In regard to education, for example, the 1952 Republican platform reads: "The tradition of popular education, tax-supported and free to all, is strong with our people. The responsibility for sustaining this system of popular education has always rested upon the local communities and the states. We subscribe fully to this principle." The corresponding Democratic plank reads in part: "Local, State, and Federal governments have shared responsibility to contribute appropriately to the pressing needs of our educational system. . . . We pledge immediate consideration for those school systems which need further legislation to provide Federal aid for new school construction, teachers' salaries and school maintenance and repair" (pp. 504, 485). See also Gerald Pomper, " 'If Elected, I Promise': American Party Platforms." Mimeo, 1966.

41. This is one of the main conclusions of Arnold Rogow, *The Labour Government and British Industry* (Oxford, 1955).

42. See Julius Turner, *Party and Constituency: Pressures on Congress* (Baltimore, 1951) and David B. Truman, *The Congressional Party* (New York, 1959).

43. See Nelson W. Polsby, *Congress and the Presidency* (Englewood Cliffs, 1964), p. 26. For a general discussion of Presidential

control, see Aaron Wildavsky, "The Two Presidencies," *Trans-action* 4 (December 1966), 7–14.

44. See Bauer, Pool, and Dexter, *American Business and Public Policy,* pp. 9–79.

Chapter 6

The Ballot and
the Political System

WE BEGAN this book by asserting that Presidential elections are important because the results are significant to us as citizens. We would now like to explore whether the act of voting in a democracy such as ours is meaningful not only in the sense that voters help choose the next President but also in the sense that their collective choice limits and shapes national policy. It seems appropriate, therefore, to begin our analysis with a brief statement of how policy outcomes are achieved in national politics. Then we shall go on to relate the act of voting in free elections to the policy process.

COALITIONS IN THE SYSTEM

In the American political system, powers and opportunities to act effectively on public policy are parceled out to the President, to Congress, to the courts, to independent regulatory agencies, to various of the Federal bureaucracies, to the political parties, and even, in some respects, to interest groups. It is clear that each of these agencies enjoys partial autonomy; but in most important areas of public policy formation, they share powers. And this means that it is possible for participants in policy mak-

269

ing to achieve their desired ends only by entering into cooperation with other participants in the system, by making coalitions.

What sorts of behavior are encouraged in a system which requires coalitions? Coalitions mean bargaining. Participants must give something in order to get something. Those who start out with the most resources to give have an advantage. But skill also counts. The prizes tend to go to those individuals and groups who are skilled in using whatever resources they have to put together and maintain coalitions. They help themselves by finding ways in which the interests of others may also be served.

The most conspicuous problem that American political parties face is to achieve a record of advocacy and accomplishment in public policy while harmonizing the interests of Presidential and Congressional wings.

The parties that convene at the national conventions do not contain the same roster of personnel, the same coalitions of interests, or the same majorities as the parties that meet in Congress. These two different types of parties, though they bear the same party labels, represent different constituencies and perspectives. The national conventions are weighted according to the winning strategy dictated by the Electoral College; Congress is still somewhat weighted according to the overrepresentation in state legislatures (which determines the shape of Congressional districts) of rural interests,[1] according to the constitutional rule giving each state two Senators regardless of population, and according to the rules of seniority that govern the House and Senate and which tend to favor one-party areas. This explains why, for example, the conservative wing of the Republican party, though dominant in that party in Congress for many years, had for many years, until 1964, failed to nominate a candidate of its own choosing at the Republican National Convention. The difference on the Democratic side between the two party coalitions was made abundantly clear in 1956 when Senator Estes Kefauver defeated Senator John Kennedy for the Vice-Presidential nomination in the convention and lost to the man from Massachusetts in the

Senate a few months later in a contest for a place on the prestige-ful Foreign Relations Committee. Obviously, the same interests and considerations were not decisive in the national convention and the Senate.

Even when a President and a Congressional majority bear the same party identification, it may be, and often is, necessary in a Presidential election campaign to adjust their varying interests on particular policies. This is done through bargaining and the creation of a coalition including interests represented in both Congressional and Presidential parties.

Although the lack of cohesion and discipline attributed to American parties can be overemphasized, it is true that on many major policies the President cannot rely on support from the full complement of his party in Congress but must seek the sup-port of at least some members of the other party. Thus, inter-party coalitions are necessary and common in American national politics.

Power within Congress is fragmented and dispersed. Bits and pieces of influence are scattered, unequally to be sure, among committee chairmen, appropriations subcommittees, the Speaker of the House, the House Rules Committee, the Senate majority and minority leaders, the President's lobbyists, and others. How is legislation passed and defeated, then, if it is not done by a central body of cohesive leaders who are able to enforce their will on Congress?

Legislative policy is approved or rejected by building a ma-jority coalition through a process of bargaining and the proposal of objectives appealing to a wide variety of interests. A series of bills may contain attractions for all; concessions may be offered, log-rolling may be attempted, and other bargaining techniques used. If the identical majority were required to pass every piece of legislation, however, and the diversity of interests in Congress prevented agreement on a comprehensive legislative program, the American political system could lead to stalemate and go the way of the French Fourth Republic. Actually, legislation in the various policy areas often requires somewhat different coalitions. Legislative politics, therefore, is largely concerned with constructing coalitions appropriate to each set of policies.

The President does not have sufficient power to accomplish all his purposes, and those the nation sets for him, by issuing orders. He must obtain the support of others. Congress holds the vital power of the purse and the general legislative authority which the President needs. But much of the time he cannot either help or harm legislators because they are nominated and elected in their own constituencies at the local and state levels. Consequently, to get some of the things he wants, the President may have to trade some top-level appointments and make policy concessions to influential interests in Congress or to interest groups or local party leaders who can exert influence in Congress.

Power is also fragmented and dispersed in the executive branch. Parts are held by bureau chiefs, department heads, interest groups, members of Congress, party leaders, coordinating committees, the Executive Office, independent regulatory commissions and, of course, by the President himself. With no central authority to dictate decisions, administrative politics require the formation of coalitions among the many dispersed centers of power.

"This does not mean," a contemporary student of the Presidency says, "that Presidents are powerless. . . ." If that were true they would have nothing with which to bargain. They do have a veto, powers over foreign policy and the armed forces, some executive authority and other resources at their disposal. "It does mean, though, that Presidential power must be exercised *ad hoc*, through the employment of whatever sources of support, whatever transient advantages can be found and put together, case by case." [2]

We may achieve some perspective on the American situation by noting how it differs from British and French experience. In Great Britain the major parties form their coalitions of interests before the national elections and, if victorious, the same coalition that won election governs in Parliament. In the Fourth Republic of France coalitions were generally not formed before, but only after the elections. Even in the Fifth Republic the alliances of convenience formed on the second ballot bear no necessary relationship to the coalition which governs France. In the United States coalitions are formed both before and after the national elections, but electoral and governing coalitions are different.

In characterizing each of our political parties as coalitions, we do not mean to suggest that they are entirely alike. In fact, they are coalitions having slightly different components, and these differences are in turn reflected in the very real differences that crop up from time to time in the platforms of the Presidential parties and in the policies the different party majorities favor in Congress.

The two political parties to a certain extent act as transmission belts for policy preferences in the general population. They perform this function partly out of choice—as partisans, party leaders know more and care more about issues—but mostly out of necessity. In order to win the great prize of the Presidency, they must gather support from a variety of groups in the population. They gain support by offering inducements to the electorate and to the organized groups which represent its various interests. By giving this support at the polls to party winners, interest groups gain opportunities to participate in party and governmental decision-making.

ELECTIONS AND PUBLIC POLICY

We would argue that free and competitive elections discourage, though they cannot provide a complete guarantee against, extreme policies and political leaders and aid in making the political system free, open, and responsive to a great variety of people and groups in the population. But it would not be correct

to say that our elections transmit unerringly the policy preferences of electorates to leaders or confer mandates upon leaders
with regard to specific policies.

It is easy to be cynical and expect too little from elections,
or to be euphoric and expect too much from them. A cynical
view would hold that the United States was ruled by a power
elite—a small group outside the democratic process. Under these
circumstances the ballot would be a sham and a delusion. What
difference can it make how voting is carried on or who wins if
the nation is actually governed by other means? On the other
hand, a euphoric view, holding that the United States was ruled
as a mass democracy with equal control over decisions by all or
most citizens, would enormously magnify the importance of the
ballot. Through the act of casting a ballot, it could be argued, a
majority of citizens would determine major national policies.
What happened at the polls would not only decide who would
occupy public office, it would also determine the content of
specific policy decisions. In a way, public office would then be a
sham because the power of decision in important matters would
be removed from the hands of public officials. A third type of
political system—a pluralist one in which numerous minorities
compete for shares in policy making within broad limits provided by free elections—has more complex implications. It suggests that balloting is important but that it does not often determine individual policy decisions. The ballot both guides and
constrains public officials who are free to act within fairly broad
limits subject to anticipated responses of the voters and to the
desires of the other active participants.

In fact, it is evident from our description of coalition politics
that the American political system is of the pluralist type. Public
officials do make major policy decisions but elections matter
in that they determine which of two competing parties holds
public office. In a competitive two-party situation such as exists
in American Presidential politics, the lively possibility of change

provides an effective incentive for political leaders to remain in touch with followers.

But it would be inaccurate to suggest that voters in Presidential elections transmit their policy preferences to elected officials with a high degree of reliability. There are few clear mandates in our political system owing to the fact that elections are fought on so many issues and in so many incompletely overlapping constituencies. Often the voters elect officials to Congress and to the Presidency who disagree on public policies. Thus, as we shall show, mandates are not only impossible to identify, but even if they could be identified they might well be impossible to enact because of inconsistency in the instructions issued to officials who must agree on legislation.[3]

Presidential elections are not referenda. The relationship between Presidential elections and policies is a great deal subtler than the relations between the outcomes of referenda and the policies they pertain to. In theory, the American political system is designed to work like this: two teams of men, one in office, the other seeking office, both attempt to get enough votes to win elections. In order to win, they go to various groups of voters and, by offering to pursue policies favored by these groups, hope to attract their votes. If there were only one office-seeking team, their incentive to respond to the policy preferences of groups in the population would diminish; if there were many such teams, the chances that any one of them could achieve a sufficient number of backers to govern would diminish. Hence the two-party system is regarded as a kind of compromise between the goals of responsiveness and effectiveness.

The proponents of a different theory would say that elections give the winning party a mandate to carry out the policies proposed during the campaign. Only in this way, they maintain, is popular rule through the ballot meaningful. A basic assumption in their argument is that the voters (or at least a majority of them) approve of all or most of the policies presented by the victorious candidate. No doubt this is plausible, but not in the sense intended because as we have seen, a vote for a Presidential candidate is usually merely an expression of a party habit and particular policy directions are not necessarily implied in the vote. Most voters in the United States are not ideologically oriented. That is, they do not see or make connections among issues. They do not seek to create or to adopt coherent systems of thought in which issues are related to one another in some logical pattern. If this is the case, then voters can hardly be said to transmit preferences for particular policies by electing candidates to public office.

Other basic objections to the idea that our elections are designed to confer mandates on specific public policies may also be raised. First, the issues debated in the campaign may not be the ones in which most voters are interested. These issues may be ones which interest the candidates, which they want to stress, or which interest segments of the press, but there is no necessary reason to believe that any particular issue is of great concern to voters just because it gets publicity. Time and time again, voting studies have demonstrated that what appear to be the major issues of a campaign turn out not to be significant for most of the electorate. In 1952, for example, three great Republican themes were Communism, Korea, and corruption. It turned out that the Communism issue, given perhaps the most publicity, had virtually no impact. Democrats simply would not believe that their party was the party of treason, and Republicans did not need that issue to make them vote the way they usually did. Korea and corruption were noticeable issues.[4] Yet how could anyone know, in the absence of a public opinion poll, which of the three issues were important to the voters and which constituted a mandate? There were, in any event, no significant policy differences between the parties on these issues—Democrats were also against Communism and corruption and also wanted an end to the war in Korea.

A second reason why voting for a candidate does not necessarily signify approval of his policies is that candidates pursue many policy interests at any one time with widely varying intensity, so that they may collect support from some voters on one issue and from other voters on another. It is possible for a candidate to get 100 per cent of the votes and still have every voter opposed to most of his policies, as well as having every one of his policies opposed by most of the voters.

Assume that there are four major issues in a campaign. Make the further, quite reasonable, assumption that the voting population is distributed in such a way that those people who care intensely about one major issue support the victorious candidate for that reason alone, although they differ with him mildly on the other three issues. Thus, voters who are deeply concerned about the problem of nuclear defense may vote for candidate Jones who prefers a minimum deterrence position, rather than Smith, who espouses the "no-city" doctrine which requires huge retaliatory forces.[5] This particular group of voters disagrees with Jones on the farm bill, on civil rights and on Federal aid to education, but they do not feel strongly about any of these matters. Another group, meanwhile, believes that farmers, the noble yeomanry, are the backbone of the nation and that if they are prosperous and strong, everything else will turn out all right. So they vote for Jones, too, although they prefer a "no-city" strategy and disagree with Jones's other policies. And so on for other groups of voters. Jones ends up with all the votes, yet each of his policies is preferred by less than a majority of the electorate. Since this is possible in any political system where many issues are debated at election time, it is hard to argue that our Presidential elections give unequivocal mandates on specific policies to the candidates who win.[6]

As we have seen, people go to the polls and vote for many reasons not directly connected with issues. They may vote on the basis of party identification alone. Party habits may be joined with a general feeling that Democrats are better for the common man or that Republicans will keep us safe—feelings too diffuse to tell us much about specific issues. Some people vote on the basis of a candidate's personality. Others follow a friend's recommendation. Still others may be thinking about policy issues but may be all wrong in their perception of where the candidates stand. It would be difficult to distinguish the votes of these people from those who know, care, and differentiate among the candidates on the basis of issues. We do know, however, that issue-oriented persons are usually in a minority while those who cast their ballots with other things in mind are generally in the majority.

Even if there is good reason to believe that a majority of voters do approve of specific policies supported by the victorious candidate, the mandate may be difficult or impossible to carry out. A man may get elected for a policy he pursued or preferred in the past which has no reference to present circumstances. One could have voted Republican because Dwight Eisenhower ended the war in Korea but this does not point to any future policy that is currently in the realm of Presidential discretion. "Corruption" in 1952 was a kind of issue where there was really no way of carrying out a supposed mandate other than determining to be honest, a course of action we may be pardoned for believing that Adlai Stevenson would have followed as well. John F. Kennedy promised in 1960 to get the nation moving. This was broad enough to cover a multitude of vague hopes and aspirations. More specifically, as President, Kennedy may dearly have wished to make good on this promise by increasing the rate of growth in the national economy, but no one was quite sure how to do this. Lyndon Johnson was able to make good many of his 1964 campaign promises on domestic policy, but saying he would be more responsible than Goldwater did not constitute a viable future policy for Vietnam.

Leaving aside all the difficulties about the content of a mandate, there is no accepted definition of what size electoral victory gives a President special popular sanction to pursue any particular policy. Would a 60% victory be sufficient? This is rarely achieved. Does 55 seem reasonable? What about 51 or 52, however, or the cases in which the winner receives less than half of the votes cast? And is it right to ignore the multitudes who do not vote and whose preferences are not directly being considered? One might ignore the nonvoters for the purpose of this analysis if they divided in their preferences between candidates in nearly the same proportions as those who do vote. But they often don't. In practice, this problem is easily solved. Whoever wins the election is allowed to pursue whatever policies he pleases, within the substantial constraints imposed by the rest of the political system. This, in the end, is all that a "mandate" is in American politics.

EXTREMISM

Among the most important things accomplished by a political system like ours is that it discourages the most extreme alternatives. Knowing that policies which would outrage significant groups in the country would result in a stream of protests leading to loss of the next election, the party in power is restrained from the worst excesses. For people in countries like America or Great Britain, this may be difficult to appreciate precisely because they rarely have occasion to witness these extremes; extreme policies are effectively ruled out by the party system and free elections. This is not so everywhere, and we can get an insight into what is possible when the ultimate restraint of free elections is missing. Imagine that in 1956 the United States repudiated its national debt on the ground that it was inflationary. Suppose that ten years previously our government had confiscated about nine-tenths of all savings by issuing new currency worth only a tenth of the old. No doubt there would have been riots in the streets, petitions galore, furious political participation by millions of formerly inactive citizens, and a complete change of government as soon as the election laws allowed. Can we conceive of a situation in which our government would ship millions of tons of wheat abroad while millions of our own people were starving? All these extreme policies have been pursued by the Soviet Union. We are more fortunate than we know if we can say that it is difficult or impossible to imagine extreme policies like these being carried out. Indeed, it is hard to imagine that anyone in a responsible position would think of such policies let alone attempt to promulgate them. Here we come to a key point. No one thinks about these things seriously, because everyone understands that they simply could not be done.

Extreme policies are discouraged in a more subtle way: Free elections discourage persons with extreme views from running for office because possible allies of such people know that they cannot win and that, if they do, their victories will last only until the next election. Extremists deprive too many people of too many of their preferred policies to win office easily. Thus we find that would-be Presidential aspirants do not get far if they are known publicly to hold bigoted views about racial or religious minorities or if they have done or said things which suggest that they are extremely hostile to large population groups such as laborers or small businessmen. Moreover, those who do attain office and wish to enjoy its benefits find that compromise and conciliation bring greater rewards than hostility and intransigence. The political system conditions those who accept the rules of free elections to moderate behavior.

PARTY COMPETITION AND POLICY

Aside from casting extremists out beyond the pale, free elections and a two-party system operate to bring governmental policy roughly in line with intense public preferences over a reasonable span of time. Through the trial and error of repeated electoral experiences, party leaders discover that certain policies must be excluded and others included if they are to have any hope of winning. The "out" party has a built-in incentive to propose policies more popular than the "in" party in order to assume office.

And the "in" party is highly motivated to respond by adopting the policy itself or by proposing others which it believes may be even more popular. Party competition for votes brings public policy into accord with private preferences. This calculus of support is far from precise; it is necessarily based more on hunch and guesswork at any point in time than on hard facts. Party leaders undoubtedly have a number of policies which they know they must include or exclude, such as Social Security and veterans' benefits. Beyond that, however, they face considerable uncertainty in determining which policies will prove to be the most popular with the largest number of voters who are in a position to help them. Policies themselves may break down, subjecting proponents to charges of ineffectiveness. There may be consequences of consequences which turn what once looked like a good thing into a disaster. John Kennedy might have been helped by a successful Cuban invasion but how was he to know that it would turn into a rout? And how could he tell that a Soviet attempt to install missiles would enable him to act decisively and recoup his fortunes? President Johnson has found it possible to do much more than previous Presidents to improve relations with Communist countries in Eastern Europe. Yet the Vietnam war has certainly created all sorts of additional difficulties in dealing with the Soviet Union. So much for the effectiveness of the policy. How about the perhaps more difficult problem in our system of discovering whether particular policies are so widely preferred as to aid one's political fortunes?

Opinion polls may help the politician, but there are always lingering doubts as to the polls' reliability; it is not certain in any event that they tell the political leader what he needs to know. People who really have no opinion may give one just to satisfy the interviewer. People who have an opinion but who care little may be counted equally with those who are intensely concerned. Many people giving opinions may have no intention of voting for some politicians who heed them, no matter what. The result may be that the politician will get no visible support from a majority who agrees with him, but instead he will get complaints from an intense minority which disagrees. The people who agree with him may not vote while those who differ may take retribution at the ballot box. Those who are pleased may be the ones who would have voted for the public official anyway. And unless the poll is carefully done, it may leave out important groups of voters, overrepresent some, underrepresent others, and otherwise give a misleading impression. Other methods of determining voter sentiment are bound to be even more unreliable. Who knows whether opinions expressed in newspaper editorials or a mail campaign are representative of the majority of the voting populace?

Let us turn the question around for a moment. Suppose a candidate loses office. What does this tell him about the policies he should have preferred? If there were one or two key issues widely debated and universally understood, the election may tell him a great deal. But this is seldom the case. More likely there were many issues and it was difficult to separate out those which did or did not garner support for his opponent. Perhaps the election was decided on the basis of personality or some events in the economic cycle or a military engagement—points which were not debated in the campaign and which may not have been within anyone's control. The losing candidate may always feel that if he continues to educate the public to favor the policies he prefers, he will eventually win out. Should he lose a series of elections, however, his party would undoubtedly try to change something—policies, candidates, organization, maybe all three—in an effort to improve its fortunes.

Let us suppose that a candidate wins an election. What does this event tell him and his party about the policies he should prefer when in office? He can take it on faith that the policies he proposed during the campaign are the popular ones. Some were undoubtedly rather vague, and specific applications of them may turn out quite differently than the campaign suggested. Others may founder on the rock of practicality; they sounded fine but they simply could not be carried out. Conditions change and policies which seemed appropriate but a few months before turn out to be irrelevant. As the time for putting policies into practice draws near, the new officeholder may discover that they generate a lot more opposition than when they were merely campaign oratory. And those policies he pursues to the end may have to be compromised considerably in order to get the support of other participants in the policy making process. Nevertheless, if he has even a minimal policy orientation, the newly elected candidate can try to carry out a few of his campaign proposals, seeking to maintain a general direction consonant with the approach that may—he cannot be entirely certain—have contributed measurably to his election.

Let us summarize. The role of Presidential elections has been found to be very important in keeping our political system open and competitive and in keeping public officials responsive to the preferences of a variety of interests in the general population. However, outcomes of these elections cannot by themselves transform the political system, nor can they register precisely all the nuances of policies preferred by the general public. In spite of this, our system of coalition politics, operating within and among the two parties, the President, Congress, state parties, and interest groups, does provide a kind of substitute for specific mandates by the electorate.

In the American political system, both inside and outside of formal government, it is necessary to receive multiple agreements and clearances from actors (bureaucrats, interest groups, legislators, the President) variously situated, having somewhat different roles to play and values to defend, in order to put new policies into effect. Alternatives which are fed into the political system and emerge as decisions are brought forth in a variety of ways, and all sorts of strategies and resources can be mobilized and focused on political decisions by interested parties. It is a system which encourages stability and discourages extremism, which sharply limits the choices available to the general public in the interests of finding agreement on only two alternatives, either of which can govern effectively. Very few people are perfectly satisfied with this framework within which our Presidential elections are held, but even fewer have devised ways of making the system better without simultaneously making it worse.

NOTES

1. *Wesberry* vs. *Sanders, Reynolds* vs. *Sims,* and the wave of reapportionment of state legislatures they set off may be expected to modify this condition somewhat over the next decade.

2. Richard Neustadt, "The Presidency at Mid-Century," *Law and Contemporary Problems* 21 (Autumn 1956), 614.

3. This parallels in many respects an argument to be found in Robert A. Dahl, *A Preface to Democratic Theory* (Chicago, 1956).

4. Angus Campbell, Philip Converse, Warren E. Miller, and Donald Stokes, *The American Voter* (New York, 1960), pp. 525–527.

5. An excellent popular treatment of this set of alternatives is contained in Richard Fryklund, *100 Million Lives* (New York, 1962).

6. See Dahl, *A Preface to Democratic Theory,* pp. 124–131.

Appendices A & B

Bibliography

Index

Appendix A

March 12	New Hampshire
April 2	Wisconsin
April 23	Pennsylvania
April 30	Massachusetts
May 7	District of Columbia
May 7	Indiana
May 7	Ohio
May 14	Nebraska
May 14	West Virginia
May 28	Oregon
May 28	Florida
June 4	California
June 4	New Jersey
June 4	South Dakota
June 11	Illinois

* In addition, Alabama and New York hold primaries to vote for unpledged convention delegates. Texas election law does not provide for Presidential primaries, but nothing in the law prohibits a political party from distributing an extra primary ballot sheet on which voters could indicate their Presidential preference. Neither state committee has yet determined whether it will conduct such a preference poll in 1968.

Appendix B

CONVENTION DELEGATES AND THE ELECTORAL COLLEGE, 1964 AND 1968

State	Convention Delegates				Electoral Votes	
	Republican		Democratic[1]			
	1964	1968	1964	1968	1964	1968
Alabama	20	26	38		10	10
Alaska	12	12	12		3	3
Arizona	16	16	19		5	5
Arkansas	12	18	32		6	6
California	86	86	154		40	40
Colorado	18	18	23		6	6
Connecticut	16	16	43		8	8
Delaware	12	12	22		3	3
Florida	34	34	51		14	14
Georgia	24	30	53		12	12
Hawaii	8	14	25		4	4
Idaho	14	14	15		4	4
Illinois	58	58	114		26	26
Indiana	32	26	51		13	13
Iowa	24	24	35		9	8
Kansas	20	20	27		7	7
Kentucky	24	24	34		9	9
Louisiana	20	26	46		10	10
Maine	14	14	16		4	4
Maryland	20	26	48		10	10
Massachusetts	34	34	69		14	14
Michigan	48	48	92		21	21
Minnesota	26	26	50		10	10
Mississippi	13	20	24		7	7

289

Convention Delegates

State	Republican 1964	Republican 1968	Democratic[1] 1964	Democratic[1] 1968	Electoral Votes 1964	Electoral Votes 1968
Missouri	24	24	58		12	12
Montana	14	14	17		4	4
Nebraska	16	16	19		5	5
Nevada	6	12	22		3	3
New Hampshire	14	8	15		4	5
New Jersey	40	40	77		17	17
New Mexico	14	14	26		4	4
New York	92	92	179		43	43
North Carolina	26	26	58		13	13
North Dakota	14	8	15		4	4
Ohio	58	58	99		26	26
Oklahoma	22	22	30		8	8
Oregon	18	18	24		6	6
Pennsylvania	64	64	125		29	29
Rhode Island	14	14	27		4	4
South Carolina	16	22	38		8	8
South Dakota	14	14	15		4	4
Tennessee	28	28	40		11	11
Texas	56	56	99		25	25
Utah	14	8	16		4	4
Vermont	12	12	12		3	3
Virginia	30	24	42		12	12
Washington	24	24	35		9	9
West Virginia	14	14	37		7	7
Wisconsin	30	30	46		12	12
Wyoming	12	12	15		3	3
Canal Zone			5		0	0
District of Columbia	9	9	16		3	3
Guam			3		0	0
Puerto Rico[2]	5	5	8		0	0
Virgin Islands[2]	3	3	5		0	0
TOTAL	1,308	1,333	2,316		538	538
Needed to nominate	655	667	1,159			
Needed to elect					270	270

[1] Figures for the 1968 Democratic National Convention are not available at this time.

[2] Puerto Rico and the Virgin Islands are entitled to participate in the National Conventions but not in the Presidential election.

Bibliography

The works listed in the footnotes should prove helpful to anyone wishing to pursue a particular line of interest in depth. However, for a start, the following may be useful. On voters and political participation, there are now several thorough inventories, for example, Robert E. Lane's *Political Life* (Glencoe, 1959), and V. O. Key, Jr.'s *Public Opinion and American Democracy* (New York, 1961). The two most intensive studies of voting behavior are *Voting* by Bernard Berelson, Paul Lazarsfeld, and William N. McPhee (Chicago, 1954), which is based on research done in Elmira, New York, during and after the 1948 Presidential campaign, and Angus Campbell and associates' *The American Voter* (New York, 1960), which is based on nationwide sample surveys conducted in 1952 and 1956. An interesting "case study" of public opinion is Herbert H. Hyman and Paul B. Sheatsley's, "The Political Appeal of President Eisenhower," *Public Opinion Quarterly* 19 (Winter 1955–56), pp. 26–39; this is reprinted in Nelson W. Polsby, Robert A. Dentler, and Paul A. Smith, eds., *Politics and Social Life* (Boston, 1963), pp. 453–464. See V. O. Key, Jr., *The Responsible Electorate* (Cambridge, Mass., 1966) for a discussion of voters in Presidential elections.

The nature of the party system in the United States has been described in a number of good texts, for example, Moisei Ostrogorski's *Democracy and the Party System in the United States* (New York, 1926), Pendleton Herring's *The Politics of Democracy* (New York, 1940), Austin Ranney and Willmoore Kendall, *Democracy and the American Party System* (New York, 1956), V. O. Key, Jr., *Politics, Parties and Pressure Groups*, 4th ed. (New York, 1958), and Fred I. Greenstein, *The American Party System and the American People* (Englewood Cliffs, N.J., 1964).

The literature on Presidential campaigns is, of course, voluminous. Two studies with historical perspective on the subject are Alexander Heard's *The Costs of Democracy* (Chapel Hill, N.C., 1960), and Eugene H. Roseboom's *A History of Presidential Elections* (New York, 1957). Among the more popular works on the 1960 campaign are Theodore H. White's *The Making of the President, 1960* (New York, 1961) and Harry Ernst's *The Primary that Made a President: West Virginia, 1960* (New York, 1962). Both of these works are highly readable, and contain a wealth of illustrations and anecdotes. More scholarly studies of the 1960 campaign include Herbert E. Alexander's *Financing the 1960 Election* (Princeton, 1962), his *Responsibility in Party Finance* (Princeton, 1963), and Sidney Kraus, ed., *The Great Debates* (Bloomington, 1962), which provide both facts and competent analysis of two important and controversial aspects of that struggle. The "official record" of the campaign, the words of the candidates themselves, is in Report 994, Parts I, II, and III, 87th Congress, 1st Session, U.S. Senate (Washington, 1961), entitled respectively *The Speeches of Senator John F. Kennedy, Presidential Campaign of 1960, The Speeches of Vice-President Richard M. Nixon, Presidential Campaign of 1960,* and *The Joint Appearances of Senator John F. Kennedy and Vice-President Richard M. Nixon, Presidential Campaign of 1960.* Two other useful analyses of the 1960 campaign are Paul T. David, ed., *The Presidential Election and Transition, 1960–1961* (Washington, 1961), and Eric Sevareid, ed., *Candidates, 1960* (New York, 1959). On the 1964 campaign, see Robert D. Novak, *The Agony of the G.O.P. 1964* (New York, 1965), Richard H. Rovere, *The Goldwater Caper* (New York, 1965), Theodore H. White, *The Making of the President, 1964* (New York, 1965), and Milton C. Cummings, Jr., *The National Election of 1964* (Washington, 1966). Finally, a dissection of one type of argument frequently used in political campaigning is contained in Aaron B. Wildavsky's "The Intelligent Citizen's Guide to the Abuses of Statistics: The Kennedy Document and the Catholic Vote," in Polsby, Dentler, and Smith, *Politics and Social Life,* pp. 825–844.

Paul T. David, Ralph M. Goldman, and Richard C. Bain's *The Politics of National Party Conventions* (Washington, 1960) gives a voluminous historical treatment of Presidential nominating conventions. See also Nelson W. Polsby and Aaron B. Wildavsky's "Uncertainty and Decision-Making at the National Conventions," in Polsby, Dentler, and Smith, *Politics and Social Life,* pp. 370–389 and Gerald Pomper, *Nominating the President: The Politics of Convention Choice* (Evanston, Ill., 1963). For material on specific conventions, see Paul Tillett, ed., *Inside Politics: The National Conventions, 1960* (Dobbs

Ferry, N.Y., 1962) and Paul T. David, Malcolm C. Moos, and Ralph M. Goldman, *Presidential Nominating Politics in 1952*, Vols. I–V (Baltimore, 1954). Information on the formal aspects of the nomination and election process can be found in *Nomination and Election of the President and Vice President of the United States, Including the Manner of Selecting Delegates to National Political Conventions*, House Document #332, 86th Congress, 2nd Session (Washington, 1960) and, with the same title, Senate item #998 (January 1964).

Finally, materials on the actual election results can be found in Richard M. Scammon, ed., *America Votes*, Vols. I–V (New York, 1956–62), and, with analytical comments, in Malcolm C. Moos, *Politics, Presidents and Coattails* (Baltimore, 1952).

Index

295